Great Big Toy Trucks

Plans & Instructions for Building 9 Giant Vehicles

Les Neufeld

The Taunton Press

The Taunton Press
Inspiration for hands-on living®

The Taunton Press, Inc., 63 South Main Street, PO Box 5506
Newtown, CT 06470-5506
e-mail: tp@taunton.com

Editors: David Heim, Peter Chapman
Copy editor: Seth Reichgott
Jacket/Cover design: Amy Griffin
Interior design: Carol Petro, Cathy Cassidy
Layout: Cathy Cassidy
Illustrator: Les Neufeld
Photographer: Les Neufeld

The following names/manufacturers appearing in *Great Big Toy Trucks* are trademarks:
Bobcat®, Forstner®, Krylon®, Krylon Fusion for Plastic®, Lee Valley®, Rockler®, Titebond III®,
Varathane®, Woodcraft®, Woodworker's Supply®

Library of Congress Cataloging-in-Publication Data

Neufeld, Les.
  Great big toy trucks : plans & instructions for building 9 giant vehicles / Les Neufeld, photographer.
    pages cm
  ISBN 978-1-62710-791-4
1. Wooden toys. 2. Trucks--Models. I. Title.
  TT174.5.W6N479 2015
  745.592--dc23
                              2015019736
Printed in the United States of America
10 9 8 7 6 5 4 3 2 1

To Corrinne,
my partner in everything

---

acknowledgments

I owe a debt of thanks to my editors, David Heim and Peter Chapman. David was a great source of advice, encouragement, and humor throughout the writing process. The book is much clearer and better written as a result of his efforts. Peter got the project going and provided oversight and advice throughout. Thank you both. My thanks to the copy editor, Seth Reichgott, for going over the text with a fine-tooth comb. The graphics department at Taunton did an amazing job of fixing my photos and upgrading the plans, turning out a beautiful product. For me, the best moment in writing a book is the first look at finished pages.

My children, Kevin, Eric, and Lisa, are now young adults. Still, they suggested valuable improvements to the toys. Kevin shared technical information about the fire truck and gave me tours of the station, trucks, and equipment. Eric helped with photographic equipment and advice. Lisa provided upbeat moral support. My thanks to each of you again.

Friends Jim K. and Dave M. donated a scrollsaw and belt sander, which proved invaluable. Dave B. let me rummage through his amazing woodshop and pick out many small pieces of hardwood.

My wife Corrinne again gave me constant support and put up with my avoiding our renovation project to spend hours in the shop building toys. Thank you, Renie. I owe you big time.

contents

Introduction 2

CHAPTER 1: Giant Loader 4

CHAPTER 2: Mining Dump Truck.......... 28

CHAPTER 3: Giant Grader.................. 44

CHAPTER 4: One Bus Four Ways 65

CHAPTER 5: Eight-Wheel
Articulating Tractor 86

CHAPTER 6: Heavy Equipment
Transporter 101

CHAPTER 7: Wheeled Crane 128

CHAPTER 8: Fire Truck 151

CHAPTER 9: Skid-Steer Loader 175

Appendix 186

Metric Equivalents 187

introduction

first and foremost, these toys are meant for kids to play with, so the designs revolve around the primary aim of giving kids some enjoyment. Coming in a close second is enjoyment for the woodworker who makes the toys. As much as possible, I have tried to choose design features that meet both of those requirements.

Unlike models, toys need to be robust. That dictates much of the design and overrides appearance in importance. For example, I have found that exhaust stacks are susceptible to breaking, so I've made them short and stubby to keep that from happening. The same goes for handles and other controls. Over time, wheels can come off if the axle pins are too short or if they are installed with a less-than-generous amount of glue. That's why I have used solid heavy axles for the larger toys. Where necessary, I make parts from Baltic birch plywood, so that grain direction does not become a weakness.

Toys also need to be attractive to kids as well as adults. Careful wood choice can provide contrast and color, and good proportion helps keeps balance. To that end, I have carefully scaled these toys from life-sized machines. Wherever possible, I have added simplified versions of real-life details, such as headlights, grills, and the many gauges and valves on the fire truck.

I hope you will feel free to change the designs, adding your own touch to each toy. You could, for instance, make everything half size if you need a smaller toy for a very young child. You could add or subtract details such as lights, bumpers, and grills. Or you could make all kinds of implements for the tractor or cargo to load on the heavy equipment transporter.

Skill Level

A novice woodworker can make these toys, and I have written the book with that in mind. However, some very accomplished woodworkers will likely make one or two of these toys. If that sounds like you, please skip over any instructions that you may not need.

Likewise, each of you will need to adapt some instructions here and there because your equipment is slightly different from mine or because you have a different way of doing things. When I was an apprentice, I came to see that different tradespeople have different ways and methods of reaching the same end. In some places, I give a couple of options for making a certain part, but in most cases I describe the method that works best for me.

Plans and Templates

I have followed common drafting conventions for the plans. In the assembly drawings, I have sometimes omitted hidden lines for the sake of clarity. However, the drawings for individual parts show all the details.

Each chapter has a few templates, which I used to simplify the layout of the more-complex curved parts. Feel free to photocopy and scale the templates. If that's not convenient for you, use the measurements in the plans to lay out the parts.

I generally print templates on heavy paper, then cut them out and trace the outlines on the wood. You can either use carbon paper to transfer the lines, or rub a soft pencil on the back side of the template, transforming it into carbon paper. When I'm working with dark wood and pencil lines are hard to see, I use an awl to "dot" the lines, making small indentations on the lines and larger indentations for the hole centers.

Wood Choice

I find that strong grain patterns take away from a vehicle's appearance, so I avoid woods like oak and ash, choosing straight-grained pieces with uniform color. The toys don't require much wood, so the costs are relatively low. You can probably use offcuts and scraps that you have on hand. Schools and cabinet shops often have hardwood scraps that they can part with cheaply or for free.

I find that if I use contrasting dark and light woods, the toys look more appealing to me as well as the kids. I have ready access to locally grown birch and maple, so I use those when I want light-colored wood; I pick through to find pieces with the lightest color and the tamest grain. Yellowheart is a good wood for the school bus and a few select parts that I would like yellow colored. I use wenge, black walnut, purpleheart, and padauk in small amounts. I use small pieces from a package of assorted veneers, as on the grill for the fire truck.

Glue Choice

I have found that wooden toys break or come apart for one of two reasons. Either some thin part protrudes too much and breaks off, or a glue joint didn't have enough glue. Good design will combat the first problem. A generous amount of a strong glue will rectify the second problem. I used Titebond III® almost exclusively for the toys in this book. It is more expensive than regular carpenter's glue, but these small projects require very little glue. Titebond says it originally developed this glue for skateboard and longboard decks, so it can take a bit of abuse, moisture, and flexing. It has the added advantage of allowing you a few extra minutes of assembly time.

When gluing small curved and angled parts, I often find clamping can be very difficult. In those instances, rubbing the part very slightly side to side or even just pressing it firmly into place for a minute or two can yield a very strong joint. I have had to remove such a glued-in part soon after it was attached and found it

difficult to dislodge after only five minutes or so. Clamping is necessary if you need extra pressure to bring the two surfaces together or if you can't hold the parts in position by hand.

Finishes

I used spray polyurethanes in aerosol containers for all the toys. These finishes are nontoxic when dry and form a hard protective coating. I prefer the Krylon® brand, primarily because the nozzles provide a flat spray pattern that works well on the toys. For a gloss finish (my overall favorite), I use Krylon Fusion for Plastic® clear gloss finish, which provides protection from ultraviolet rays and is much more resistant to runs than any other spray I have found so far. This is a great benefit when spraying into the small corners and odd-shaped parts on these toys.

I sand the parts as I assemble them, usually working up to 220-grit for the final sanding in places that will not be easy to sand after assembly. I sand lightly with 220-grit or 320-grit paper between coats, especially after the first coat. I generally apply three or four coats of finish, with more on areas that will be handled a lot.

Wheels and Axles

Several of the larger toys have wheels that cannot be purchased, and part of the challenge is making these large wheels. Although you can make all the wheels in the shop, factory-made treaded wheels are so inexpensive that I think they are worth buying. For a couple of the toys you will saw extra cross treads in those purchased wheels.

Factory-made axle pins are a good purchase, too, but only for the smaller wheels and only when the pin will fit into a hole more than an inch deep. Otherwise, the axle pins become a weak point and can work loose over time.

The 1¾-in. wheels used on the fire truck and one version of the school bus can be hard to find. I have listed a couple of suppliers in the Appendix.

CHAPTER 1

Giant Loader

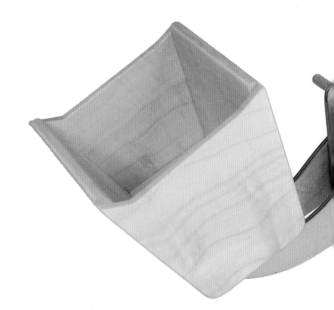

Several heavy equipment manufacturers make huge loaders similar to this design. This one is intended to work with the mining dump truck in the next chapter and the grader in Chapter 3. While you may not want these toys outside in the mud, there are endless things kids will move with the loader, such as blocks, dominoes, and other small toys.

The loader has lots of small parts, but basically it is a large block for the rear body pinned to a small block for the front frame. Attached to the rear body are the cab, bumper, exhaust, ladders, and two wheels. The front frame holds the bucket assembly and the other two wheels. The 4-in. wheels are identical to the ones used on the mining truck and the giant grader. I've used contrasting woods for the wheels, fenders, and cab to make the toy look sharper, but kids will enjoy it just as well if you make all the parts from the same wood.

The loader articulates in the center in order to steer. The bucket swivels to dump and load, and a lever raises and lowers the whole bucket assembly. The child using the toy can hold the bucket up by slipping the lever mechanism into notches on the bucket arms. That way, he or she can drive around with the bucket kept at the desired height.

Top View

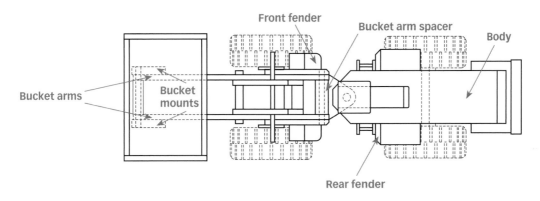

Front fender

Bucket arm spacer

Body

Bucket arms

Bucket mounts

Rear fender

Side View

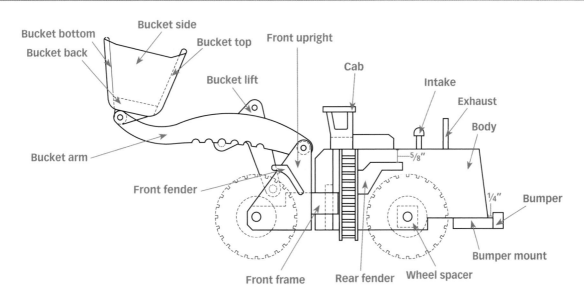

Bucket bottom

Bucket side

Bucket back

Bucket top

Front upright

Bucket lift

Cab

Intake

Exhaust

Body

Bucket arm

5/8"

Front fender

1/4"

Bumper

Front frame

Rear fender

Wheel spacer

Bumper mount

PART NAME	FINISH DIMENSIONS L × W × T, IN.	NO. REQ'D.	NOTES
Wheels	4 dia. ¾ thick per half	4	Need 8 halves to make 4 wheels.
Body	8½ × 3¾ × 2½	1	
Wheel spacers	1 × 1 × ⅛	2	
Cab base	3 × 1 × ¾	1	
Cab sides	1¾ × 1¼ × ¼	2	Note grain direction.
Cab roof	1¾ × 1½ × ¼	1	Note grain direction.
Cab back	1 × 1 × ¼	1	Drill before cutting.
Bumper	3½ × ½ × ¾	1	
Bumper mount	3⅜ × 2 × ½	1	
Front fenders	1⁹⁄₁₆ × 1⅜ × 1	2	Can be ⅞ in. or ¾ in. thick.
Rear fenders	2¼ × 1½ × 1	2	Can be ⅞ in. or ¾ in. thick.
Ladder sides	4⅜ × ½ × ⅛	4	Baltic birch plywood
Ladder rungs	⅛ dowel × ⅞ long	22	Cut overlong, trim after assembly.
Front frame	4½ × 2⅛ × 1¾	1	
Front uprights	4¼ × 3⅛ × ¼	2	Solid wood or Baltic birch plywood. Cut overlong, trim after assembly.
Bucket arms	9¾ × 1¾ × ¼	2	Baltic birch plywood
Bucket arm spacers	⅝ dowel × 1⅝ long	2	Check length against front upright spacing.
Bucket lifts	4¹¹⁄₁₆ × 2¹¹⁄₁₆ × ¼	2	Baltic birch plywood. Cut about ½ oversize.
Arm support dowel	⅜ dowel × 2¼ long	1	
Lift mount dowel	⅜ dowel × 2⅝ long	1	Cut ⅛ in. overlong.
Lift handle	¼ dowel × 4¼ long	1	
Bucket arm dowel	¼ dowel × 2⅝ long	1	Cut ⅛ in. overlong.
Bucket pivot dowel	¼ dowel × 2¾ long	1	Cut ⅛ in. overlong.
Bucket back	5½ × 2³⁄₁₆ × ½	1	
Bucket bottom and top	5½ × 3⅜ × ¼	2	Cut ¹⁄₁₆ in. overlong.
Bucket sides	3¹⁵⁄₁₆ × 3⅞ × ¼	2	Solid wood or Baltic birch plywood
Bucket mounts	1⅝ × ¹¹⁄₁₆ × ⅜	2	Solid wood or Baltic birch plywood
Exhaust	¼ dowel × 2 long	1	
Intake	⅜ axle pin, factory made	1	Cut 1⅝ in. long including head.
Articulation pin	⅜ dowel × 2¾ long	1	Cut ¹⁄₁₆ in. overlong, sand after installation.
Axles	½ dowel × 5½ long	2	Measure exact length from loader.
Wheel hubs	1 dia. wheel, factory made	4	
Plastic washers	To fit	2–10	Optional. Use for wheels and articulation joint.

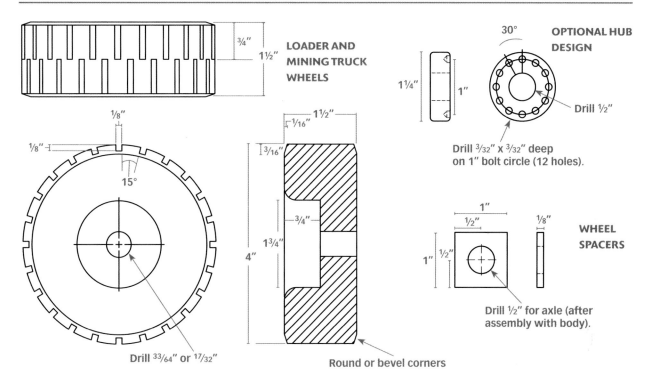

LOADER AND MINING TRUCK WHEELS

OPTIONAL HUB DESIGN

Drill ¹/₂"

Drill ³/₃₂" x ³/₃₂" deep on 1" bolt circle (12 holes).

Drill ³³/₆₄" or ¹⁷/₃₂"

Round or bevel corners

WHEEL SPACERS

Drill ¹/₂" for axle (after assembly with body).

Wheels

Making these wheels takes a bit of time, but they look great and are not that difficult to do. Make the four wheels in eight halves, cut the treads, and then glue the halves together. The four outside halves need to be donut-shaped, and the four inside halves have no center cutouts.

There are two ways to cut the treads. One option is to use a bandsaw and shape the treads a little. The other option is to use a tablesaw. The wheels still come out pretty nice, and it is much faster, but the bandsaw is a friendlier, safer machine. I will describe both methods.

Preparing the Disks

1. Lay out 8 disks. Keep an eye on the center mark from your compass, as you will use it a few times. Mark the location with pencil in case the tiny indentation disappears.

Use wood that is close to ¾ in. thick. I tend to use dark wood for the wheels, but that's only because I like the look better.

2. Lay out a circle that is ¼ in. smaller in diameter than the outside diameter. This line will be for the tread bottoms.

3. Bandsaw the disks just a tiny bit oversize (¹/₃₂ in.), then disk-sand them exactly to the line. Do this carefully, as you want the wheels both round and concentric to the center compass mark.

Lay out the treads on the "bad" side of the disk, if there are any appearance differences side to side. The "good" side of the wheel will have chipout, but this will be removed later when you bevel the corner. The "bad" side tread ends will have clean corners that will be visible later, but the rest of the surface will be glued to the mating disk to form the herringbone treads.

4. Lay out the 24 treads, using the template on p. 27. It seems to be easiest in this case to cut out a photocopy of the template (use paper as thick as the copier will take). For the bandsaw method of tread cutting, each tread is cut to a "V" shape on the template. This makes it easier to cut the template and trace the pattern onto the wood and gives the treads a little nicer shape. The circle drawn earlier provides the layout for the bottom of the treads.

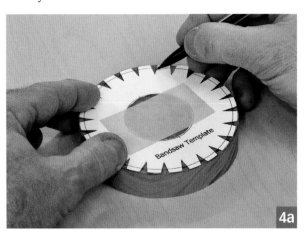

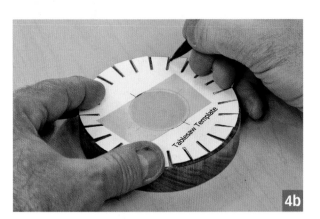

For the tablesaw method, cut out the slots in the template and use them to mark 24 lines on the disks. A rectangular carpenter's pencil works a bit better for these slots than a regular pencil.

5. Drill a 1¾-in. hole in the center of four disks. I use a Forstner® bit for this because it leaves a smoother finish.

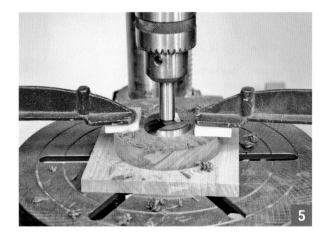

6. Round the edges of the large hole. Do this now if you are doing it by hand; it's harder after the wheel halves are glued together. File a little with a round or half-round file, then sand. The hole needs only a small radius; you can decide what looks good (about a ⅛-in. radius is good enough).

It works well to use a router mounted in a table, with a ⅛-in. or ¼-in. roundover bit, but it is safest to do that after the wheel halves are glued together.

TIP

You aren't limited to cutting square treads in these wheels. If you angle the miter fence on the tablesaw, you can cut angled treads. If you try this, pay attention to the wheels' orientation. The left and right wheels have to be mirror images, so you will need to angle the miter gauge in the opposite direction.

Cutting the Treads

Bandsaw method:

1. Don't rotate the wheel as you cut a given tread. Instead, cut the two angled lines and then use the bandsaw as a sort of motorized file, carving out the treads. Pull up a stool; it will take a while to cut all the treads in all eight disks.

You can set up two stops to keep the blank centered on the blade and control the depth of cut. This will make the cutting go a little faster (see inset photo below).

2. File with a small file and sand as needed to clean up the treads.

Tablesaw method:

Begin by attaching a long auxiliary fence to the miter gauge. If you normally use a thin-kerf blade, switch to one that's ⅛ in. thick. It will make better-looking treads.

1. Clamp a stop in place to locate the wheel so the tablesaw blade cuts on center to the wheel. Mark a line on the table in line with the blade center and measure from it. For these 4-in. wheels, the stop will be set exactly 2 in. from the blade center.

2. Set the blade to cut ⅛ in. deep and cut on each line. Don't worry if you get a little chipout at the

end of the cut. Make that side the outside of the wheel when gluing the halves together. The outside corners are beveled after assembly, so the chipout will disappear.

3. File a bevel on each tread.

Wheel Assembly

Whichever method you used to cut the threads, it is now time to glue the halves together. Each finished wheel will have one drilled disk glued to one solid disk.

1. Before glue-up, drill the axle holes in the four solid disks. Rather than use ⅜-in. factory-made axle pins, it's a little better to go with ½-in. dowel. That means the holes need to be about 1/32 in. larger than the dowel to allow the wheel to spin freely. I use a 33/64-in. or 17/32-in. drill. It is very important to center these holes as accurately as possible.

TIP

Drilling a hole exactly on center is one of the more difficult operations. One old machinist's method is to draw a $\frac{1}{16}$-in. oversize circle around the compass centerpoint, then enlarge the compass center mark with an awl. Fit the drill press with a small bit ($\frac{1}{8}$ in. or smaller). This makes it easier to align the drill with the center mark. If the spinning bit is off-center, it will flex a little when it is lightly touched to the center mark. You will be able to spot that right away and move the workpiece a tiny amount to compensate. Align the workpiece until the bit does not flex when gently touched to the center mark. Clamp it down and drill the pilot hole. Then change bits and drill the large one without moving the workpiece.

I hold the wheel using C-clamps, but a parallel clamp or a drill-press vise would also work. Later, if you try the wheels on the loader and find that one wheel doesn't quite touch the ground, you may have to drill out the hole with a slightly larger bit, or enlarge it by hand with a round file.

2. Use glue sparingly. It's hard to remove if it squeezes out into the treads or the center hole.

Sand to break the sharp corners of the best edges of the treads, then put these edges together with the worst ones to the outside. The outsides get beveled anyway, so chipped edges just disappear. Align the circumferences as closely as possible.

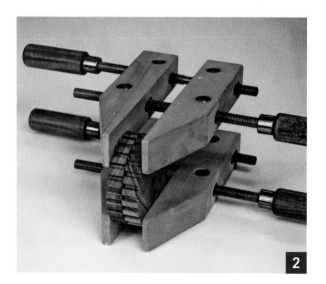

3. Bevel the outside corners with a disk sander, rotating the wheel carefully by hand. Clamp a wedge-shaped guide to the sander's table, which will help you keep the bevel reasonably consistent all the way around. Do the inside edges first for practice, as they are not easily seen.

4. Lightly run the treaded surface of the wheels over the sander to smooth the faces if there is a noticeable step where the two halves meet.

Body

1. Laminate stock if you need to. Square up this block to the dimensions given in the cut list on p. 6.

2. Lay out the outline for the top and side. Locate the holes for the intake, exhaust, and articulation pivot now. Save the axle hole for later, after you have glued on the wheel spacers.

3. Drill the various holes. The $\frac{3}{8}$-in. dowel hole on the bottom (for the articulation pivot) should be a snug fit on a $\frac{3}{8}$-in. dowel. In this case, I had to use a $\frac{25}{64}$-in. bit because the dowel was oversize. The $\frac{1}{4}$-in. hole on the top for the exhaust required a slightly oversize drill too, in this case an "F" drill,

Body

Bumper Assembly

TOP VIEW

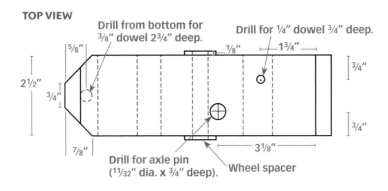

Drill from bottom for ³⁄₈" dowel 2³⁄₄" deep.

Drill for ¼" dowel ¾" deep.

5/8"

2½"

3/4"

7/8"

1/8"

1³⁄₄"

3/4"

3/4"

Drill for axle pin (¹¹⁄₃₂" dia. x ¾" deep).

Wheel spacer

3⅛"

TOP VIEW

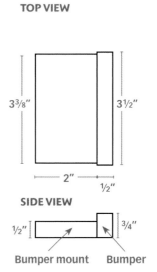

3³⁄₈"

3½"

2"

½"

SIDE VIEW (showing location of wheel spacers)

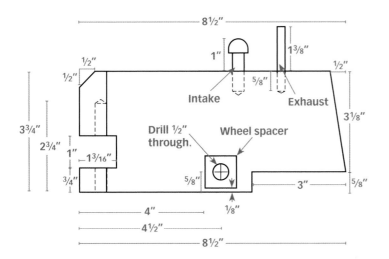

SIDE VIEW

½"

½"

¾"

Bumper mount

Bumper

8½"

1"

1³⁄₈"

½"

½"

5/8"

Intake

Exhaust

3⅛"

3¾"

2³⁄₄"

1"

1³⁄₁₆"

Drill ½" through.

Wheel spacer

5/8"

3/4"

5/8"

3"

5/8"

4"

1/8"

4½"

8½"

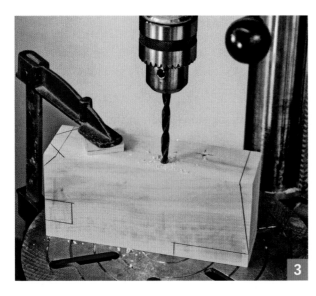

which is 0.007 in. larger than ¼ in. The ¹¹⁄₃₂-in. intake hole is for a standard axle pin, used as an air intake.

4. Cut the side contour using a bandsaw. Cut the 1-in. by 1³⁄₁₆-in. articulation notch carefully, right to the line. This will leave a minimum of filing and fitting later.

5. Cut the top contour—the angles at the front. You will have to redraw the layout lines, as the ends were cut off when you made the side contour.

6. Sand as needed, removing any sharp corners.

7. Cut the dowel for the exhaust and the axle pin for the intake to length. The cut list gives measurements for those pieces, but lengths aren't critical.

8. Use a toothpick to put glue in the exhaust and intake holes, then push or tap the dowels into place.

Wheel Spacers

These spacers are just that. They move the wheels away from the body so that they don't rub on the sides. I have not used them on the front wheels of the loader; they have less tendency to rub because most of the wheel protrudes past the frame. If you want spacers on the front wheels, a thin plastic washer can be used as a spacer and wear plate.

1. Cut the 1-in. by 1-in. squares of 1/8-in.-thick wood (see the drawing on p. 7). I used an offcut here, but Baltic birch plywood also works very well.

2. Glue the spacers to the body, positioning them according to the measurements on the drawing on p. 11.

3. When the glue has dried, locate and mark the center of the axle hole.

4. Drill the hole.

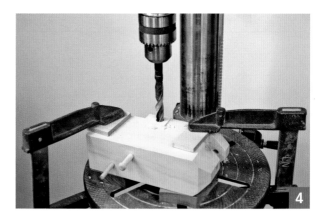

Cab

To assemble the cab, you first attach the cab base to the top of the body, then glue the cab sides in place, followed by the roof and the back. The sizes are not critical; you could vary the length or width a little. However, a contrasting wood enhances the toy's appearance.

Cab Base

1. Lay out the base and cut it to shape. It's a good idea to cut the cab back out now, too, because it is the same width as the base.

2. Sand as needed. Bevel the corners that are not covered by the sides.

3. Glue the base to the body. I think it looks best if the front of the base is about 3/4 in. from the front of the body.

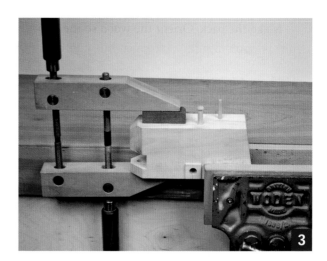

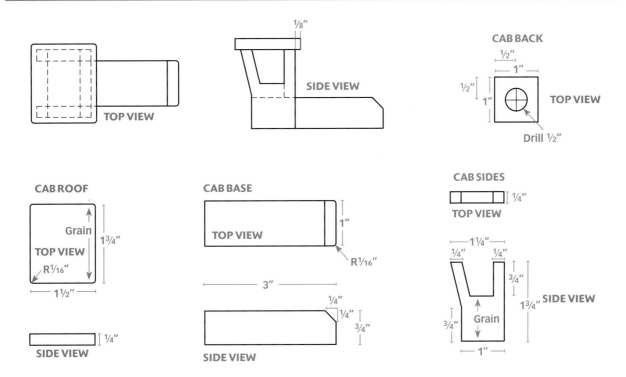

1/8"

SIDE VIEW

CAB BACK

1/2"
1"

1/2" | 1"

TOP VIEW

Drill 1/2"

CAB ROOF

Grain

TOP VIEW

R1/16"

1 3/4"

1 1/2"

SIDE VIEW

1/4"

CAB BASE

TOP VIEW

1"

R1/16"

3"

1/4"
1/4"
3/4"

SIDE VIEW

CAB SIDES

1/4"

TOP VIEW

1 1/4"

1/4" | 1/4"

3/4"

3/4" | Grain

1 3/4" **SIDE VIEW**

1"

Cab Sides and Back

The sides should have the grain running vertically to strengthen the window posts.

1. Lay out the sides on ¼-in. wood. To be sure they are identical, lay out one side, then attach the two pieces with double-sided tape and cut both pieces at once.

2. Saw to shape at the bandsaw, and then file and sand all surfaces.

3. Make the back. Orient the wood so the grain runs horizontally for a stronger glue joint. Drill the

window hole first, then cut the piece to size. Make the width a hair oversized.

4. Glue the sides to the cab base. Have all the surfaces flush at the front. Glue the cab back in place at the same time. When the glue has dried, sand the back flush with the sides.

5. Glue a piece of sandpaper to a small flat board and use that to hand-sand the cab top flat, ready for the roof. You can do this with a disk sander if you are very careful. Don't remove any more wood than you need to.

Roof

The roof is just a rectangle of ¼-in. wood attached to the top of the cab.

1. Cut the roof to size. It should overhang the cab by about ⅛ in. all around. Sand and bevel all sharp corners.

2. Apply glue to the top of the cab, then attach the roof. Use a weight to act as a clamp, or gently clamp the roof in place.

Bumper

The bumper consists of the bumper mount and the bumper itself (see the drawing on p. 11). Glue them together, and then attach the assembly to the loader.

1. Cut the two pieces of ½-in. wood. Sand all surfaces, except where the two pieces join.

2. Glue the two pieces together, then bevel or round off all sharp corners.

3. Glue the assembly to the underside of the loader, leaving about ¼ in. between the bumper and the back of the loader.

Ladders

The ladders take a little time to make and are a bit tricky to assemble, but they help to give a sense of the scale of this huge loader. I have found that the best way to make these identical components is to rough-cut the ladder sides about 1 in. too long and tack them together. Once you have drilled the holes for the rungs in all the sides at once, you cut them to length.

The ladders are glued to the sides of the loader, and the rear fenders butt against them as reinforcement.

1. Cut four pieces of ⅛-in. plywood to about 5½ in. long.

2. Put small dots of glue at the very ends and clamp all four sides together.

3. Lay out and drill the holes for the rungs. Check on a piece of scrap wood to find a bit that fits your ⅛-in. dowel (it may be 9⁄64 in.).

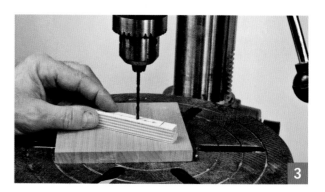

Ladders

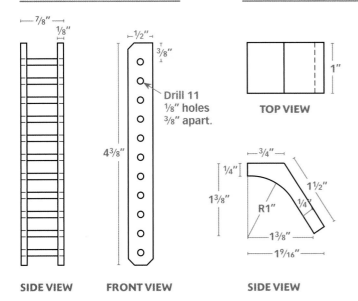

— 7/8" —
1/8"

— 1/2" —
3/8"

Drill 11
1/8" holes
3/8" apart.

4 3/8"

SIDE VIEW   FRONT VIEW

Front Fenders

1"

TOP VIEW

— 3/4" —

1/4"

1 1/2"

1 3/8"   1/4"

R1"

1 3/8"

1 9/16"

SIDE VIEW

Rear Fenders

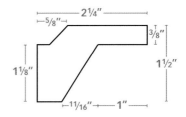

1"

TOP VIEW

— 2 1/4" —
— 5/8" —

3/8"

1 1/8"   1 1/2"

— 11/16" — 1" —

SIDE VIEW

TIP

The technique for cutting and drilling the ladder sides will also work for other parts of the toy. In fact, any time you need two or more identical small parts, consider stacking the blanks and shaping all of them at once. Use drops of glue or double-sided tape to hold the pieces together.

4. Sand all the edges even.

5. Mark the edges so you will know which ends are up and which sides will face each other on each ladder.

6. Cut the sides to their final 4 3/8-in. length.

7. Cut 22 pieces of 1/8-in. dowel, making them about 1 in. long, which is 1/8 in. more than their finished length. You'll sand off the excess after assembly.

8. Dry-fit the ladders. Slide all the rungs into one side piece, then slip on the other side. Start at one end and work your way to the other end, fitting the rungs in the holes as you go. This can be difficult if the dowels are a little tight, but it is manageable.

9. Disassemble the ladders. Use a toothpick to put glue in the holes on one of the sides and install the

dowels. Have them protrude about 1/16 in. Apply glue to the holes in the second side and press it in place. Make sure the alignment marks face each other correctly.

Try to get the sides parallel and straight. I rest one ladder side on top of a vise that is opened about 1/4 in., then tap very gently with a small mallet until the sides are parallel. Get them within 1/32 in. or, better yet, within 1/64 in. You can also squeeze the sides together with a digital caliper, which reads the size as it gently presses the sides to the correct spacing (see inset photo above).

10. When the glue has dried, sand away the excess dowel. Sand the edges flat so that the ladder will make good contact with the side of the loader body. You can do this with a sheet of sandpaper glued to a flat backing board. Or, if you are brave, on a stationary belt sander with a fine-grit belt.

11. I glue the ladders in place when I attach the fenders. It seems a bit easier to align everything that way. So, on to the fenders.

Fenders

The rear fenders fit on the side of the loader and up against the ladder. Make the front fenders now, too, following the same procedures and using the same wood.

1. Lay out the fenders on 1-in.-thick wood. If you don't have wood that thick, you can use ¾-in. or ⅞-in. material instead.

2. Cut the pieces to shape and sand as needed. Use the disk sander to get a good flat surface on the rear fenders, where they contact the ladder. Check this fit and adjust as needed. Ideally, it is a 90-degree corner, but you never know.

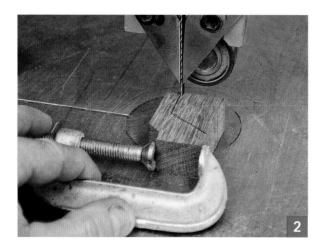

3. Sand to remove all sharp corners.

4. Set the front fenders aside. I install them when the loader nears completion.

5. Check the position of the rear fenders by temporarily installing the wheels. There should be about ½ in. between the top of the body and the top of the fenders.

6. Glue one ladder and one rear fender to the loader. Put a small amount of glue along the edges of the ladder and press it gently into place. Check that the ladder is square to the body, moving it as needed. The top of the ladder should be even with the top of the body.

Glue the fender to the body and the side of the ladder. Make sure there is about ¼ in. of space between the fender and the wheel.

Clamping these pieces is fine, but it's a bit tricky to keep everything straight. I have had no problem without clamps, provided the parts fit tight.

7. When the glue has dried, attach the other ladder and fender.

Plastic Washers

You don't really need the washers if it bothers you to have a nonwood component. However, the washers make the larger moving parts work more smoothly and reduce wear, so I use them with these large wheels. You can place the washers between the body and the wheels, between the wheels and the hubs, and in the articulation joint. I make the washers from the lid of a plastic container, like a coffee can.

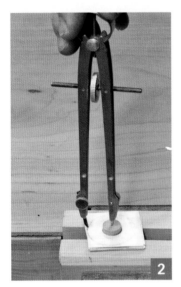

Front Frame

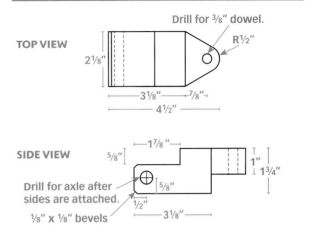

TOP VIEW

Drill for ⅜″ dowel.

R½″

2⅛″

3⅛″ — ⅞″

4½″

SIDE VIEW

1⅞″

⅝″

1″

1¾″

Drill for axle after sides are attached.

⅝″

½″

⅛″ x ⅛″ bevels

3⅛″

Front Uprights

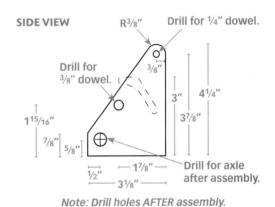

SIDE VIEW

R⅜″

Drill for ¼″ dowel.

Drill for ⅜″ dowel.

⅜″

3″

4¼″

3⅞″

1¹⁵⁄₁₆″

⅞″

⅝″

Drill for axle after assembly.

½″

1⅞″

3⅛″

Note: Drill holes AFTER assembly.

1. Cut 10 squares of plastic about ½ in. larger than the finished washer. Stack them and clamp them between two pieces of wood. Drill the appropriate hole size through the assembly (about ⁹⁄₁₆ in. for the axle washers and ⁷⁄₁₆ in. for the articulation pin) in the approximate center of the plastic stack.

2. Take apart the stack and cut the washers to the desired shape and size. Put the washer over a scrap axle dowel that you've clamped in a vise. Draw a circle on the washer so you can trim it neatly. Round washers are great, but hexagonal or octagonal ones are fine too. The toy looks best if the washers are small enough to be inconspicuous.

Front Frame

This is the core of the front section of the loader. You glue ¼-in.-thick uprights to this frame, and then mount the bucket arms to the uprights. A hole drilled in the back part of this frame holds the pivot pin that allows the loader to steer (see Front Frame drawing above).

1. Cut the frame block from 1¾-in.-thick wood. Laminate pieces if you need to.

2. Lay out the side and top profiles. The 1-in.-thick section (with the ⅜-in. hole) should fit into the 1-in. slot in the body to form the articulation joint. I install plastic washers to make this joint smoother and more durable. If you plan to do the same, factor the washers' thickness into your measurements.

3. Drill the hole to fit a ⅜-in. dowel, and make it about 1¼ in. deep. The frame will pivot on this dowel, so you don't want it to be a tight fit. If the dowel is a bit oversize, use a ²⁵⁄₆₄-in. drill.

4. Saw the side profile, then the top profile.

5. Sand as needed. Keep the sides as flat and parallel as possible, because the front uprights will be attached here.

Front Uprights

1. Lay out the uprights on ¼-in.-thick wood. I used solid wood for these parts, but Baltic birch plywood is also fine. Mark centers for the three holes on one upright, but drill the holes after assembly.

2. Cut the uprights to size on the bandsaw.

3. Sand to break all sharp edges.

4. Glue the uprights to the front frame. Have the front of the uprights even with the front of the frame, or even protruding a little.

5. Drill the three holes. The dowels should slide into these holes with a minimum of tapping and pushing, so you may need to drill oversize. To find out, make test holes on some scrap before you drill through the uprights. (Drilling the ¼-in. hole as shown in the photo may produce some tearout, but the bucket arms will hide it. If you want to make the toy as neat as can be, put masking tape over the inside edges of the uprights or drill through a scrap block placed between the two uprights.)

Bucket Arms

Don't cut the arms to their finished shape right away. Leave extra wood in the area where the holes go (see the phantom dashed line on the template), then trim the arms after drilling those holes. The arm assembly holds the bucket at one end and mounts to the uprights at the other end. Use the same general method as you did on the ladder sides to make both arms at the same time. I think Baltic birch plywood is the best material for these parts.

1. Use the template to lay out the shape on one piece of ¼-in. plywood. I scribbled on the back of the template with a carpenter's pencil to transform the template into carbon paper, lined up the dashed straight line on the template with a straightedge on the plywood, and traced the outline.

Use an awl to mark the centers of all the holes. The last hole on the right is optional, used only if you want extra-high lift on the bucket. If you want that, you will have to modify the lift mechanism as well. I ended up drilling the hole anyway, because it

Bucket Arms

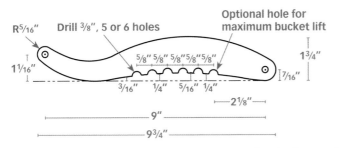

R⁵/₁₆" Drill ³/₈", 5 or 6 holes

Optional hole for maximum bucket lift

1¹/₁₆"

5/8" 5/8" 5/8" 5/8" 5/8"

1³/₄"

7/₁₆"

3/₁₆" 1/₄" 5/₁₆" 1/₄"

2¹/₈"

9"

9³/₄"

Note: A template is also provided at the end of the chapter

Bucket Arm Spacers

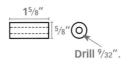

1⁵/₈"

5/8"

Drill ⁹/₃₂".

Lift Assembly

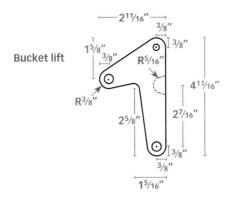

2¹¹/₁₆"

3/₈"

3/₈"

Bucket lift

1⁵/₈"

3/₈"

R⁵/₁₆"

R³/₈"

4¹¹/₁₆"

2⁷/₁₆"

2⁵/₈"

3/₈"

3/₈"

1⁵/₁₆"

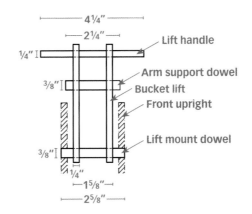

4¹/₄"

2¹/₄"

1/₄"

Lift handle

3/₈"

Arm support dowel

Bucket lift

Front upright

Lift mount dowel

3/₈"

1/₄"

1⁵/₈"

2⁵/₈"

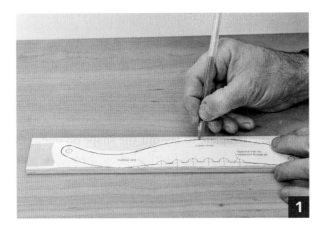

1

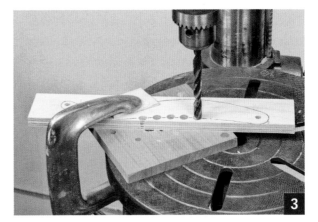

3

is hard to do later, but I don't really plan for the extra high lift.

2. Attach the two blanks for the bucket arms with a dab of glue at each end, as you did with the ladder sides.

3. Drill the holes. The ³/₈-in. holes are exact size. The end holes need to fit a ¼-in. dowel, and may need to be slightly oversize.

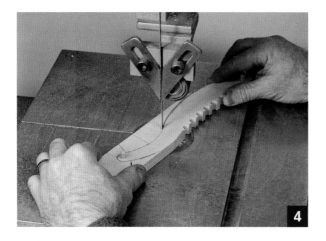

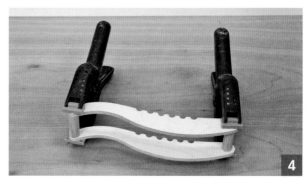

4. Cut the final contour with the arms still together. Saw through the ³⁄₈-in. holes to make the notches for the bucket lift.

5. Pin the arms together with short pieces of ¼-in. dowel in the end holes. File and sand the edges.

6. Separate the arms and sand all the sharp corners. Later, when assembling the bucket and arms, you will shape the notches to ensure that the mechanism works properly.

Bucket Arm Spacers

These spacers go between the bucket arms at the ends to keep the arms spaced correctly. You glue them to the arms to make the assembly a little more rigid.

1. Cut the spacers from ⁵⁄₈-in. dowel, making sure the ends are square. Determine the length by measuring the distance between the outside edges of the front uprights and adding ¹⁄₁₆ in.

2. Drill through the center of the spacers with a ¹⁷⁄₆₄-in. or ⁹⁄₃₂-in. bit. This will allow the ¼-in. arm dowels to slide through easily.

3. To glue the spacers to the arms, cut some ¼-in. dowel to use to align the holes.

4. Assemble the parts dry first. Align the arms and spacers, using the ¼-in. dowel. Separate the pieces and add glue sparingly to the ends of the spacers. Clamp the pieces gently, or hold them tight by hand while you slip out the locating dowels. Place clamps directly over the spacers.

Bucket Lift

This assembly pivots on the middle hole of the front uprights. The top hole holds a ¼-in. dowel for the handle. The lift mount and arm support holes hold ³⁄₈-in. dowels. The arm support dowel rests in the notches on the arms. This allows the operator to drive around with the bucket off the ground. Make the bucket lift assembly the same way you did the arms and the uprights.

1. Cut two Baltic birch plywood blanks. Lay out the bucket lift shape on one blank and attach it to the second with dabs of glue on areas that will be trimmed off later.

2. Drill the holes and saw the blanks to shape.

3. Pin the parts together with short pieces of dowel so you can file and sand the edges.

4. Glue the arm support dowel in place, but leave out the other two dowels for now. Have the long edges sitting flat so you can align them easily. Make a spacer 1 in. thick to fit between the lift sides to keep them parallel, and then check the spacing by sliding the lift assembly between the bucket arms. The photo shows a couple of walnut dowels keeping the other holes aligned while I glue in the arm support dowel.

5. Cut the lift mount dowel, which holds the lift to the front uprights. Make it 2¾ in. long, or about ⅛ in. longer than its finished size.

6. Slide the lift mount dowel into place, but don't glue it yet. The lift assembly pivots on this dowel.

7. Cut the bucket arm dowel and the bucket pivot dowel. Make them about 1/16 in. overlong; you'll trim them after installation. Use one right now to mount the bucket arms to the front uprights. Set the other dowel aside; you'll use it later to mount the bucket to the arm.

8. Slide the bucket arm dowel into place, pinning the bucket arms to the uprights so they can pivot.

9. Cut the dowel lift handle and slide it into place.

10. Check that the mechanism works. Does the arm support dowel catch on the half-holes? (At this point only one dowel is glued; the others are still floating in position just to check out the mechanism.) These notches will need to be rounded a little to make the bucket easier to lift. I also like to sand a little off the contour curve so that a little less than half of each hole remains (see the inset photo at right).

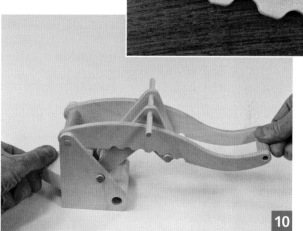

Round the corners just enough so that if you pull on the lift the bucket arms rise without jamming; if you lower the lift, the arm support dowel should come free of the arms, allowing the arms to drop. However, if you press on the bucket to simulate a load, the arms should remain locked in position.

11. When the mechanism works, glue the dowels in place into the uprights. Here's what I do to keep glue from being smeared along the dowel: Put glue in the two holes on one upright only. Slide the dowels in through the unglued holes, but stop with about ¼ in. to go. Put glue on this last ¼ in., and then tap in the dowels. This keeps glue on each end, but none in the middle.

12. Install the handle, but don't use any glue until it has only about ¼ in. to go to be in position. Then put glue on the dowel in two places near the lift sides, on the outside of one lift side and on the inside of the other lift, and tap it in the last ¼ in.

Make sure there is clearance (1/32 in. to 1/16 in.) between lifter and arms, so the parts can move freely. Check this before the glue hardens; if the parts bind you will need to remake the part. Here, the fit is better too loose than too tight.

13. When the glue has dried, sand the dowels flush with the uprights.

Bucket

The bucket is made up of five main parts: the two sides, the back, the bottom, and the top. Start with the back, cut the angles on the edges, glue on the top and bottom, and finish with the sides. Use solid wood for all these parts. There is a certain amount of sanding and planing needed to get all the edges even, and you would likely end up removing the veneer if you used plywood.

Bucket Back

1. Cut the back slightly oversize and trim it later. If you are using a tablesaw, cut the 15-degree angles before trimming the piece to length. The tablesaw cuts will be easier and safer if the wood is about 12 in. long. Or, if you plane the angles by hand, it will be easier to do that if the wood is extra-long.

2. If you aren't using a tablesaw, lay out the angles with a protractor or trace them from the template at the end of the chapter. Plane the angles. Check that the final edges are parallel and the angles are as close as possible to 75 degrees.

3. Cut the bucket back to length, then sand the wide surface that will be on the inside of the bucket.

Bucket Bottom and Top

1. Cut the two parts about 1/16 in. over their finished length and width.

Bucket Assembly

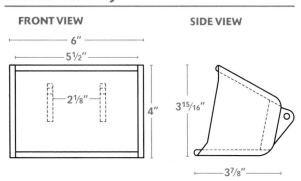

Bucket Top and Bottom

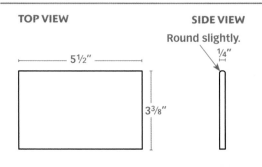

Bucket Back

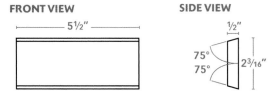

Bucket Mounts

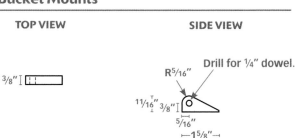

2. Round one edge of each part. These edges will form the front edges of the bucket. The amount of rounding is not critical.

3. Sand the faces. Don't worry about the ends or back edges; you'll sand them after assembly.

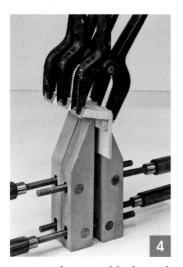

4. Glue either the top or bottom to the bucket back. This is tricky to clamp, but it can be done. I clamped a block of scrap to the top/bottom part to keep the back from sliding forward when clamped and to keep the parts square. The scrap block needs to be removed soon after clamping, in case some excess glue has squeezed out and sticks to it. Or you could plane a small bevel on the offending corner of the block to provide a little clearance channel for the squeezed-out glue.

TIP

Resist the temptation to nail the bucket bottom to the back. The nail heads will create problems when you try to sand and round over that joint.

5. Glue the other top/bottom part in place, again using the scrap block. When the glue has dried, sand the bucket ends even and flat so you can attach the sides.

Bucket Sides

Cut these pieces a fair bit oversize, in case the angles on the bucket so far do not exactly match the drawing. Trim the edges after you glue on the sides.

1. Lay out the sides using the template on p. 27. Place the bucket assembly onto the layout to be sure it will fit. If need be, trace around the bucket assembly and add about $\frac{1}{16}$ in. all around.

2. Saw the pieces on a bandsaw, leaving $\frac{1}{16}$ in. to $\frac{1}{8}$ in. extra on the top, bottom, and back. Cut the front edges close to the line. File and sand those front edges now.

3. Finish-sand both faces, especially the surface that will be the inside of the bucket.

4. Glue the sides to the bucket assembly.

5. When the glue has dried, sand around the bucket sides to make them flush with the rest of the bucket. I do most of this with a disk sander and belt sander, but I do the final sanding by hand. Finally, plane and sand the rounded corners and finish-sand the whole bucket.

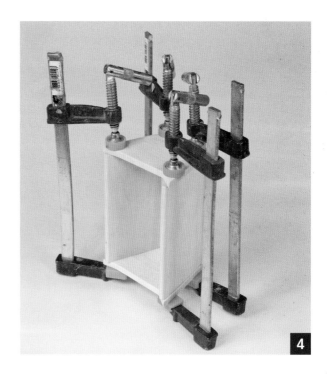

Bucket Mounts

The mounts are attached to the bottom of the bucket, and a pivot dowel pins the bucket assembly to the ends of the bucket arms.

1. Lay out the mounts on ⅜-in.-thick wood, but don't cut them out yet.

2. Drill the holes before cutting, while the parts are still easily clamped to the drill press table.

3. Saw the pieces to shape, leaving them ¹⁄₃₂ in. to ¹⁄₁₆ in. oversize all around.

4. Pin the mounts together with a short dowel.

5. Sand the mounts to exact shape. It's most important to keep the ⅜-in. distance from hole center to bottom from going undersize; otherwise, the bucket may rub on the bucket arms when it tries to pivot.

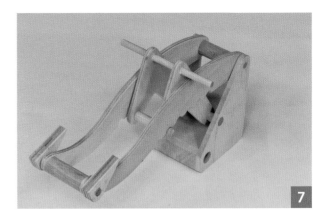

6. Cut the bucket dowel, making it ⅛ in. overlong. Slide it into the end of the bucket arms but don't glue it yet.

7. Put glue in the holes in each bucket mount, and then slip them over the ends of the dowel. Make sure you align the flats on the mounts by pressing them onto a flat surface.

8. When the glue has dried, sand away the excess dowel. It is okay if the mounts are a bit stiff when they pivot on the dowel.

9. Put glue on the flat edges of the mounts and press the bucket into place, centering it carefully. Use a combination square to make sure the bucket is perpendicular to the loader arms. Check that the bucket is facing the correct way, with the bottom of the bucket farthest away from the loader arm. Clamp gently, or use a weight to press the mounts against the bucket.

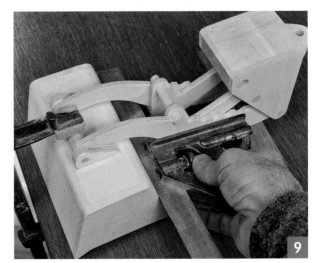

Major Assembly

The end is near. You're ready to assemble the remaining parts. You will pin the front assembly to the loader body, creating the articulation joint, and add the front fenders. After that, you may want to apply the finish before the wheels go on, although you could put the wheels on first if you wanted.

1. Test the fit of the articulation joint, using a plastic washer on each side of the front frame. Use a piece of ⅜-in. dowel 5 in. to 6 in. long to check the pivot action. (The long dowel is easy to remove.) If need be, file and sand the projection on the front frame to get a good fit into the slot in the loader body. If the joint is too loose, add a washer.

2. When it all fits nicely, remove the long dowel and put paste wax into the pivot hole in the front frame, using a cotton swab.

3. Install the dowel for the articulation joint. Mark the length and cut it about ¹⁄₁₆ in. too long. Sand the ends and bevel them slightly.

4. Put glue in the upper part of the hole in the body. Don't put any below the notch, or glue will be dragged into the hole in the front frame, seizing up the joint.

5. Tap in the dowel until there is only about ½ in. to go. Put glue on this ½ in., and then tap the dowel in until only ¹⁄₁₆ in. protrudes.

6. When the glue has dried, file and sand this dowel flush if you wish. However, there's no harm in leaving this dowel slightly long.

7. Glue the front fenders in place, positioning them so the 4-in. wheels have about ¼ in. of clearance. Check this as you did with the rear wheels, using a wheel temporarily in place.

Finish

Finish as desired. See the section on finishing (p. 3) for some options. It is a little easier to finish the wheels separately from the rest of the loader, especially if you are using a spray finish. When spraying the loader, put scrap dowel or small pieces of cloth in the axle holes to keep out stray finish.

Wheel and Axle Assembly

The wheels turn freely on the axle dowels, and the dowels can spin in the body and frame as well. "Hubs" made from small treaded wheels cap the ends of the axle dowels. This makes for a very robust wheel mechanism.

1. For the hubs, I use 1-in.-diameter factory-made wheels. They come with a ½-in. counterbore, which is very easily and accurately drilled out to fit the axle dowel. Install these with the flat side out and they look better than other hubs I have tried.

You can also use slices of 1-in. dowel, or rounds cut out with a 1-in. or 1¼-in. hole saw, or rounded factory-made dowel caps.

5. Round the ends of the dowels or bevel them to make them look a bit better. Sand the ends smooth and then brush or spray some finish on them. During assembly, some glue will get on the ends of the dowel; the finish makes it much easier to remove excess glue.

6. Temporarily assemble the wheels and plastic washers onto the dowel and into the loader body. Mark where the hubs will go by drawing a small line where the dowel protrudes from the wheel. Also, check that all the wheels turn when on a flat surface. If one wheel is not touching, drill the axle hole in all four wheels a little larger. Better that the wheels are looser than tighter.

2. Whatever hub material you choose, drill out the centers to fit snugly on the axle dowel.

3. If you decide to do so, drill the small holes on the hubs to simulate a bolt circle (see the Optional Hub Design drawing on p. 7). Use the template on the facing page to lay out the holes. Make them about $3/32$ in. diameter by $1/16$ in. deep.

7. Glue one hub to each axle dowel. I generally rub some paraffin on the dowel, except where glue will be applied for the hubs.

8. When these glue joints are dry, install the axles, wheels, and washers, and then glue the other two hubs in place. Make sure the wheels spin freely, a bit loose if anything. I use a small wrench-shaped spacer made of plastic, cut from the same container lid that I used to make the washers (see the top left photo on the facing page). If I don't use the spacer in place between wheel and frame, occasionally I tap a snug-fitting hub into place a bit too tightly and the wheels refuse to turn freely even with washers in place. At this point it is very difficult to remove that hub, short of drilling it out. After assembly, remove the spacer wrench and the wheels will spin easily.

The smaller spacer is for $3/8$-in. axles, and the larger one is for $1/2$-in. axles. Exact sizes are not important.

TIP

If you expect to make a fair number of hubs, drill the holes in a steel washer that has a $1/2$-in. hole and use it as a jig to guide the drill bit. It makes the process much faster.

4. Cut the axle dowel to length. It should be long enough to go through the loader, two wheels, two hubs, and the plastic washers, and protrude past the hubs by $1/16$ in. to $1/8$ in. on each side. I put a washer between the body and the wheels, and sometimes between the wheel and the hub, too.

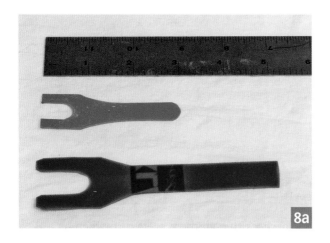

8a

8b

Templates

For full-size template, enlarge by 162%.

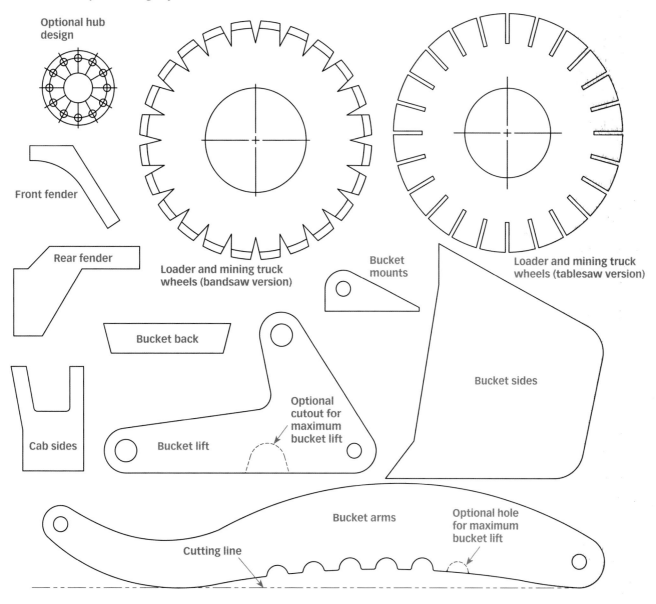

Optional hub design

Front fender

Rear fender

Cab sides

Loader and mining truck wheels (bandsaw version)

Bucket back

Bucket lift

Optional cutout for maximum bucket lift

Bucket mounts

Loader and mining truck wheels (tablesaw version)

Bucket sides

Bucket arms

Optional hole for maximum bucket lift

Cutting line

CHAPTER 2

Mining Dump Truck

i f you have ever walked up close to one of these giant trucks, no doubt you were impressed. I know I was when our family had a chance to walk around "The World's Largest" truck, which is powered by a locomotive engine. These gargantuan vehicles are fascinating to young and old.

The Mining Dump Truck is relatively simple to build, although it can be tricky to get the dump box assembled and squared up. The wheels will take a little time, too, but they are not difficult to make. You laminate three blocks of wood to make up the substantial frame, then perch the cab on top and attach the large dump box to a hinge on the back. The truck rolls on six large wheels, the same ones used on the Giant Loader.

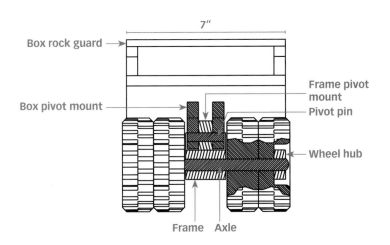

Back View

Side View

Box side

Box front

Compressed-air tank

Power-steering oil tank

Box rock guard

Cab

3/4"

Deck

Air intake

Fender

Ladder

Bumper

Box bottom

Box pivot mount

Fuel and oil side tank

Frame

Wheel hub

Axle

Frame pivot mount

Front View

Compressed-air tank

Power-steering oil tank

Cab

Box rock guard

Deck

Air intake

1 1/8"

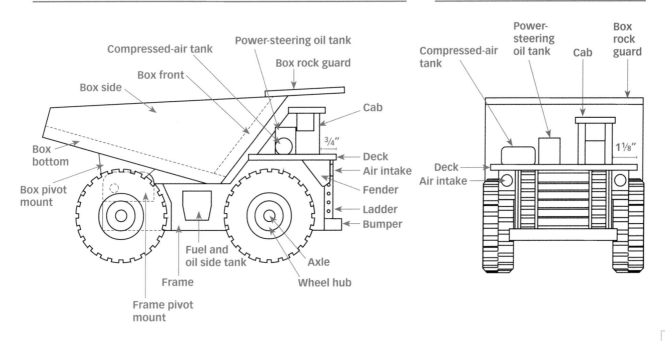

PART NAME	FINISH DIMENSIONS L × W × T, IN.	NO. REQ'D.	NOTES
Wheels	4 dia. × ¾ thick per half	6	Need 12 halves to make 6 wheels.
Frame	9¾ × 3 × 1¾	1	
Frame sides	7⅛ × 3 × 1¼	2	
Deck	6½ × 3⅞ × ¼	1	Solid wood or Baltic birch plywood
Cab base	2½ × 1¾ × 1	1	Contrasting wood
Cab sides	2½ × 1¾ × ¼	2	Contrasting wood or Baltic birch plywood
Cab roof	1¾ × 1⅝ × ¼	1	Contrasting wood; note grain direction
Grill	2¼ × 2¼ × ¼	1	Contrasting wood
Bumper	4¾ × ¾ × ½	1	Contrasting wood
Fenders	1¼ × 1⅛ × ¾	2	Contrasting wood
Air intakes	½ dowel × ⅜ long	2	
Compressed-air tank	¾ dowel × 1½ long	1	
Power-steering oil tank	1⅛ × 1 × ¾	1	
Box sides	10 × 4½ × ⅜	2	
Box bottom	8¼ × 6¼ × ½	1	
Box front	6¼ × 4⅝ × ½	1	
Box rock guard	7 × 3½ × ¼	1	
Box pivot mounts	2⅝ × 1¾ × ½	2	
Frame pivot mount	2¼ × 1¼ × ⅝	1	
Box pivot dowel	⅜ dowel × 1⅝ long	1	Cut overlong, trim after installation.
Fuel and oil side tanks	1¼ × 1¼ × ½	2	Contrasting wood
Ladder sides	2½ × ⅜ × ⅛	4	Baltic birch plywood
Ladder rungs	⅛ dowel × ⅞ long	14	Cut overlong, trim after installation.
Wheel hubs	1 dia. wheel, factory made	4	
Plastic washers	To fit	2–10	Optional (see Chapter 1); use for wheels.
Front axle	½ dowel × 7 long	1	Cut to fit truck.
Rear axle	½ dowel × 7¼ long	1	Cut to fit truck.

Wheels

Follow the drawings and instructions in Chapter 1, p. 7, to make the wheels. The wheel hubs are also identical to those on the Giant Loader. You can make them from store-bought wheels or cut your own. See Chapter 1, p. 25, for the details.

Set the wheels and hubs aside until it is time to assemble the truck.

Frame and Frame Sides

The frame is the block of wood that forms the core of the truck. You glue the frame sides to this core to widen the front section while leaving the back narrow for the big dual wheels. You attach the wheels, dump box, and other parts to the finished frame.

1. If you don't have wood that is 1¾ in. thick, laminate pieces. When the glue has dried, square up the block and plane or sand it to the proper thickness.

2. Lay out the side contour and cut it on the bandsaw.

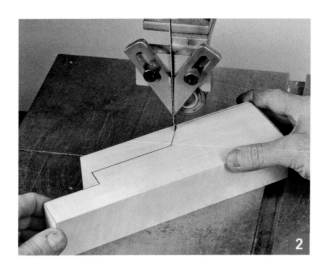

Frame

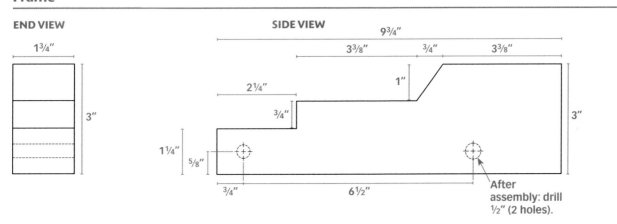

Frame Sides

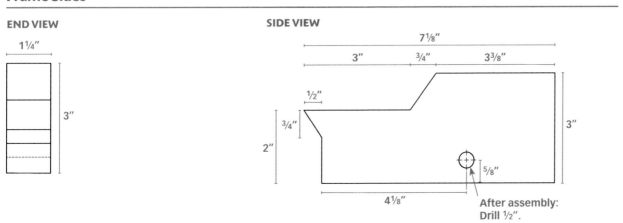

3. Lay out the frame sides on pieces of 1¼-in. stock and cut them on the bandsaw. File and sand the back end of the sides now, as that will be hard to do after you assemble the parts.

4. If you want to reduce the toy's weight, drill out the thick frame piece. I used a 1¾-in. Forstner bit on the end hole, then a series of 1½-in.-diameter, slightly overlapping holes. If you do this, mark the location of the axle holes and trace the outline of the frame side on the frame, so you don't inadvertently drill in the wrong places.

5. Glue the frame sides to the frame.

6. File and sand all the surfaces smooth. Take care to make the front quite flat, where the grill will be attached. I sand the front on a disk sander, making sure the table is exactly square to the disk.

7. Mark the centers for the two axle holes. The centers of the two holes should be ⅝ in. up from the bottom.

8. Drill the ½-in.-diameter axle holes. The axle dowel will need to fit into this hole and can be a little loose. If necessary, you can enlarge the hole a little with a ³³⁄₆₄-in. or ¹⁷⁄₃₂-in. drill bit, or you can sand the dowel down slightly.

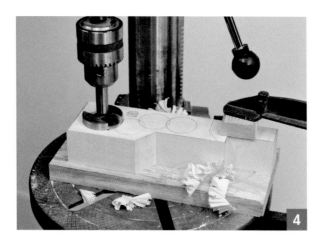

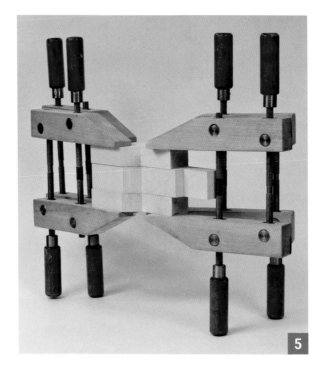

TIP

Using the right drill bits can make a difference. For very large holes, I use Forstner bits instead of hole saws, because the Forstners leave very smooth-sided holes. For smaller holes, I prefer brad-point bits because they are easier to center on the hole locations.

Deck

This piece is a small rectangular board that sits on the frame. I tend to use a wood that contrasts with the frame, but that is entirely up to you. Later, you will attach the cab to the deck.

1. Cut the deck to size, sand it smooth, and bevel all sharp corners.

2. Glue the deck to the frame. It should project ⅜ in. past the front of the frame and be centered from side to side. The fit at the back is not critical.

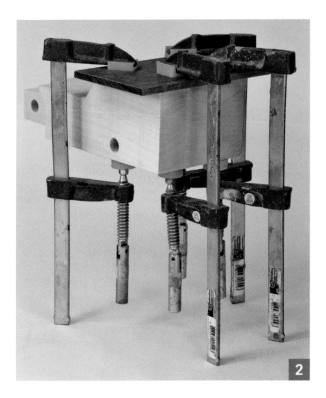

Cab

The cab has four main parts: the base, the roof, and two sides. The base also provides the angled back surface. You attach the sides to the base and set the roof on top. Then you attach the completed cab to the deck. The size of the cab is not critical; you can vary the length or width if you like.

Cab Base

1. Outline the cab base on a block of 1-in.-thick wood. In a pinch, ¾-in.-thick wood will work.

Cab Assembly

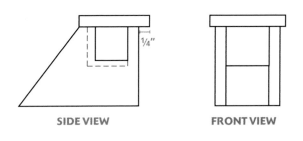

SIDE VIEW   FRONT VIEW

Cab Base

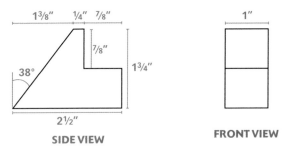

SIDE VIEW   FRONT VIEW

Cab Sides

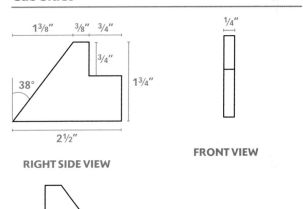

RIGHT SIDE VIEW   FRONT VIEW

LEFT SIDE VIEW

Cab Roof

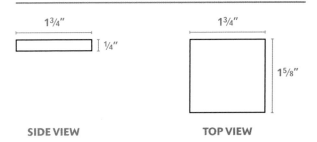

SIDE VIEW   TOP VIEW

2. Saw to the lines, and then file and sand. However, leave the bottom unsanded and as flat as possible.

Cab Sides

1. Use dabs of glue or double-sided tape to stick two pieces of ¼-in.-thick wood together. Lay out the sides on these blanks, making sure that the grain runs vertically for the strength of the window posts. This means you will glue to end grain when the roof goes on, but it will be strong enough for a nonstructural joint. Baltic birch plywood is also a good material for the sides.

2. Saw the sides to shape at the bandsaw, and then file and sand all surfaces.

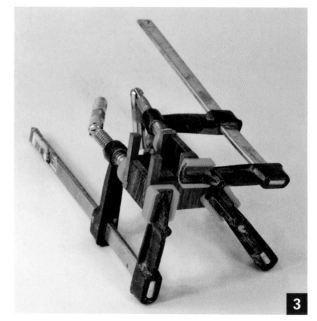

3. Glue the cab sides to the cab base. Make sure that all the surfaces are flush on the front and bottom.

4. Sand the top and bottom lightly and carefully to get them exactly flat. The best way is to glue a piece of sandpaper to a small flat piece of plywood or medium-density fiberboard (MDF) and use that. Don't remove any more wood than you need to.

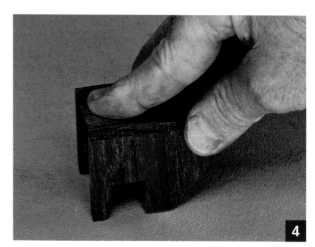

Cab Roof and Attachment

1. Cut the roof piece to size. It should overhang the cab by about ¼ in. front and back, and ⅛ in. on the sides.

2. Sand and bevel all sharp corners.

3. Put a drop of glue on the top of each cab window post and along the top back edge of the base. Attach the roof and gently clamp it in place.

4. Glue the assembled cab to the deck. Use the position shown in the drawing on p. 29 as a starting point; the exact location is not critical. Position the cab where you think it looks best.

Grill

The grill is a thin square slab of wood with a few decorative grooves (see the drawing on p. 37). I used purpleheart for the grill, as I did for the deck.

1. Cut the grill to size. There are several rectangular shapes close together at the front of the truck, so keep the corners square or they will looked skewed when assembled. Sand the piece as needed.

2. Mark the position of the grooves. I spaced them ⅜ in. apart, but that is not a critical measurement.

3. To cut the grooves, I attached the grill to a squared-up block of scrap wood with double-sided tape, which makes it easier and safer to cut. I cut a kerf in another piece of scrap and clamped it to the bandsaw table as a stop block. I just push the grill into the blade until it touches the stop block, making all the grooves the same depth.

4. Glue the grill to the frame. The top of the grill should be ⅛ in. below the deck overhang; a ⅛-in.

spacer is handy here, as you can see in the photo. Center the grill side to side.

Bumper

1. Cut the bumper to size (see the drawing on p. 37). This is another piece that can be made from a contrasting wood, if you like.

2. Sand as needed, removing all sharp corners.

3. Glue the bumper to the front of the frame, ⅛ in. from the bottom of the grill. Be sure the overhang is equal on each end.

Fenders

These triangular pieces (see the drawing on the facing page) provide some protection to the front of the wheel; they also provide a location for the air intakes (they look somewhat like headlights) that you will install next.

1. Use a piece of ¾-in.-thick wood that's about 3 in. wide and at least 3 in. long; that's large enough to fit the two fenders with enough extra to clamp and hold.

2. Outline the shape of the fenders on opposite sides of the blank. On the edges, locate the centers for the holes for the air intakes.

3. Drill the holes for the ½-in. dowel that represents the air intakes. Drill only ¼ in. deep.

4. Cut out the fenders on the bandsaw. Sand as needed. Bevel the outside corners but not the corners that will be glued against the frame sides.

TIP

Wrap a piece of blue painter's tape around the drill bit to mark the depth of the hole. When the tape touches the wood, you know it's time to stop drilling.

Air Intakes

1. Make sure the dowel for the air intake fits in the holes in the fender without having to force it.

2. Mark the length of the dowel for the air intakes but don't cut to length yet. Sand and bevel the end while the dowel is longer and easier to hold, and then cut to length.

3. Put a little glue in the holes and install the air intakes into the fenders.

4. Glue the assemblies in place so that the front of the fender is about ⅛ in. proud of the front of the frame.

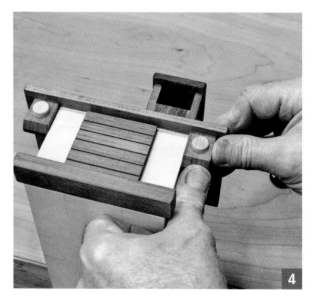

Deck

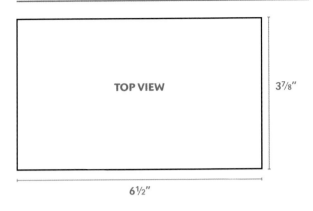

TOP VIEW

3⅞"

6½"

FRONT VIEW

¼"

Grill

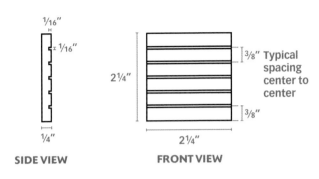

1/16"

1/16"

¼"

SIDE VIEW

2¼"

⅜" Typical spacing center to center

⅜"

2¼"

FRONT VIEW

Front Bumper

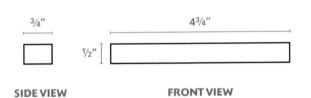

¾"

4¾"

½"

SIDE VIEW

FRONT VIEW

Fenders/Air Intakes

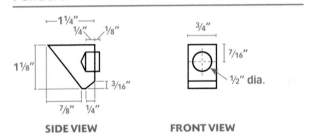

1¼"

¼"

⅛"

1⅛"

3/16"

⅞"

¼"

SIDE VIEW

¾"

7/16"

½" dia.

FRONT VIEW

Ladders

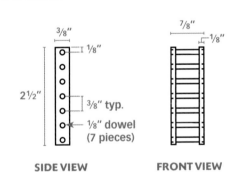

⅜"

⅛"

2½"

⅜" typ.

⅛" dowel
(7 pieces)

SIDE VIEW

⅞"

⅛"

FRONT VIEW

Tank Locations

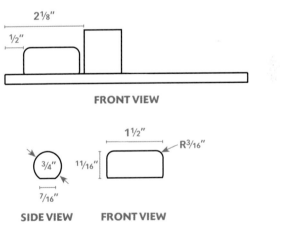

2⅛"

½"

FRONT VIEW

1½"

11/16"

R3/16"

¾"

7/16"

SIDE VIEW   FRONT VIEW

COMPRESSED-AIR TANK

Fuel and Oil Side Tanks

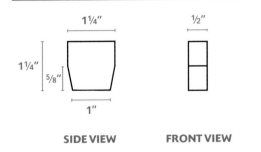

1¼"

½"

1¼"

⅝"

1"

SIDE VIEW

FRONT VIEW

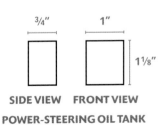

¾"

1"

1⅛"

SIDE VIEW   FRONT VIEW

POWER-STEERING OIL TANK

Ladders

Two short ladders (see the drawing on p. 37) flank the grill at the front of the truck. You make them just like the ladders on the Giant Loader (see Chapter 1, p. 14).

Two Tanks

Make the compressed-air tank from a short piece of dowel; the power-steering oil tank, from a rectangular block. Glue both pieces to the deck, near the cab. The drawing at the beginning of the chapter shows a location for both, but their exact placement isn't critical.

1. Cut a piece of dowel to length. I've specified a ¾-in. dowel, but it can be a little larger or smaller, depending on what you have on hand.

2. Bevel or round the ends. I use a disk sander, then a file and sandpaper, for this.

3. Sand the flat, as shown in the drawing on p. 37. This provides a better gluing surface; here, too, the exact size is not critical. Glue the compressed air tank to the deck.

4. Cut the small block for the power-steering oil tank to size.

5. Sand the faces and round over the edges. Glue the tank to the deck.

TIP

You can save a little time building this model if you use a store-bought wood barrel for the compressed-air tank. All you need to do is sand the flat to make a gluing surface. You may find other ready-made parts at the hobby shop that you can adapt for your models.

Fuel and Oil Side Tanks

These blocks are glued to the frame, centered between the wheels.

1. Lay out the tanks (see the drawing on p. 37) and cut them on the bandsaw.

2. Sand as needed, breaking the sharp corners on the outside surfaces.

3. Glue the tanks to the frame. I did not clamp them, but that would not be too hard to do, especially if you glued one tank at a time.

Dump Box

The dump box consists of four main parts: two sides, the bottom, and the front. You attach the rock guard and pivot parts later.

1. Lay out the sides. You can use ½-in.-thick solid wood or Baltic birch plywood that's ¼ in. or ⅜ in. thick. This truck has ⅜-in. Baltic birch plywood sides, but I have used ½-in. solid wood on other trucks. If you decide to use ½-in. wood for the sides, make the bottom and front ¼ in. narrower so the final outside dimension remains the same. At this stage, have the bottom and front edges of the sides come to a point; you will create that short flat on the bottom after you have assembled the dump box.

Box Sides

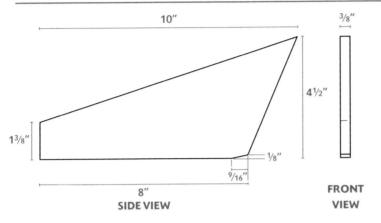

10"

3/8"

4½"

1³/₈"

⅛"

9/16"

8"

SIDE VIEW

FRONT VIEW

Box Front

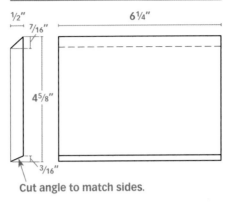

½"

7/16"

6¼"

4⁵/₈"

3/16"

Cut angle to match sides.

SIDE VIEW   FRONT VIEW

Box Bottom

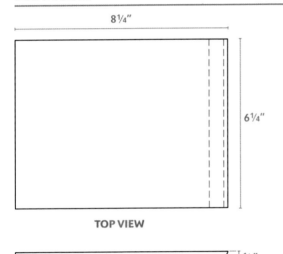

8¼"

6¼"

TOP VIEW

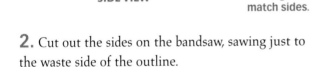

½"

SIDE VIEW

Cut angle to match sides.

Box Rock Guard

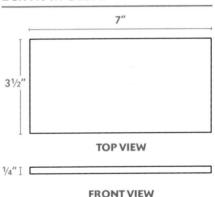

7"

3½"

TOP VIEW

¼" I

FRONT VIEW

2. Cut out the sides on the bandsaw, sawing just to the waste side of the outline.

3. Hold the sides together with clamps or double-sided tape and sand the edges up to the lines. Making the sides identical now will make assembly more accurate when it's time for you to attach the bottom and front.

4. Make the box bottom and box front. I use ½-in.-thick solid wood. Baltic birch plywood is an option, but it is harder to sand the sides flush with the ends later, because you could sand through the veneer in places. Cut a piece to width (6¼ in. if using ⅜-in. sides) and long enough for both parts, so that both will be exactly the same width. If you

decide to plane the angles on the ends, cut each piece now, making them slightly longer than the finish size. But if you want to use a miter saw or tablesaw to cut the angles, cut them while the board is long and easier to hold safely.

5. Cut or plane the angles. Cut the same angle on the front of the bottom and the bottom of the front. Use the dump box side to gauge the angle (see the top photo on p. 40).

6. Test the joint where the bottom and front meet by holding the pieces in place on a side. Sand or file the angle as needed until you see a minimal gap. This joint is hard to force together by clamping. Sand the inside faces of the bottom and front.

7. Dry-clamp the box parts. If possible, the sides should protrude a little past the bottom and front. That will make it easier to sand the parts flush later. When you think you have this psychiatric test under control, glue the edges and clamp the pieces in place. Tap the front down tight onto the bottom. There doesn't seem to be any good way to clamp those two parts together.

If clamping doesn't work for you, don't hesitate to use a 23-gauge pin nailer if you have access to one. If not, you can use finishing nails to hold the pieces tight as the glue dries. However, you have to plane or sand the small flat on the bottom, so you will have to remove or set the nails and fill the small holes.

8. When the glue has dried, plane and sand the small flat on the bottom. Then plane and sand all the surfaces flush. Take your time to get the surfaces as square and parallel as possible. This is easy to say, but all the angles make it a bit of work and may involve some compromises.

9. Cut the rock guard, taking its size directly from the width of the dump box. It should be about 7 in. long. Sand it smooth. If needed, plane or sand the top of the dump box so that the rock guard sits flat.

10. Make sure that the rock guard is square to the box and protrudes the same distance on each side. Glue the rock guard in place.

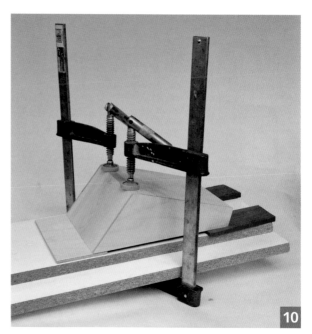

Dump Box Pivot Mounts

The pivot for the dump box tilt has three parts: a frame mount and two box mounts. Make the frame pivot mount first, followed by the box pivot mounts, and then assemble them.

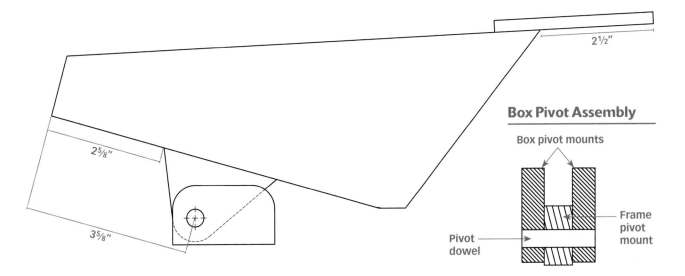

Box Pivot Assembly

Box pivot mounts

Frame pivot mount

Pivot dowel

2½"

2⅝"

3⅝"

Frame Pivot Mount

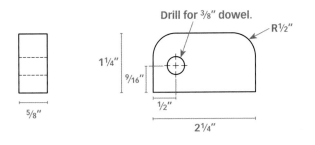

Drill for ⅜" dowel.

R½"

1¼"

9/16"

½"

2¼"

⅝"

Box Pivot Mounts

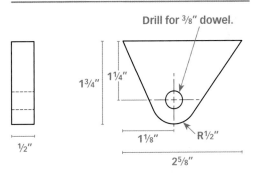

Drill for ⅜" dowel.

1¾"

1¼"

½"

1⅛"

R½"

2⅝"

Frame Pivot Mount

1. Lay out the frame pivot mount on a piece of ⅝-in.-thick wood, but don't cut it out yet. If you don't have a piece of ⅝-in.-thick wood handy, you can use ½-in. material. Don't use ¾-in. wood, though, because it would make the pivot assembly rub on the rear wheels.

2. Drill the hole for the ⅜-in. dowel. It will need to spin in this hole, so you want a close fit, but not one so tight that the dowel cannot move.

3. Cut out the frame pivot mount. Sand it as needed, but keep the bottom glue surface flat.

Box Pivot Mounts

1. Lay out the two parts, but don't cut them out until you have drilled the holes. (You can lay them out side by side, as shown in the top photo on p. 42, or you can cut two pieces and stick them together, so you can drill and cut both parts at once.) The 1⅛-in. dimension from the back of the mount to the hole center could be a little bigger, but don't make it smaller or the wheels may not have enough clearance.

2. Drill the holes, aiming for a snug fit on a ³⁄₈-in. dowel.

3. Cut the parts to size and shape. If you have cut them separately, pin the parts together with a short piece of ³⁄₈-in. dowel so you can sand the edges.

4. Assemble the box and frame pivot mounts. Cut the ³⁄₈-in. dowel to length (for now, make it about ¹⁄₈ in. too long). Wax the center ¹⁄₂ in. or so of the dowel with paraffin or other wax and then slide the dowel into the hole in the frame pivot mount. The wax not only helps the box move, but it also keeps glue off the center of the dowel.

Put glue in the holes in the box pivot mounts and slide them onto the dowel. Twist the box pivot mounts and press them against a flat board or table top to align the ends. They should be snug against the frame pivot mount.

5. When the glue has dried, sand the ends of the dowel flush with the box pivot mounts.

6. Glue the frame pivot mount to the frame. Be sure it is centered left to right on the frame. If necessary, sand the end of the mount so it fits exactly into the notch in the frame, as shown in the photo below. Clamping this piece is a bit tricky. I used a spacer of ¹⁄₂-in.-thick wood (walnut in the photo) to provide clamping pressure directly to the frame and frame pivot mount.

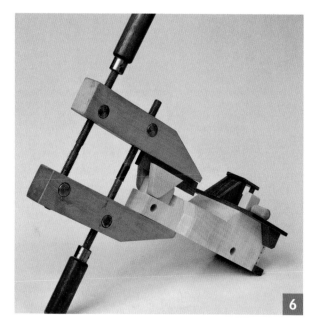

7. Prepare to glue the box to the box pivot mounts. To do this, place the truck upside down. Center the box side to side and check the alignment of the box to the frame at the front. Make the parts look square and centered when you check them by eye, even if the measurements are a tiny bit off. Mark the location of the mounts on the bottom of the box.

8. Clamp a scrap to the box to provide a stop for the mounts. They tend to slide when clamped because of the angles involved.

9. Dry-fit the box mount assembly to the box. To make sure the box won't hit the wheels later, measure to check that there is at least 2¹⁄₄ in. from the center of the axle hole to the closest part of the

Finish

At this point you can apply a finish to the truck, or you could wait until you have attached the wheels. I prefer to finish the wheels before I attach them. You may want to read the section on finishing, on p. 3. If you decide to apply a finish now, remember to stuff the axle holes with some tissue or cloth to prevent finish from building up in them.

Wheel Assembly

The wheels, axles, and their assembly procedures are the same as for the Giant Loader in Chapter 1; see p. 25 and follow those instructions. It's best to glue the double wheels together and handle them as an extra-wide wheel; see p. 89.

box bottom. If for some reason this dimension is too small, you will need to glue shim strips to the base of the mounts and then reassemble.

Spread glue on the box pivot mounts and press the assembly onto the box. Check the alignment of the box and frame again.

CHAPTER 3

Giant Grader

i based this grader on the extremely heavy duty versions used in mining operations to maintain the wide gravel roads used by the real-life versions of the huge trucks and loaders covered in the first two chapters. With this toy, a child can make and grade toy-sized roads.

The grader follows the design of an actual one: It has articulated steering and an engine section that is very similar to the loader's. It also has a blade that raises, lowers, and swivels. The toy has a large wood block for the rear engine housing, which pivots on the longer, slender front frame. The engine housing also holds four rear wheels. The front frame holds the cab, ladders, and the two front wheels. The blade mechanism is under the front frame. The 3-in. wheels are a bit smaller than the ones used on the mining truck and the giant loader, but otherwise are the same.

Wheels

Like the larger wheels used on other vehicles, the wheels on the Giant Grader take a bit of time, but they look great and are not all that hard to make. As a time-saving alternative, you can modify factory-made 3-in. treaded wheels. If you cut angled grooves in the perimeter, the wheels will look similar to those on the Heavy Equipment Transporter in Chapter 6. The factory-made wheels are only 1 in. wide, however, but they might look good as duals.

You do not have to make the wheels first. You can wait, but you will need the wheels before drilling the holes for the axle pins. To make the wheels, follow the

Top View

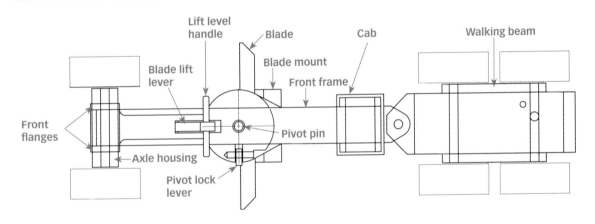

Lift level handle

Blade

Cab

Walking beam

Blade lift lever

Blade mount

Front frame

Front flanges

Pivot pin

Axle housing

Pivot lock lever

Side View

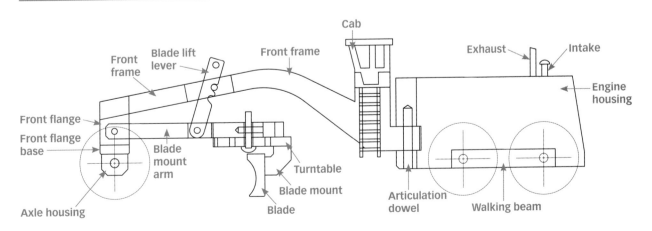

Cab

Front frame

Exhaust

Intake

Front frame

Blade lift lever

Engine housing

Front flange

Front flange base

Blade mount arm

Turntable

Axle housing

Blade mount

Blade

Articulation dowel

Walking beam

PART NAME	FINISH DIMENSIONS L × W × T, IN.	NO. REQ'D.	NOTES
Wheels	3 dia. × ¾ thick per half	6	Need 12 halves to make 6 wheels.
Engine housing	8⅛ × 3¾ × 2½	1	
Exhaust	¼ dowel × 1½ long	1	
Intake	⅜ axle pin, factory made	1	Cut to 1⅝ in. long, including head.
Walking beams	4½ × ¾ × ¼	2	
Front frame	13¹¹⁄₁₆ × 3⁷⁄₁₆ × 1½	1	Cut to 13¾ × 3½ × 1½, then use template.
Cab sides	1¾ × 1¾ × ¼	2	Can use contrasting wood.
Cab roof	2½ × 2 × ¼	1	Can use contrasting wood.
Cab back	1½ × 1⅛ × ¼	1	Can use contrasting wood.
Ladder sides	2¾ × ⅜ × ⅛	4	Baltic birch plywood; cut to 3¾ in. long, trim later.
Ladder rungs	⅛ dowel × ⅞ long	14	Cut 1 in. long, trim after assembly.
Front flanges	2⅜ × 1¼ × ¼	2	Cut to 2¾ in. long, trim later.
Front flange base	1½ × 1¼ × ¼	1	Note grain direction on drawing.
Blade mount arm	7½ × 3 × ½	1	
Turntable	3⅜ × 3 × ¼	1	Baltic birch plywood
Blade mount	3 × 1¼ × 1⅛	1	
Mount arm dowel	¼ dowel × 2 long	1	Cut to 2⅛ in. long, trim after assembly.
Blade	8¼ × 1¾ × ¾	1	Use ½-in. thick wood if not milling the curve.
Pivot lock lever	1¼ × ⅝ × ¼	1	Baltic birch plywood
Pivot lock lever dowel	¼ dowel × 1⅛ long	1	Cut to 1¼ in. long, trim after assembly.
Pivot pin	⅜ axle pin, factory made	1	
Blade lift lever	3½ × ⅝ × ⅜	1	Baltic birch plywood
Blade lift handle	¼ dowel × 2½ long	1	
Lift lever anchor dowel	¼ dowel × 1 long	1	Cut to 1⅛ in. long, trim after assembly.
Lift lever catch dowel	¼ dowel × 1½ long	1	Cut to 1⅝ in. long, trim after assembly.
Axle housing	3¼ × 1⅛ × ¾	1	
Articulation dowel	⅜ dowel × 2½ long	1	
Axle pins	⅜ axle pin, factory made	6	Use 2½-in. long pins, cut length to fit.

TOP VIEW

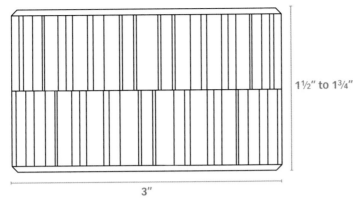

1½" to 1¾"

3"

SIDE VIEW

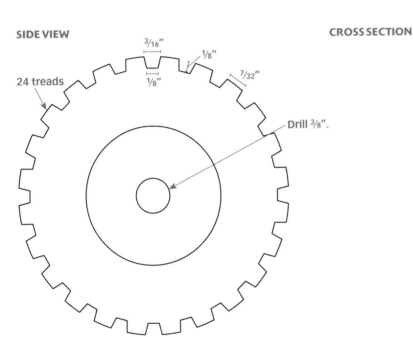

3/16"

1/8"

1/8"

7/32"

24 treads

Drill ⅜".

CROSS SECTION

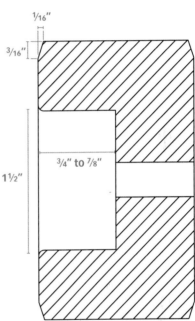

1/16"

3/16"

¾" to ⅞"

1½"

instructions in Chapter 1 but adjust the sizes according to the drawing above. You will need twelve halves to make six identical wheels.

Engine Housing

This part of the grader consists of a large block for the engine housing and two thin "walking beams" attached to the sides of the housing (see the drawing on p. 48). The beams allow the wheels to stand away from the housing.

I used a readily available wood variously known as box elder, maple ash, or Manitoba maple. I suspect you may use something different.

1. Rough out the wood block (laminate stock if necessary). Square it up to its length, width, and thickness.

2. Lay out the outline of the articulation joint at the front, the angles at the front and rear, and the three vertical holes. Don't mark the axle holes yet; wait until you have attached the walking beams.

TOP VIEW

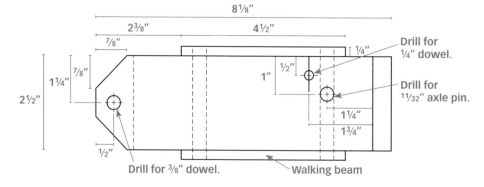

8⅛″
2⅜″   4½″
⅞″
¼″
½″
1″
1¼″   ⅞″
2½″
½″

Drill for ¼″ dowel.

Drill for ¹¹⁄₃₂″ axle pin.

1¼″
1¾″

Drill for ⅜″ dowel.   Walking beam

SIDE VIEW

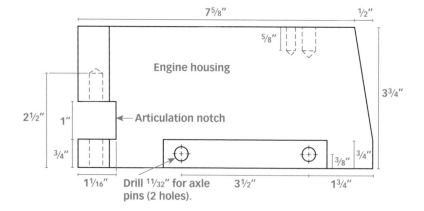
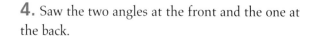

7⅝″   ½″
⅝″
Engine housing
3¾″
2½″   1″
Articulation notch
¾″
⅜″   ¾″
1¹⁄₁₆″   Drill ¹¹⁄₃₂″ for axle pins (2 holes).
3½″   1¾″

3. Saw out the articulation notch carefully. Cut right to the line to give yourself a minimum of filing and fitting later.

4. Saw the two angles at the front and the one at the back.

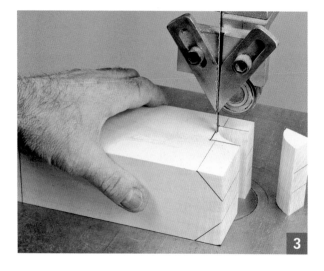

5. File and sand the angles and notch. Make sure the articulation notch is as straight and square as possible. The size of the notch is not critical because you can size the front frame tenon to fit.

6. Drill the two holes in the top. The larger hole is for a standard axle pin, which is used as an air intake. Dowel size varies, so bore test holes on a piece of scrap to get a good fit. The location of these two holes is not at all critical. Put them where you think they look best.

7. Drill the hole for the articulation joint. The ⅜-in. hole should provide a snug fit on a ⅜-in. dowel. Drill test holes until you're satisfied with the fit. Drill right through this part of the engine housing, but make sure the setup is secure and square to the table and drill bit. Don't worry if you get some tear-out; it will be hidden when you assemble the grader.

8. Sand all surfaces to around 120-grit, removing any sharp edges and corners. Parts get a bit scratched as you make the rest of the toy, so it's probably best to leave the final sanding till the end.

9. Cut the walking beams to size. Glue them to the engine housing, one at a time.

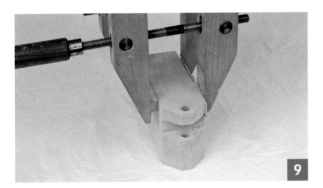

Front Frame

The front frame is the backbone of the grader. I used a good local birch for this part, but you could also laminate it using three strips of solid wood or Baltic birch plywood. I have used those materials in the past.

TIP

The front frame has a slot for the lever that lifts the blade. If you laminate the frame in three layers, you can make the slot in the bargain, with no drilling or cutting later. Just make the middle layer of the lamination in two pieces, with space for the slot between them.

---

1. Use the template on p. 64 to trace the shape. You can lay out the frame from the drawing, but that gets pretty complicated.

2. Saw the frame to shape and sand all surfaces smooth.

3. Lay out the articulation hole and the angles beside the hole.

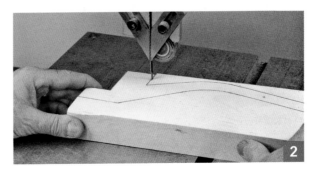

TOP VIEW

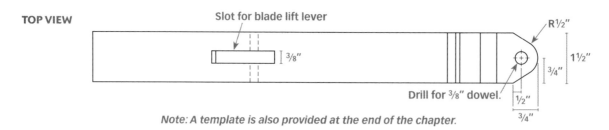

Slot for blade lift lever

R½"

3/8"

1½"

3/4"

Drill for 3/8" dowel.

1/2"

3/4"

Note: A template is also provided at the end of the chapter.

SIDE VIEW

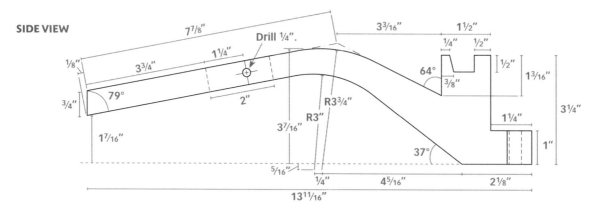

7⅞"

Drill ¼".

3³/₁₆"

1½"

¼"   ½"

1/8"

3¾"

1¼"

64°

1/2"

1³/₁₆"

3/8"

3/4"

79°

2"

R3¾"

R3"

1¼"

3¼"

1⁷/₁₆"

3⁷/₁₆"

37°

1"

5/16"

¼"   4⁵/₁₆"   2⅛"

13¹¹/₁₆"

4. Drill the articulation hole to fit the ⅜-in. dowel. Take care with this setup; the hole needs to be quite accurate as well as exactly square to the frame. Clamp the frame directly to the drill press table to ensure that this part of the frame is flat on the table. Check that the sides of the frame are square to the table and parallel to the drill bit. I added a second clamp to prevent the frame from pivoting or moving sideways.

5. Fit the articulation joint tenon into the engine housing, aiming for a snug fit. Allow for plastic wear washers (see Chapter 1, p. 16) if you decide to use them, as I did. Keep the tenon as straight and square as possible. I use small files and sandpaper to refine the fit of this joint.

6. Cut the angles on the articulation joint.

7. Lay out the slot for the blade lift lever (unless, of course, you've created the slot by laminating three layers). Either take the measurements from the drawing or transfer the location from the lines on the template.

8. Cut the slot. I drilled a ²⁵/₆₄-in. hole at each end, sawed out the waste with a coping saw, and cleaned up the slot with chisels, files, and sandpaper.

Cab

The cab sides should have the grain running vertically to make the window posts strong. The cab back needs the grain running horizontally for a better glue joint with the roof. I used a contrasting wood on this grader, but you could use Baltic birch plywood instead.

TIP

Here are a couple of other ways to cut the slot for the blade lift lever. Drill a series of closely spaced holes, and then chop out the waste with a chisel. Or use a small trim router, with scrap blocks clamped to the sides of the frame to support the router base; square up the ends of the slot with a chisel.

Cab Roof

TOP VIEW

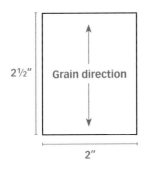

SIDE VIEW

Assembled Cab (Showing location on front frame)

SIDE VIEW

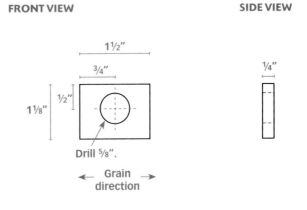

Cab Sides

FRONT VIEW   **SIDE VIEW**

Cab Back

FRONT VIEW   **SIDE VIEW**

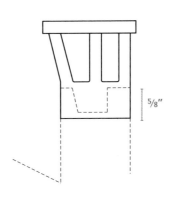

Drill 5/8".

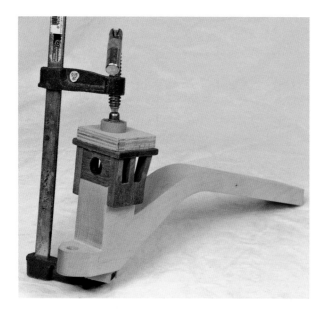

Making the cab follows the same process used for the loader cab, so refer to Chapter 1, p. 12, for the instructions; use the dimensions shown on p. 51. Glue the cab to the front frame, as shown in the photo above.

Ladders

The ladders help give a sense of the scale, as they do on the mining truck and the huge loader. To make these, use the dimensions in the drawing on the facing page but follow the instructions from Chapter 1, p. 14.

Glue the ladders on with their tops touching the bottom edges of the cab sides. I set them back between ⅛ in. and ¼ in. from the front of the cab, as shown on the assembly drawing. The exact measurement isn't critical.

Front Flanges

The flanges drop down from the front of the frame and provide mounting points for the blade mechanism and the front axle housing. Cut them a bit long now and trim them after you dry-fit the engine housing and front frame.

1. Use ¼-in. solid wood or Baltic birch plywood. Lay out the shape, but saw the parts between ¼ in. and ½ in. too long for now. Sand the surfaces.

2. Glue the flanges to the frame. Have the top edge protrude slightly (about ¹⁄₃₂ in.) so you can sand it flush later.

3. Drill the ¼-in. pivot hole through both front flanges. Also drill the pivot hole through the slot in the frame for the lift lever handle.

4. Dry-fit the engine housing and front frame, using washers in the articulation joint if needed. Leave the articulation pivot dowel a bit long so that you can remove it later. The front frame should pivot easily but not swing freely. When you are satisfied with the assembly, block it up using two blocks under the engine housing. Make a spacer to support the front frame and take any slack out of the articulation joint (see the top photo on p. 54).

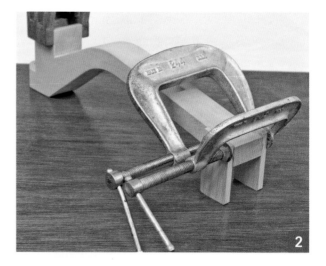

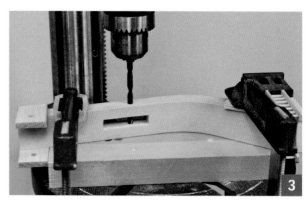

Ladder

FRONT VIEW   **SIDE VIEW**

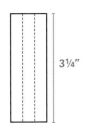

3/16″
3/8″
1/4″
2³/₄″
3/8″ typ.
1/4″
Drill for ¹/₈″ dowel (7 holes).

1/8″
7/8″
¹/₈″ dowel

Front Flanges

TOP VIEW   **SIDE VIEW**

  ⊥ 1/4″

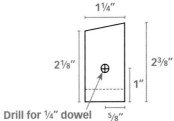

1¼″
2¹/₈″
2³/₈″
1″
5/8″
Drill for ¼″ dowel after assembly.

Axle Housing

TOP VIEW

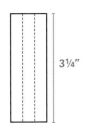

3¼″

SIDE VIEW

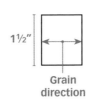

1¹/₈″
9/16″
3/4″
1/2″
3/8″
1/4″
Drill ¹¹/₃₂″ after assembly.

Front Flange Base

TOP VIEW

1½″

Grain direction

SIDE VIEW

1¼″
3/8″

Blade Lift Lever

TOP VIEW

 ⊥ 3/8″

SIDE VIEW

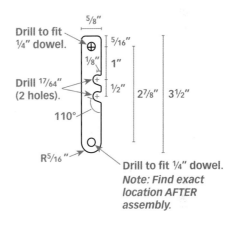

5/8″
5/16″
Drill to fit ¼″ dowel.
1/8″
1″
Drill ¹⁷/₆₄″ (2 holes).
1/2″
2⁷/₈″
3½″
110°
R⁵/₁₆″
Drill to fit ¼″ dowel.
Note: Find exact location AFTER assembly.

Lift Lever Handle

TOP VIEW

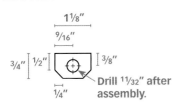 ← ¼″ dowel

SIDE VIEW

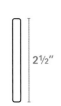

2½″

Exhaust

TOP VIEW

○ ← ¼″ dowel

SIDE VIEW

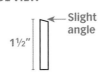

1½″
← Slight angle

Intake

TOP VIEW

 ← ³/₈″ axle pin

SIDE VIEW

1¹/₈″

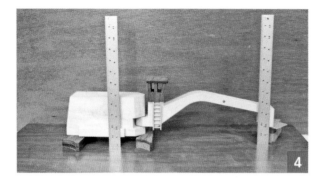

5. Mark the length of the front flanges. The bottom of the flanges should be the same height as the top edge of the walking beams.

6. Saw the flanges to their final length. Sand the top and front edges flush with the front frame.

Axle Housing

The axle housing is a small beam attached to the front of the grader, with holes in the ends to allow the axle pins to hold the wheels in place. Choose a wood with uniform grain, as the drill bit tends to wander a little when going through end grain. Drill these holes after assembly, when you can determine the correct height of the holes.

1. Cut the axle housing to size.

2. Use a block plane to bevel two edges' corners. Aim for a 45-degree bevel, but the exact angle and size are not critical.

Front Flange Base

This small piece (see the drawing on p. 53) fits between the front flanges, at the bottom. It provides a gluing surface for the axle housing, which needs to be firmly attached. The grain for the flange base runs perpendicular to the front frame to provide the best glue strength for attaching the axle housing and front flanges.

1. Cut the small block to the same width as the front frame. It should be very close to 1½ in. long, 1¼ in. wide, and ¼ in. thick.

2. Glue the block to the axle housing, making sure it is centered on the length and width.

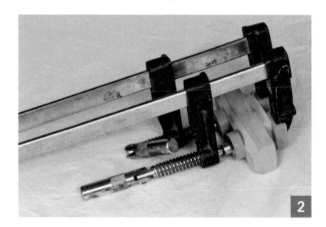

3. When that glue has dried, glue the axle housing assembly between the front flanges, flush with their bottom and sides.

Axle Pin Locations

You find the location of the axle pin holes as part of a dry-fit, much the way you laid out the length of the front flanges.

1. Dry-fit the engine housing and front frame again. Work on a flat surface, such as a tablesaw table. Set the assembly on two blocks under the ends of the engine housing. Rest the end of the front frame on a spacer (I made a rough wedge) to hold some weight and take the slack out of the articulation joint.

2. Mark the center height of all six holes. I do this with a carpenter's pencil (the flat shape is ideal) and a block of wood just thick enough to hold the pencil at the center height of the walking beam. Mark vertical lines to locate the centerpoints of the holes.

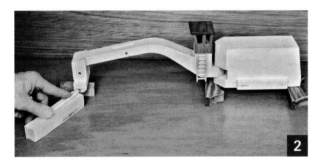

3. Drill the holes, but as always, make test holes first to be sure the drill bit you use actually fits the axle pins you have. When drilling the real holes, make sure the engine housing is square to the table and drill bit. Use the same drill press setup as for the front flanges (see p. 52). The drill is less likely to wander if it is sharp and you don't push it into the wood too fast.

TIP

A drill bit can sometimes veer off-center as it goes through a thick block of hardwood, especially when boring into end grain. To minimize this, I do a careful layout and drill from each side. Often this is the most accurate way to drill axle pins into end grain.

Blade Mount Arm

The blade mount arm pivots at the front of the grader and holds the blade in place under the back of the lever (see the drawing on p. 56). In the middle is the blade lift mechanism that locks the blade at the desired height.

1. Lay out the shape on ½-in.-thick wood, either with the template on p. 64 (certainly the easiest method) or by taking measurements from the drawing.

2. Lay out the slot and the pivot hole. If you plan to cut this slot using the same method you used on the front arm, then mark the centers for two holes at the ends of the slot.

3. Bandsaw the blade mount arm to shape and then sand the edges to the lines. At this point, the only critical measurement is the 1½-in. width at the front, where the arm fits between the front flanges. The arm needs room to pivot freely, with a little extra room to compensate for the finish later. In all, aim for ¹⁄₃₂ in. clearance for now.

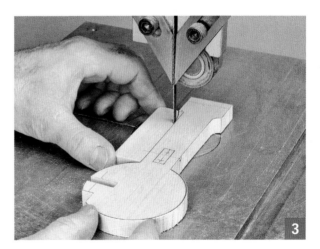

4. Cut the slot, using whatever method you favor. Square the ends and file or chisel the sides so the slot will fit ⅜-in.-thick Baltic birch plywood, used for the blade lift lever. Widen the slot by about ¹⁄₃₂ in. to allow a little clearance for the finish (see the top photo on p. 57).

Blade Mount Assembly

TOP VIEW

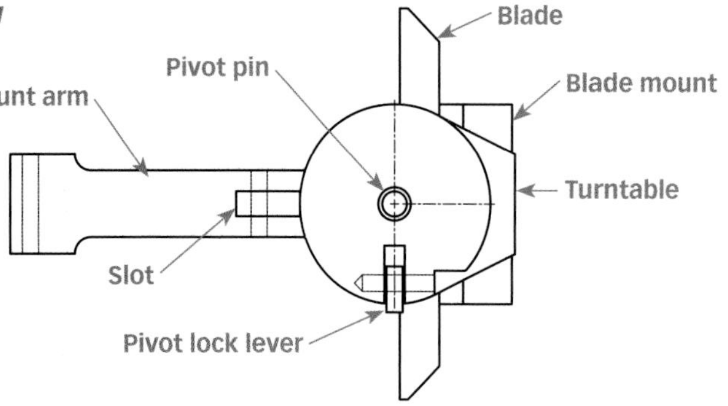
Blade
Blade mount
Pivot pin
Blade mount arm
Turntable
Slot
Pivot lock lever

SIDE VIEW

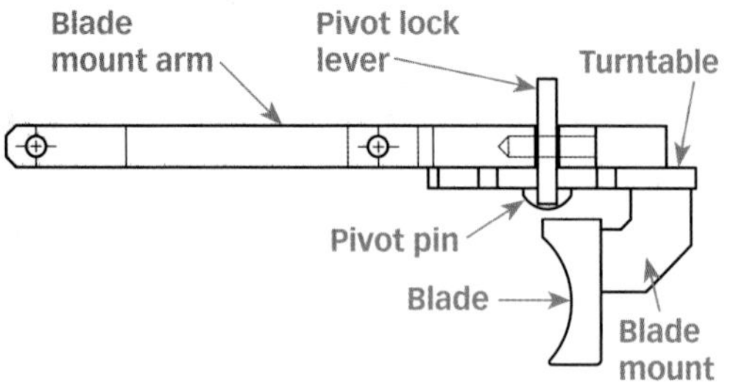
Blade
mount arm
Pivot lock
lever
Turntable
Pivot pin
Blade
Blade
mount

FRONT VIEW

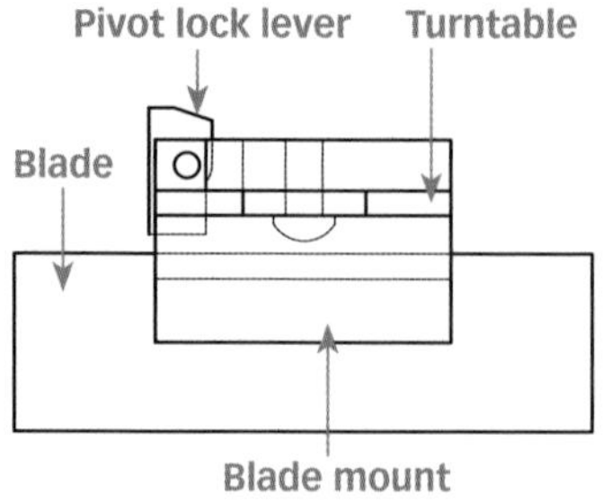
Pivot lock lever
Turntable
Blade
Blade mount

Pivot Lock Lever

FRONT VIEW **SIDE VIEW**

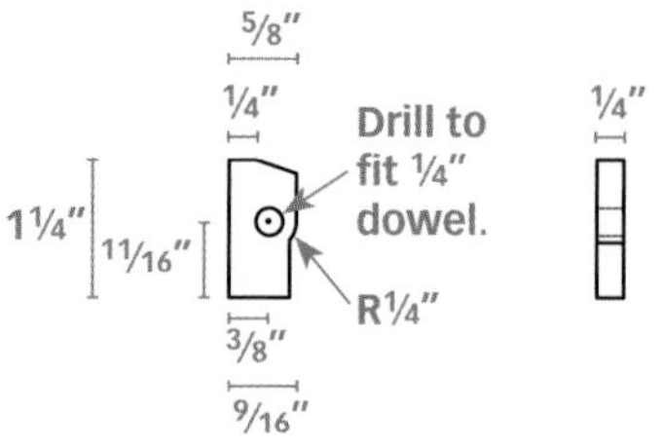
5/8"
1/4"
Drill to
fit 1/4"
dowel.
1 1/4"
11/16"
R1/4"
3/8"
9/16"
1/4"

Blade

TOP VIEW

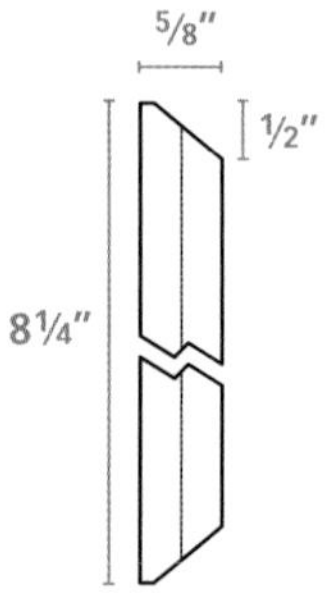
5/8"
1/2"
8 1/4"

SIDE VIEW

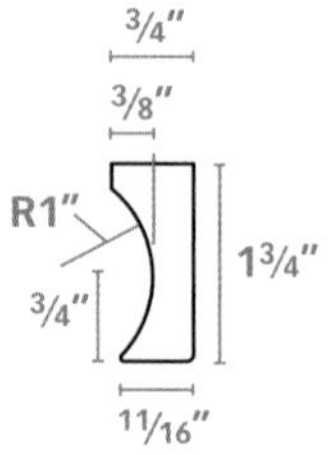
3/4"
3/8"
R1"
1 3/4"
3/4"
11/16"

Blade Mount Arm

TOP VIEW

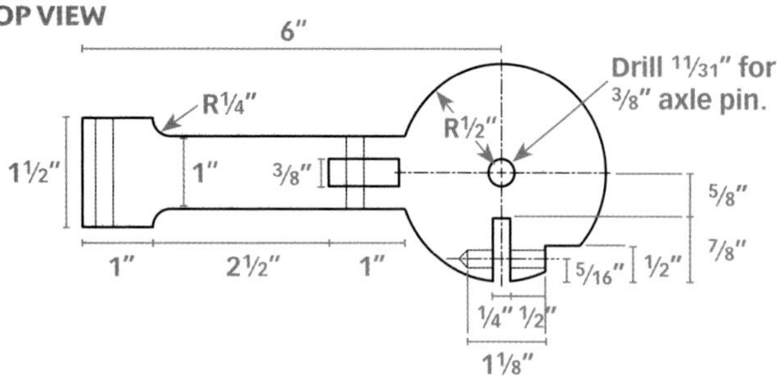
6"
Drill 11/31" for
3/8" axle pin.
R1/4"
R1/2"
1 1/2"
1"
3/8"
5/8"
7/8"
1"
2 1/2"
1"
5/16"
1/2"
1/4" 1/2"
1 1/8"

SIDE VIEW

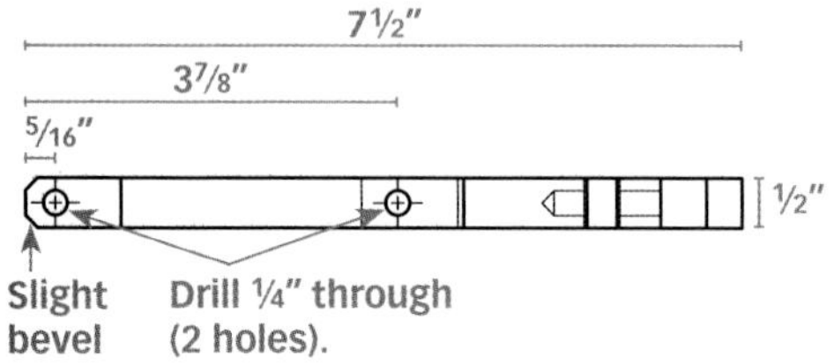
7 1/2"
3 7/8"
5/16"
1/2"
Slight
bevel
Drill 1/4" through
(2 holes).

FRONT VIEW

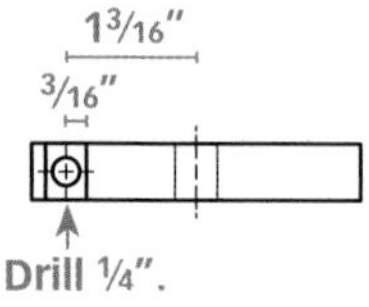
1 3/16"
3/16"
Drill 1/4".

Blade Mount

FRONT VIEW

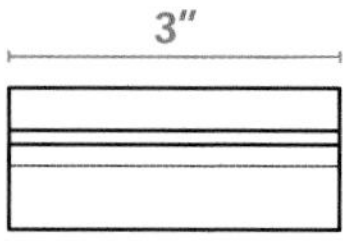
3"

SIDE VIEW

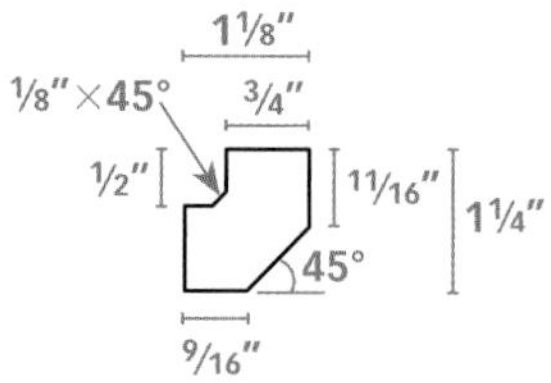
1 1/8"
1/8"×45°
3/4"
1/2"
11/16"
1 1/4"
45°
9/16"

Turntable

TOP VIEW

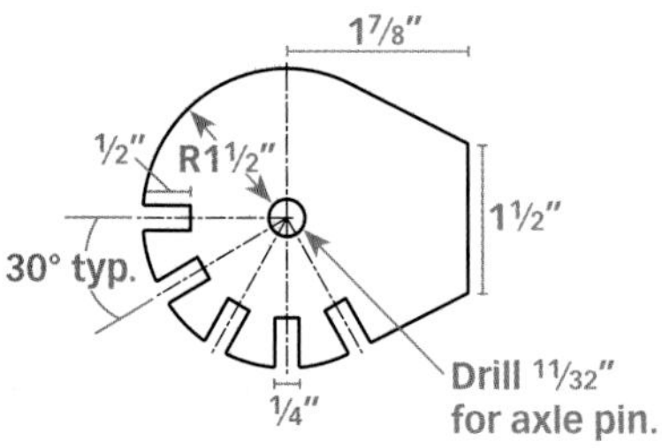
1 7/8"
1/2"
R1 1/2"
1 1/2"
30° typ.
1/4"
Drill 11/32"
for axle pin.

SIDE VIEW

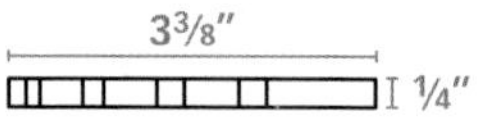
3 3/8"
1/4"

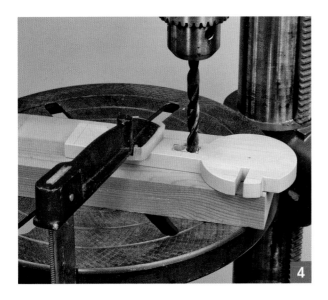

5. Drill the $^{11}/_{32}$-in. pivot hole for an axle pin.

6. Now lay out the three ¼-in. holes—one at the front, one through the slot, and a third drilled through the notch on the round portion—for the lock lever. A ¼-in. dowel needs to slide in freely but not rattle, so pick the drill that best fits your dowel.

7. Hold the arm on edge and drill the two holes through the side.

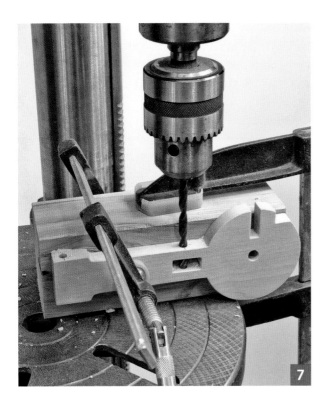

8. Hold the arm on end, clamped to a scrap block, and drill the lock lever hole.

Turntable

The turntable holds the blade and pivots to angle the blade. It has slots for the lock lever to locate the blade angle and lock it into place (see the drawing on the facing page). Make the turntable from Baltic birch plywood for strength around the notches.

1. Lay out the turntable and drill the center pivot hole.

2. Cut the piece to size and sand it to the lines. I saw the notches at the bandsaw, making several cuts to nibble out the shape. The pivot lock lever (which you will make shortly, from ¼-in. plywood) should fit snugly into the slots; allow about ⅟₆₄ in. of clearance to account for the thickness of the finish. With the notches cut, sand to break all the sharp edges.

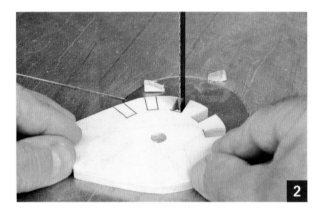

Blade Lift Lever

The blade lift lever (see the drawing on p. 53) allows the blade to be positioned just above ground level for grading and positioned well up from the ground at other times.

1. Lay out the profile and the hole on ⅜-in.-thick Baltic birch plywood. Make the piece at least ⅛ in. oversize in width so you can drill the notch holes.

2. Drill the two notch holes. Saw the lever to its final ⅝-in. width, and then saw, file, and sand the notches to shape.

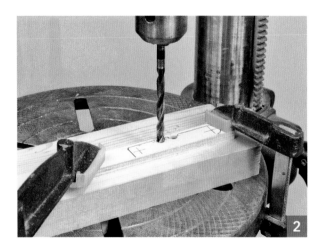

3. Dry-fit the grader, using temporary dowels to pin the parts together. Use scrap blocks to hold the blade mount arm approximately level.

4. Hook the top notch of the lift lever over the dowel in the frame. Stick a pencil through the hole in the blade mount arm to mark the hole location for the bottom pivot point in the lift lever. Also check that the handle hole at the top is above the frame. If it isn't, move the parts slightly until the handle clears the frame. Mark through the front frame to locate the hole for the top pivot point.

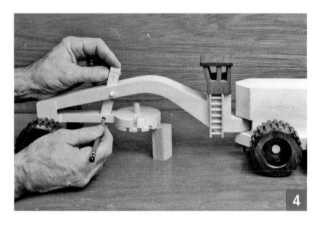

TIP
Mark the holes in the lift lever with a brad-point drill bit that's the same size as the one used for the holes in the blade mount arm and front frame. The bit's point will mark the center of the hole. Move the centerpoint left or right as needed to center the holes on the lever's width.

5. Drill the holes to fit a ¼-in. dowel where you have marked the lift lever. Be sure to center the holes on the lever's ⅝-in. width.

6. Sand the rounded end to make it concentric with the pivot hole.

7. Check that both notches fit over the dowel in the frame and are secure enough not to slip off until you move the lever up or down. File and shape the notches as needed until the lever resembles the one shown in the top photo on the facing page.

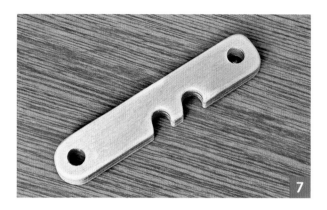

8. Leave the grader assembled, at least for now.

Pivot Lock Lever

Attach this small lever to the blade mount arm with a short dowel. It swivels down into the slots on the turntable to lock the blade at an angle.

1. Lay out the lever's profile and mounting hole on Baltic birch plywood (see the drawing on p. 56).

2. Drill the hole to fit a ¼-in. dowel. Saw the profile, and then sand the edges smooth.

3. Use a long scrap dowel to mount the lever in the notch in the blade mount arm. Check that the lever fits into the turntable notches with minimal clearance and pivots freely. If it seems tight, lightly sand the faces.

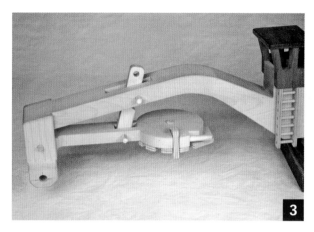

Blade

Now it's time to start working on the blade (see the drawing on p. 56). To me, this block of wood looks best with a curved, or coved, front. However, it takes a bit of work to mill that shape, using the tablesaw to cut the cove. If you don't have a tablesaw, it's OK to give the blade a rectangular cross section. I built a grader with a plain rectangular blade for my children years ago. They had lots of fun with it, and I never heard a comment about the plain blade.

These instructions explain how to make a blade with a curved front. If you decide to omit the curve, just follow steps 1, 7, and 9. If you are not familiar with cutting a cove on the tablesaw, watch this excellent video from *Fine Woodworking* magazine: www.finewoodworking.com/how-to/video/how-to-cut-coves-on-the-tablesaw.aspx.

1. Rough out the blade as well as an identical piece from scrap, for trial cuts. Make them at least 12 in. long, because longer pieces are easier and safer to saw.

2. Set the tablesaw blade to a ⅜-in. height. You will make the first cut at a lower setting; use this height for set-up purposes.

3. Clamp a fence to the saw table at a 17-degree angle, with the edge of the fence board ⅛ in. away from the blade edge.

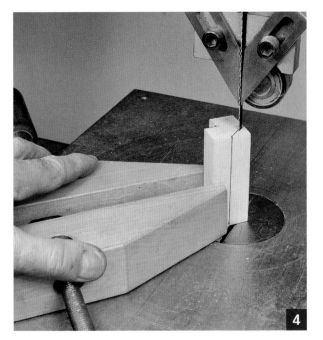

4. Clamp on a second fence so that the blade material slides smoothly between them.

5. Set the blade height to 1/16 in. and take the first cut. Use push sticks to guide the wood over the blade.

6. Make a series of similar cuts, raising the blade no more than 1/16 in. each time. Continue until the cove is 3/8 in. deep and 1¼ in. wide.

7. Cut the blade to length.

8. Sand the radius, using a 1½-in. to 2-in. dowel as a sanding block. Or use a gooseneck cabinet scraper.

9. Cut the bevels at the ends.

Blade Mount

The blade mount is a 3-in.-long block that connects the blade to the turntable (see the drawing on p. 56).

1. Cut the wood to size. Square up the two surfaces that will be glued to the turntable and blade. I use a disk sander for this.

2. Lay out the profile on one end.

3. Use a clamp to hold the block on end, and cut the notch on the bandsaw.

4. Move the clamp and cut the angle opposite the notch.

5. Finish-sand everything but the glue surfaces.

Assembly: First Stage

You're now ready to connect all the arms and levers that fit on the front frame. You'll also add some details to the engine housing and glue the blade into place.

Blade Lift and Pivot Lock Levers

1. Leave the lift lever anchor dowel at least 1/8 in. overlong for now. Install it dry until it has about 3/8 in. to go. Put glue in the empty flange hole with a toothpick, and put a little glue on the end of the dowel where it is about to enter the flange. This tends to keep glue from entering the pivoting part of the hinge joint. Tap or push in the dowel until it protrudes about 1/16 in.

2. Saw, file, or sand the dowel flush.

3. Use the same method to install the lift lever catch dowel in the frame. File and sand the ends flush.

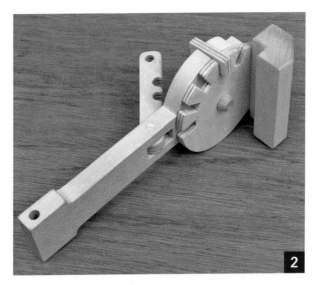

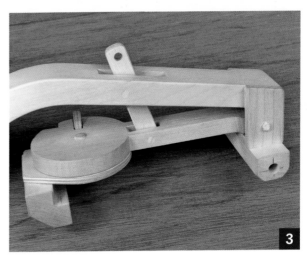

4. Install the pivot lock lever exactly as you did the blade lift lever, and then cut off the excess dowel. File and sand the dowel flush with the surface in the small notch.

Blade Mount and Turntable

1. Glue the blade mount to the turntable. Make sure it is centered, although that is mainly for appearance, not function. The parts are a bit awkward to clamp, but because there is a fairly good amount of glue surface I just hold the parts together firmly for between three and five minutes and then set the assembly aside to cure.

2. Cut an axle pin to length. Put glue in the hole in the blade mount arm, then slip the pin through the turntable and up into the hole in the blade mount

arm. Have a piece of softwood and a mallet handy to tap the pin into place if needed. The turntable needs to be able to pivot but can be fairly snug.

3. Use the mount arm dowel to pin the blade mount arm assembly to the frame. Again, push the dowel in partway dry, and then put glue in the dowel hole as well as on the other end of the dowel. Push or tap the dowel in until it just protrudes.

4. Trim the dowel to length. File and sand it flush.

Lift Lever Handle

1. Cut the lift lever handle to length. Bevel the ends to break the sharp corners (see the drawing on p. 53).

2. Push the dowel into the lever until it protrudes ½ in., and then put glue on the dowel for about ¼ in. of its length, just where it is about to enter the lever. Push or tap it in the rest of the way, centering it on the lift lever.

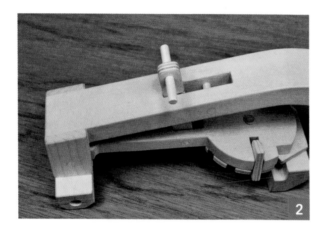

Intake and Exhaust

1. Cut the exhaust dowel and intake axle pin to length. Sand a slight bevel on one end of the exhaust if desired (see the drawing on p. 53).

2. Put glue in the holes on the top of the engine housing and tap the exhaust and intake into place. Their exact height is not important.

Position the Blade

1. Dry-fit the articulation joint again.

2. Temporarily install the wheels, without glue. They need to be in place to get the height of the blade correct, and then removed for finishing.

3. Rest the grader on a flat surface (I used an old door) and put the blade in place; use ¹⁄₃₂-in. shims to hold it off the surface. Make sure the lift lever is firmly in place on the frame dowel so the blade mechanism is at its final grading height.

4. Center the blade on the blade mount and make sure you can hold it firmly in place for three or four minutes. When the position looks good and you have a grip figured out, put glue on the face of the blade mount and press the blade firmly against the mount. Holding it for three or four minutes will likely do. Leave it alone until the glue has cured.

Finishing and Second-Stage Assembly

Finish the grader as desired. It is a little easier to finish the wheels separately from the rest of the grader, and also a bit easier to spray the front and engine housing sections separately. That's how I proceeded with this grader.

Finish the Wood

1. First, plug holes with a length of dowel or small pieces of paper towel. In my experience, spray-finishing doesn't affect the assembled pins and pivots.

2. Apply the finish. I used a fast-drying satin Varathane® varnish.

3. Finish the heads of the axle pins now. Use pins that are as long as possible, as short pins tend to come out after a while.

4. Sand lightly between coats and apply as many coats as is appropriate. I generally use four coats.

Articulation Joint and Wheels

1. After the final coat of finish is good and hard, assemble the front and rear halves at the articulation joint, if you have not already done so. I used small plastic washers (see Chapter 1, p. 16) in the articulation joint. Dry-fit the parts to make sure they still fit after you have applied the finish. Sand as necessary.

2. Cover the workbench or table with a soft rag to protect the finished parts as you rotate the grader and tap the pivot pin into place.

3. Use a long thin dowel to put some glue in the upper part of the engine housing part of the joint. Install the dowel until you have only about ½ in. to go and put some glue on that final ½ in. of dowel. Tap the dowel in the rest of the way.

4. Saw and file to remove the excess dowel. It does not have to be exactly flush. It's fine if it protrudes even ⅛ in.; it's also easier on the finish than trying to sand it all flush.

Wheel Assembly Check

1. I used small plastic washers between the wheels and the grader to keep them slightly away from the grader and to have them spin a little more freely. Make these washers if you'd like.

2. Pre-assemble the wheels and axles without glue. Make sure that all six wheels rotate when the grader rolls along. If necessary, you can drill the axle holes ⅟₃₂ in. oversize for a little leeway. If that's not enough, go ⅟₁₆ in. oversize.

TIP

Wheels should not be tight. That's not an issue when a child rolls the grader over carpet or rugs, but it is on a hard surface. One of my two sons was always bothered if a wheel didn't spin, so I learned to watch for this flaw.

---

3. Use the axle pins that you have already cut to length. Rub a little wax on each pin's shaft, just below the head. This will allow the wheel to spin a bit more freely.

4. Put a little wax on the end of the axle housing on the front frame, but try not to get wax into the hole.

5. Have a softwood punch ready, in case a pin gets a bit stuck and needs gentle persuasion. Put a soft rag on the table so you won't scratch the grader as you lay it on its side.

6. Make a small horseshoe-shaped piece of plastic that's ⅟₆₄ in. to ⅟₃₂ in. thick (see the top left photo on p. 27). You can slide it between the wheel and the axle housing for installation, then slip it out afterward to provide a set amount of clearance for the wheel to spin freely.

7. Put glue into an axle hole, using a toothpick. Be generous and use good-quality glue. Put the axle pin into the wheel, then apply a small amount of glue to the last ½ in. or so of the axle pin. I have had axle pins loosen after lots of play time, so I'm more generous with glue than I was originally. However, be prepared for some squeeze-out.

8. Gently push or tap the axle pin into place, leaving the plastic horseshoe spacer in place under the wheel.

9. As soon as the pin is in all the way, let the glue cure for two or three minutes before removing the horseshoe spacer and installing the next wheel. Repeat for the remaining wheels.

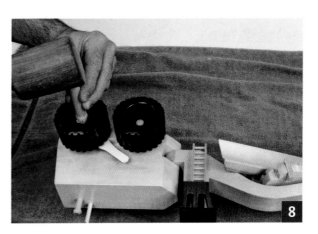

Templates

For full-size template, enlarge by 203%.

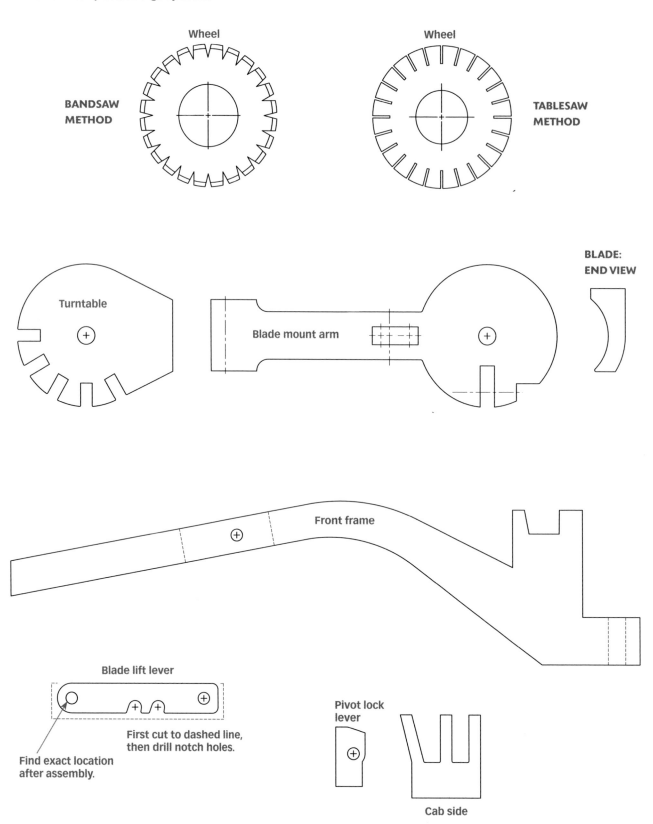

Wheel

Wheel

BANDSAW METHOD

TABLESAW METHOD

BLADE: END VIEW

Turntable

Blade mount arm

Front frame

Blade lift lever

First cut to dashed line, then drill notch holes.

Find exact location after assembly.

Pivot lock lever

Cab side

CHAPTER 4

One Bus Four Ways

t *oy school buses* are an all-time best seller, popular
for many generations. You can make this bus four different
ways: with a solid body or one made from a laminated blank;
with monster wheels or normal wheels. I think the bus looks
best with a body made from a solid block of wood, so the grain
runs in one direction. However, that requires a block 3¾ in. square, which
may be expensive or hard to find. So for the bus shown here I laminated
a hollow block from pieces of yellowheart. I also chose monster wheels to
take the bus out of the realm of the ordinary.

If you want to make a solid-body bus or use conventional wheels,
you'll find instructions in the sidebars at the end of the chapter
(see pp. 84–85).

Wheels

Making the wheels for the bus involves the same general procedures used for
the Giant Loader's wheels in Chapter 1, p. 7. These monster wheels are 2¾ in.
in diameter and have angled treads, so there are a couple of manufacturing
differences.

There are many treads to cut when making four wheels, so I use the tablesaw,
which is faster than using the bandsaw. However, if you need to use a bandsaw
you can. You will have to make a simple fixture first, unless your bandsaw table
tilts in two directions.

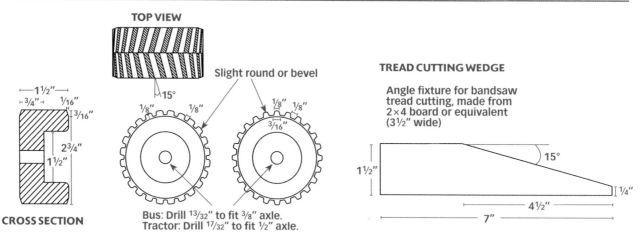

One Bus Four Ways Plan

Rear bumper

Front bumper

Fender

Roof light

Roof lights

Hood

Grill

Fender

Fender

Grill

Bumper

Body

Rear axle housing

Driveshaft assembly

Front axle housing

Front axle housing

Wheels for Bus (or Tractor)

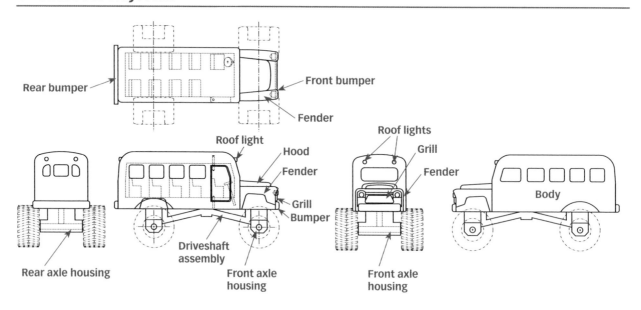

TOP VIEW

15°

Slight round or bevel

1½"

¾"

1/16"

3/16"

1/8"

1/8"

1/8"

1/8"

3/16"

2¾"

1½"

CROSS SECTION

Bus: Drill 13/32" to fit 3/8" axle.
Tractor: Drill 17/32" to fit 1/2" axle.

TABLESAW CUT TREADS   **BANDSAW CUT TREADS**

TREAD CUTTING WEDGE

Angle fixture for bandsaw tread cutting, made from 2×4 board or equivalent (3½" wide)

15°

1½"

¼"

4½"

7"

ONE BUS FOUR WAYS **CUT LIST**

PART NAME	FINISH DIMENSIONS L × W × T, IN.	NO. REQ'D.	NOTES
Needed for all versions			
Door	2¼ × 1¼ × ⅜	1	
Door hinge pins	⅛ dowel × 1 long	2	Cut overlong, trim after assembly.
Seats	1⅛ × 1¼ × ¾	9	Contrasting wood; cut from piece 12 in. long.
Steering wheel	⅝ dowel × ⅛ long	1	
Steering column	⅛ dowel × 1⅝ long	1	
Fenders	2⅝ × 1½ × ¾	2	
Front bumper	2⅞ × ½ × ¼	1	
Rear bumper	3⅛ × ½ × ¼	1	
Grill	2⅛ × ½ × ⅛	1	Can also use 1⁄16-in. thick veneer.
Headlights	⅜ dowel × ⅜ long	2	
Roof lights	¼ dowel × ⅜ long	4	Use reddish contrasting wood if possible.
Needed for laminated-body version			
Laminated body blank	8⅜ × 2⅞ × 3¾	1	Laid up from pieces cut from ¾-in.-thick stock
Frame	27 × 2⅞ × ¾	1	Frame itself is 10⅞-in. long. Remainder of piece used to cut back, front, and roof.
Body sides	8⅜ × 3¾ × ⅜	2	Only for laminated body
Hood	2 9⁄16 × 2⅜ × 1⅛	1	Only for laminated body
Needed for solid-body version			
Solid body blank	11⅜ × 3¾ × 3¾	1	
Needed for monster-wheel version			
Wheels	2¾ dia. × ¾ thick per half	4	Need 8 halves to make 4 wheels.
Driveshaft assembly	6⅛ × 1 × ⅜	1	Baltic birch plywood. Cut to fit between axle housings.
Front axle housing	2¾ × 1 9⁄16 × 1⅛	1	Use only with monster wheels.
Rear axle housing	3 × 1 9⁄16 × 1⅛	1	Use only with monster wheels.
Front axle	½ dowel × 5¾ long	1	
Rear axle	⅜ dowel × 6 long	1	
Wheel hubs	⅜ factory dowel end caps	4	
Needed for small-wheel version			
Small wheels	1¾ dia. wheels	4	Factory-made parts
Small wheel axle pins	11⁄32 pins, 1½ long	4	Factory-made parts
Front axle housing	2¾ × 1⅛ × ⅝	1	
Rear axle housing	3 × 1⅛ × ⅝	1	

1. Make the wedge shown in the drawing on p. 66 from a short length of 2×4 construction lumber or other scrap. The exact angle is not critical.

Make the stop block from another piece of scrap and bandsaw a ¼-in.-deep slot in the end. Position the block so that the blade will plunge about ⅛ in. deep into the wheel.

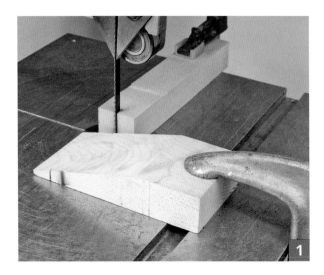

2. Cut the treads. You want the bandsaw blade to be centered on the wheel, but because the cut is at an angle it will start to one side of center on the top surface of the wheel and then exit the bottom on the opposite side of center. So hold the wheel about ⅛ in. off center when making the cuts. If you do that, the cut will be the same depth on both sides of the wheel disk. Practice on an extra disk to get the hang of it.

Cut half the disks with the wedge on the left of the blade. Reverse the wedge, so it's on the right side of the blade, to cut the remaining disks.

3. File with a small file and sand as needed to clean up the treads.

Bus Frame

If you are making the bus body from a solid block, skip this section.

The frame is a ¾-in.-thick board that runs the length of the bus and holds the hood, cab, and axles. The plans call for using ⅜-in. wood for the bus sides. You can use either ¼-in.- or ½-in.-thick wood instead, but you have to adjust the width of the frame accordingly: It needs to be 3 in. wide if you use ¼-in. sides; 2⅝ in. wide if you use ½-in.-thick sides. The front angled surfaces of the frame remain the same size.

1. Cut the frame from a piece of wood long enough for the frame as well as the back, front, and roof. The piece should be about 27 in. long in all.

2. Lay out the profile of the frame.

3. Cut the piece to length and rip it to width, but leave it rectangular. Do not cut the front angles yet.

4. Sand one face (the "floor") before attaching the seats.

Interior Assembly

The bus has nine seats, which are glued to the frame and aligned with the windows. A simple steering wheel goes in front of the driver's seat. You attach all the seats and the steering wheel before assembling the sides and roof.

Seats

Begin by cutting a strip of wood about 12 in. long by 1¼ in. wide and ¾ in. thick. If you like, the seats could certainly be made from ⅞-in.- or even 1-in.-thick wood. You can cut the seats on either the tablesaw or the bandsaw.

Bus Frame

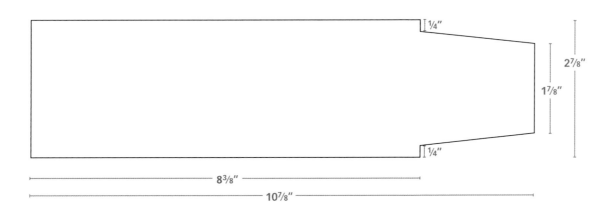

Seats

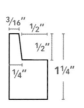

TOP VIEW **SIDE VIEW**

Front Bumper

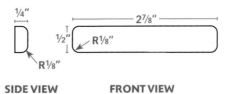

SIDE VIEW **FRONT VIEW**

(Rear bumper is 3⅛" long.)

Roof Lights

Steering Wheel Assembly

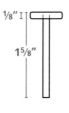

TOP VIEW **SIDE VIEW**

Grill

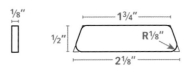

SIDE VIEW **FRONT VIEW**

Headlights

Tablesaw method:

1. Set the blade for a 7-degree tilt to make the angled surface of the backrest. Make the cut the length of the strip.

2. Set the blade for a ½-in. height and the rip fence ⅝ in. from the edge of the blade. Cut the blank along its length to make the seat surface.

TIP

Work safe when cutting small parts like the bus seats. Outfit the tablesaw with a zero-clearance insert so that offcuts won't get trapped, and use push sticks to move the wood over the blade.

3. Cut the individual seats from the resulting strip.

Bandsaw method:

1. Cut individual seat blanks from the 12-in. strip.

2. Lay out the seat and backrest on the end of each blank, and then make the cuts.

Bus Body

TOP VIEW

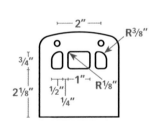

Drill floor ⁹⁄₆₄" (at 16° to 18°) for steering column.

R¼"

R³⁄₁₆"

³⁄₁₆"

Drill ⁹⁄₆₄" with door in place.

RIGHT SIDE VIEW

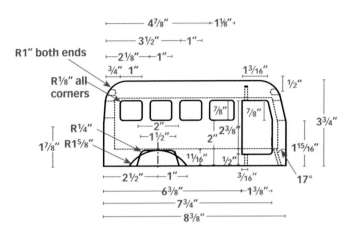

R1" both ends

R⅛" all corners

R¼"

R1⅝"

REAR VIEW

2"

R³⁄₈"

¾"

2⅛"

½"

1"

¼"

R⅛"

FRONT VIEW

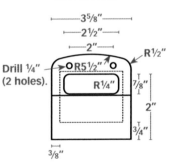

3⅝"

2½"

2"

R½"

Drill ¼" (2 holes).

R5½"

R¼"

⅞"

2"

¾"

⅜"

LEFT SIDE VIEW

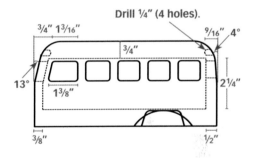

Drill ¼" (4 holes).

¾" 1³⁄₁₆"

¾"

⁹⁄₁₆" 4°

13°

1³⁄₈"

2¼"

⅜"

½"

Seat Assembly

1. Sand the seats and break all sharp corners.

2. Lay out the seat locations on the frame, using the drawing on p. 66 as a guide. Use small pencil marks.

3. Glue the seats to the frame. I press them in place firmly but don't find it necessary to clamp them.

3

Steering Wheel

1. Drill the angled hole for the steering column in the frame (floor) of the bus. The exact angle is not critical.

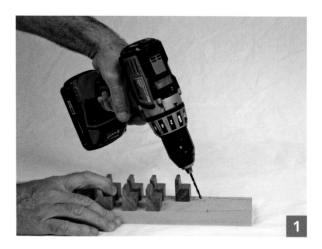

2. Make the steering wheel. Sand the end of a short piece of ⅝-in. dowel chucked in the drill press.

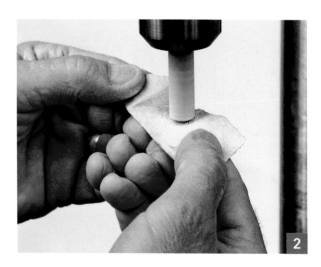

TIP

The drill press can double as a small vertical lathe, especially for light shaping and sanding of dowels. Grip the dowel only hand tight so the chuck jaws do not mar the surface. Sanding the flat end of a dowel with coarse sandpaper leaves a pattern of concentric circles that show the center location accurately.

3. Remove the dowel from the chuck, mark the center, and drill the end for a ⅛-in. dowel, about ¼ in. deep. Carefully saw off a slice a little more than ⅛ in. thick.

4. Glue a 1⅝-in.-long piece of ⅛-in. dowel into the steering wheel. When the glue is dry, grip the thin dowel in the drill press and sand to round the sharp corner of the steering wheel. Sand the dowel flush with the steering wheel on the other side. Glue the steering wheel in place once you have assembled the front and cut the inside contour.

Body Front, Back, and Roof

1. Use the piece left over from cutting the frame. Cut pieces that are ⅝ in. and ⅞ in. long (three each) to stack up to the 2¼-in. interior height of the body. Cut the roof piece, making it about ½ in. overlong.

2. Glue the end blocks together to form the front and back. Make sure the blocks are flush on one face—especially at the back—which will be the inside surface. Keep the ends of the blocks flush, too, because you will glue the bus sides to them later.

3. Sand the inside surface of the back. I use a disk sander and finish sanding by hand. Sand the inside surface of the roof, too. Be sure to keep the surface flat, especially at the ends, where it will join the front and backs.

4. Assemble the body front, roof, and back. Do not glue the front to the frame yet.

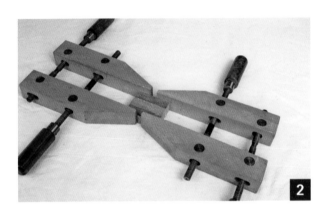

5. Pry up the top slightly so you can slip the band-saw blade in between the frame and the front to make the interior contour cuts.

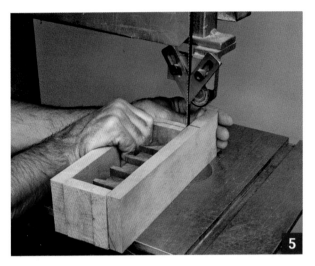

6. Saw the interior angle on the front surface. I begin this cut at the top, where the front meets the roof, and saw as accurately as possible to reduce filing and sanding later.

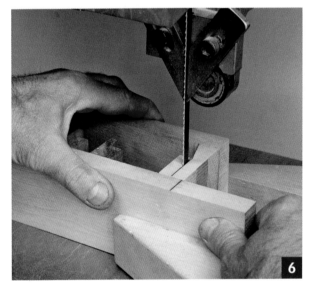

7. Slip some glue into the joint where the front meets the frame, and clamp. Make sure to align the edges.

8. File and sand as needed to finish the inside surfaces. Then glue the steering wheel assembly in place.

9. Saw the front and back surface flat and square to make it easy to drill holes for the windows and for the dowels representing flashing lights. Sand the sides flat. I use a sanding board for this. It's an old section of sanding belt glued to a piece of medium-density fiberboard.

10. Lay out the holes for the lights and windows on the front and the back. Use the templates for this (see the drawing at the end of the chapter), marking the centers clearly with an awl.

11. Drill the holes very carefully with a hand drill or a drill press. A brad-point drill or Forstner bit makes accurate alignment a bit easier.

12. Draw the contours of the windows using the holes as guides, or use the templates on p. 83. The exact contour is not critical.

13. Use a coping saw to cut out the windows. Be careful not to nick the rounded corners with the sawblade. This is a bit awkward with the roof in place, but not impossible. File and sand the front and back windows to their final shapes.

Body Sides

Glue the sides to the body, then attach the door and round the corners. When cutting out the sides, save a small piece for the door.

1. Use the templates to lay out the front and back contours and the centers for the holes that form the corners of the windows and door.

2. Drill the corner holes for the windows and door. Put a piece of scrap wood under the workpieces to help reduce the amount of tearout as the drill breaks through.

3. Use a coping saw to cut all the window openings. Alternatively, a scrollsaw would be great for this step, if you have access to one. Cut just to the waste side of the lines.

4. File a slight bevel on the rough edges to reduce the tearout when you file the openings.

5. File and sand the openings to the layout lines. I use 6-in. bastard-cut and smooth-cut flat files for this, so I have to do very little sanding later. Touch up the corners with a ¼-in. round file.

6. Saw and sand the wheel wells.

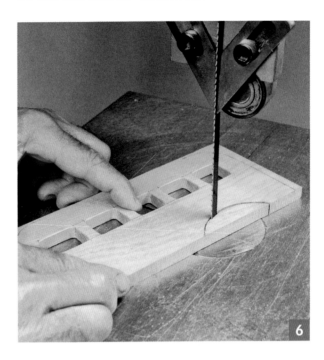

7. Trace the door opening onto a piece of the wood you used for the sides. Saw the door to shape, and then sand the edges so you have a ½₂-in. to ½₆-in. gap all around the door when in place.

8. Lay out the holes for the door's dowel hinges. These locations are important, so make them as accurate and aligned as possible.

9. Clamp the door in place to keep it centered. Drill the holes for the hinge dowels. The dowels will need to be a sliding fit in the hole, so drill a test hole in a scrap of wood to check the fit.

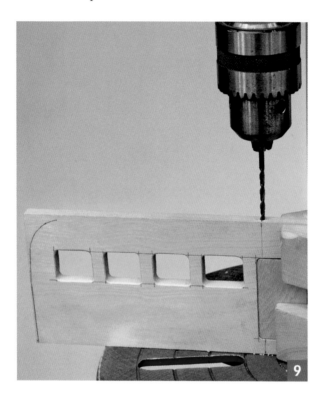

10. Cut the ⅛-in. dowels to create the door hinge pins, making them about ¼ in. overlong. You'll trim them after assembly.

11. Give the hinged side of the door a roundover with a ³⁄₁₆-in. radius so that it will pivot. Assemble the door and door hinge pins to check that the door opens freely. At this point, you can drill window holes into the door if you wish. You can leave them round or cut and file them into rectangles.

12. Wax the ends of the pins where they fit into the door. The door will rotate on the pins, and the pins will be glued into the side of the bus.

13. Install each pin about ⅜ in. deep into the side, and then spread glue around the section of the pin that is still exposed. Tap it in the rest of the way, making sure the door still opens.

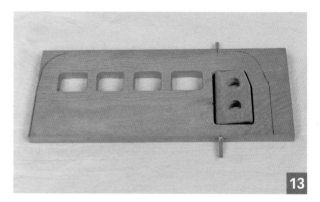

14. Carefully cut the sides to length, following the line for the straight vertical section at the front. These edges will fit against the rear edge of the front fenders. Sand these edges smooth and square now, when it is easy to smooth them.

15. Roundover the outside corner of this vertical section, strictly for appearances. A ⅛-in. or ³⁄₁₆-in. radius is fine.

16. Glue the sides to the body, one at a time. Check the alignment carefully. Look inside to be sure the spaces between the tops of the windows and the roof surface are even.

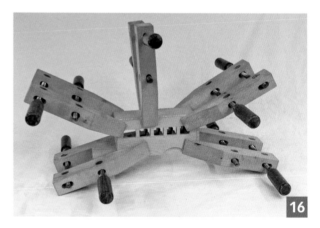

17. When the glue is dry, saw the angles and curves at the front and rear of the bus. Sand the edges roughly flush with the body. You'll do the final sanding after you round the corners.

18. File and sand the front of the body (the fire-wall area) as flat and smooth as you can. The back of the hood will attach here.

Body Roundovers

Older buses have very few sharp corners, so the idea here is to round everything. The corners along the sides of the roof have a ½-in. radius, the front and back have a 1-in. radius, and the top of the roof has a radius of 5 in. to 6 in. I don't measure any of these, though. I just round them until they look about right and generally match the drawings (see the drawing on p. 71).

I use a hand plane, disk sander, and belt sander to rough out the roundovers. Then I file them to even up any uneven areas. When I am satisfied with the general appearance, I hand-sand.

The photos in the rest of the chapter show the bus from many angles, so you can take a peek ahead and get an idea of the amount of rounding required on each surface.

Hood

The front section of the bus has the hood in the center with a fender on each side. All three parts are tapered on the sides, and have all the visible surfaces rounded to some degree.

Hood

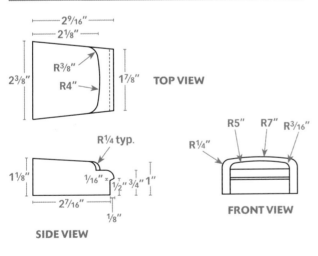

TOP VIEW

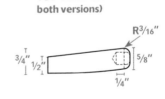

FRONT VIEW

SIDE VIEW

Fenders

TOP VIEW (common to both versions)

FENDER (for small-wheel version)

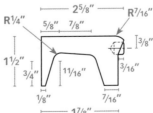

FENDER (for monster-wheel version)

Drill ¼" deep for ⅜" dowel headlights.

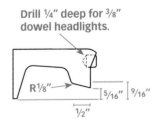

1. Square up a piece of wood at least 1⅛ in. thick, 2⅜ in. wide, and 2⁹⁄₁₆ in. long.

2. Lay out the side and top profile. I use the template (p. 83), but measuring it out will work also.

3. Saw the top and front profiles.

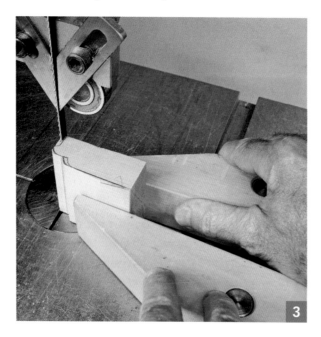

4. Lay out the side angles and saw them about 1⁄32 in. oversize. This makes it easier to align the hood and frame surfaces after assembly.

5. Shape the front of the hood. The exact sizes of the roundovers are not critical, as long as they look even and smooth and appear to match the drawings. I do all this shaping by eye, so every bus looks a little different.

6. When you are satisfied with the shape of the hood, fit it to the front of the body. If the surfaces of both pieces are exactly flat and square, the fit will be perfect. Usually, though, I have to do a little bit of trimming to get a pretty good fit, especially where the hood meets the firewall area. Slight gaps are okay where the fenders will be attached. When the fit is as good as you can get it, glue the hood to the frame and body.

Tip

I find that the best time to clean up glue squeeze-out is when the glue has just begun to harden, probably 20 to 40 minutes after assembly. The glue is still quite soft and easy to remove with a chisel. However, it is sometimes difficult to reach all the squeeze-out that way. The alternative is to immediately wipe away the squeeze-out with a slightly damp cloth. That can leave a smeared residue of glue that only becomes visible when finishing. Getting the wood too damp can weaken the glue joint.

7. Carefully disk sand or file the angled sides of the hood to ensure they are flat, square, and flush with the frame. The fenders attach to these surfaces.

Fenders

1. Use the template on p. 83 to lay out the fenders side by side on a strip of wood. Mark the centers and drill the ½-in.-diameter holes that define the curves on the wheel wells.

2. Mark the centers of the headlight holes and drill them to fit a ⅜-in. dowel. Check the size ahead of time.

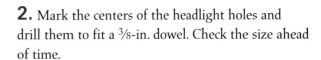

3. Saw out the wheel wells and sand them smooth. This is easier to do before sawing the angles on the fenders.

4. Saw the fenders to rough shape, including the front contour and the angled surface.

5. Hold a fender against the hood and trace the hood's shape on it, then file and sand to the line to give the fenders their rounded profile. At the front, match up the top surface as it meets the top surface of the hood. Get this as close as you can before assembly, and then touch it up a little after you have glued on the fenders.

6. When the fit is close all around, glue the fenders to the hood. I press them firmly into place, without clamping.

7. After the glue has dried, smooth the transitions between the fender front and the hood front.

Bumpers, Grill, and Lights

1. Cut a strip of wood long enough for both bumpers. Cut the bumpers to length and smooth the corners. Glue the bumpers to the ends of the frame, with each bumper centered left to right and flush with the bottom of the frame.

2. Cut a thin strip of wood for the grill. I used yellowheart for this bus, but other solid wood is fine, as is ⅛-in. Baltic birch plywood. For the bus with conventional wheels, I used a small piece of veneer; it works well and looks less bulky. Glue the grill in place.

3. The headlights are pretty straightforward. Round and smooth the ends of a piece of ⅜-in. dowel, then cut it to length and glue it in place.

4. For the roof lights, cut two lengths of ¼-in. dowel, each about 1½ in. long. I didn't have any reddish wood dowels, so I used a ¼-in. plug cutter and made some padauk plugs ⅜ in. long. Before cutting the roof lights to length, sand to round the ends of the dowel stock. Use the drill press for this as you did with the steering wheel.

Tip
You can make dowels on the drill press. Chuck a short, square length that's slightly larger than the finished diameter of the dowel you want. Use a file to turn the wood round, and finish with sandpaper. To size the dowel precisely, use calipers or even an open-end wrench as a gauge.

5. Cut the dowels to length and sand off the rough end to smooth the corners slightly. Put glue in the holes and push or tap the light dowels into place.

Axle Housings and Driveshaft

1. Cut a strip of 1⅛-in.-thick wood about 6 in. long, which is enough for both monster-bus axle housings.

2. Cut the housings to their finished length. As the drawing below shows, the rear housing is 3 in. long; the front housing, 2¾ in. long. Don't cut the ½-in. by ¾-in. notches yet.

3. Lay out and drill the holes to fit factory-made ⅜-in. dowel axles. Dowel diameters vary a bit, so drill a test hole in scrap wood to check the fit.

Monster-Bus Axle Housings

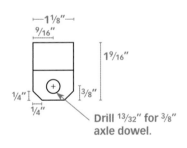

—1⅛"—
9/16"
1 9/16"
¼"
3/8"
¼"
Drill 13/32" for ⅜"
axle dowel.

SIDE VIEW

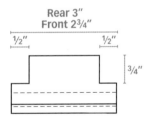

Rear 3"
Front 2¾"
½"   ½"
¾"

FRONT VIEW

Monster-Bus Driveshafts

TOP VIEW

⅜"

FRONT VIEW

7/8"   2¼"   ⅜"
½"
3/8"
½"
1"

To fit between axle
housings (about 6⅛")

4. Cut the notches and bevels and sand away all the sawmarks. Break all the sharp corners except on the surface that will contact the frame.

5. Mark the axle housing locations on the underside of the frame. Center the wheels under the wheel wells.

6. Glue and clamp one axle housing in place, checking it for square as well as for position. Clamp the second one in place without glue.

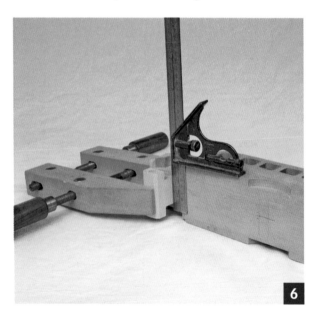

7. Cut the driveshaft blank to length so it fits tight between the housings. Cut the driveshaft shape, and then sand it to remove sawmarks and any sharp corners.

8. Glue the driveshaft and the second axle housing on at the same time to ensure that the parts all fit snugly. As usual, it is a good idea to dry-fit the parts together first.

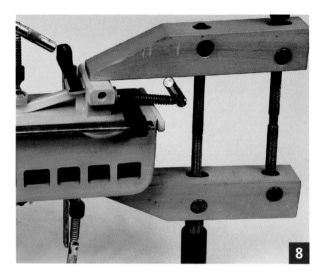

9. Remove any excess glue and finish-sand the bus.

Finishing and Assembly

This bus has monster wheels, so I spray-finish them separately from the bus body. See the notes on finishing, p. 3.

Put the bus together when the finish has dried. Assemble the wheels, axles, and hubs, following the procedure covered in Chapter 1, p. 25. There's no need for plastic washers on the axles, though. I used factory-made dowel caps for the hubs, but you could make your own, as described on p. 25.

Templates

For full-size template, enlarge by 295%.

FENDER (small wheels)

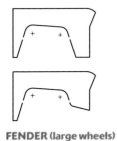

FENDER (large wheels)

HOOD

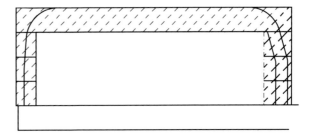

RIGHT SIDE

Interior outlined by phantom line

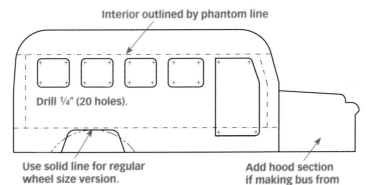

Drill ¼" (20 holes).

Use solid line for regular
wheel size version.

Add hood section
if making bus from
one solid block.

LEFT (DRIVER'S) SIDE

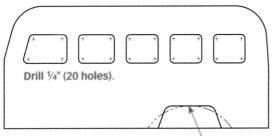

Drill ¼" (20 holes).

Use solid line for regular
wheel size version.

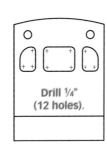

Drill ¼"
(12 holes).

REAR WINDOW

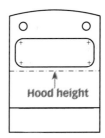

Hood height

FRONT WINDOW

Wheel

TABLESAW METHOD

Wheel

BANDSAW METHOD

How to make a solid-block *Body*

As MUCH AS I LIKE THE COLOR of the yellowheart monster bus, sometimes the color and grain of a solid block yield a better look. To make a bus body from a solid block, rough out the exterior shape, saw pieces from each side, cut the windows, bandsaw the interior from the remaining block, and reassemble everything for its final shaping. Here are the specifics.

1. Square up the wood to its final 3¾-in. by 3¾-in. by 11⅜-in. size. Lay out the side profile but leave the front and back windshield areas square to the length of the blank. This will allow more accurate drilling for the window and roof light holes.

2. Saw the front profile, defining where the headlights and grill will go. **(PHOTO 1)**

3. Lay out the top profile of the hood. Carefully make those cuts to define the angled hood. **(PHOTO 2)**

4. Cut away a slab on each side. Mark lines ⅜ in. in along the sides. Saw carefully on the inside of the lines, leaving the sides about 1/32 in. oversize. **(PHOTO 3)**

5. Use the template on p. 83 to mark the four holes for the interior cut and the profile lines for the interior cutout. Then drill the holes. **(PHOTO 4)**

6. To hollow the interior, begin by marking an entry line for the bandsaw blade. I use a spot that will be covered by the rear bumper, because it is about the only place that will be invisible later. Cut away the interior, staying as close to the lines as you can. **(PHOTO 5)**

7. Glue the bus body closed. Glue a piece of veneer into the entry cut to close that gap. You may need a double thickness. Orient the veneer grain along the width of the bus to make it easier to conform to the sawn curve. **(PHOTO 6)**

8. Sand the sawn faces of the body sides and the side slabs on a belt sander, then finish the flattening process with a sanding board, as shown on p. 74. I use a large flat file to remove the sawmarks and flatten the interior surfaces as much as possible (especially the floor), then switch to a large smooth file and finally sandpaper. Most of the interior surfaces are not readily visible, but the floor should be flat enough to allow the seats to glue into place.

9. Lay out and drill the steering wheel hole up from the underside of the bus. The remaining steps—cutting windows and windshield, fitting the door, shaping the fenders, adding the bumpers and grill, and rounding over the edges—are the same as for the laminated body (see pp. 75–79). **(PHOTO 7)**

How to make conventional *Wheels*

I USED 1¾-IN. FACTORY-MADE WHEELS for the bus shown here. They came with only ¼-in. holes, so I drilled them out to ⅜ in., which allowed me to use the stronger ¹¹⁄₃₂-in. axle pins.

1⅛"
9/16"
5/16"
¼"
¼"
Drill ¹¹⁄₃₂" for axle pins

Rear 3"
Front 2¾"
5/8"

You can easily make conventional wheels instead, although they lack a bit of the detail that factory-made ones have. The conventional wheels also require slightly different axle housings, as shown in the drawing.

1. Use a holesaw to make the blanks. Set the drill press to its lowest speed. The wheel will be about ³⁄₁₆ in. smaller in diameter than the nominal size of the holesaw.

2. Cut the head off a bolt that fits the center hole left by the holesaw; a bolt that's ¼-in. diameter and at least 2 in. long usually works. Grip the shank of the bolt in the drill press, leaving the threads exposed. Put the wood wheel blank onto the bolt, then a washer, and

tighten it in place with a nut. If there's room, put a washer between the wheel and the chuck.

3. With the drill press still at a slow speed, file and sand the sawn circumference. Round over the corners to suit. You could play with adding a few grooves in the periphery to produce treads.

4. Remove the wheel and drill out the center to the axle or pin size. Counterbore one end of the hole to a size suitable for the axle pin head or the dowel cap.

5. To assemble the wheels, use the wrench-shaped spacer described in Chapter 1 (pp. 26–27). Apply glue to the axle housing hole and tap in the axle pin. Remove the spacer and the wheels will spin freely.

CHAPTER 5

Eight-Wheel Articulating Tractor

*Y*ou can often see these huge tractors working on large farms and road construction. They have articulated steering and typically roll on eight large tires— sometimes twelve. In real life, they are more than 15 ft. wide and 12 ft. tall.

This toy also has an articulated steering joint and eight monster wheels. The front section, made from a narrow block, has the cab on top and four wheels mounted on a solid axle. The smaller rear section has another axle and a hitch for implements. In keeping with the theme of this book, I have made a pair of roller compactors, the kind used on heavy construction in real life. However, you could instead make any variety of wagons, trailers, or farm implements.

I used purpleheart for the body sections and birch for the wheels. But feel free to reverse the color scheme, depending on what you have in your wood supply.

Eight-Wheel Articulating Tractor Plans

TOP VIEW

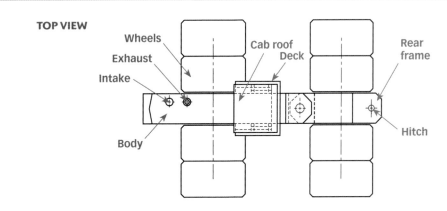

Wheels

Exhaust

Intake

Body

Cab roof

Deck

Rear frame

Hitch

FRONT VIEW

Cab roof

Cab side

Body

Deck

Wheel hub

Axle

SIDE VIEW

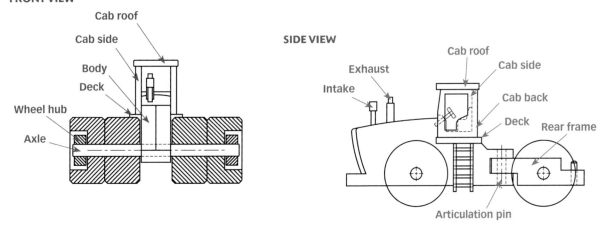

Exhaust

Intake

Cab roof

Cab side

Cab back

Deck

Rear frame

Articulation pin

EIGHT-WHEEL ARTICULATING TRACTOR CUT LIST

PART NAME	FINISH DIMENSIONS L × W × T, IN.	NO. REQ'D.	NOTES
Wheels	2¾ dia. × ¾ thick per half	8	Need 16 halves to make 8 wheels.
Body	7¼ × 2⅞ × 1¼	1	
Rear frame	4 × 1⅛ × 1¼	1	Use same wood as for body.
Cab base	1½ × ¹⁵/₁₆ × 1¼	1	Contrasting wood
Cab sides	2 × 1¾ × ¼	2	Contrasting wood. Cut oversize to start.
Cab roof	1⅞ × 1⅞ × ¼	1	Contrasting wood
Cab back	2 × 1¼ × ¼	1	Contrasting wood. Cut oversize to start.
Deck	2¼ × 2 × ¼	1	Contrasting wood
Seat	⅞ × 1 × ⅝	1	
Steering wheel	½ dowel × ⅛ long	1	Cut from longer piece after shaping.
Steering column	⅛ dowel × 1 long	1	
Ladder sides	2⁵/₁₆ × ⅜ × ⅛	4	Baltic birch plywood
Ladder rungs	⅛ dowel × ⅞ long	10	Cut 1 in. overlong, trim after assembly.
Exhaust pipe	⅜ dowel × 1¾ long	1	Cut ½ in. overlong, trim before installation.
Exhaust tip	¼ dowel × 1 long	1	
Intake	¼ dowel × 1⅞ long	1	
Intake cap	⅜ dowel × ½ long	1	Cut ½ in. overlong, trim before installation.
Hitch pin	¼ dowel × 1⅛ long	1	
Articulation pin	⅜ dowel × 1½ long	1	Cut ¼ in. overlong, trim after installation.
Axles	½ dowel × 7⅛ long	2	Measure precise length from tractor.
Wheel hubs	1 dia. wheel, factory made	4	
Plastic washers	To fit	2–10	Optional for wheels and articulation joint
Compactor frames	7 × 4⅞ × ¼	2	Baltic birch plywood
Compactor skirts	3 × 1 × ¼	4	Baltic birch plywood
Rollers	2 dowel × 4 long	2	Stock dowel from building supply
Roller axles	½ dowel × 5 long	2	Trim after assembly.
Compactor hitches	1¾ × ⅞ × ¼	2	Baltic birch plywood
Compactor hitch pins	¼ dowel × ⅝ long	2	
Optional weight	4⅝ × 1½ × ½	2	Use dense, heavy hardwood.

Wheels

The tractor wheels are identical to the monster wheels on the school bus in Chapter 4.

1. See pp. 7–9 for details on how to cut the treads with a tablesaw or bandsaw.

2. When the wheels are complete, glue them together in pairs to make dual wheels. This will ensure that both wheels spin when kids push or pull the toy. Put a bit of masking tape over a ½-in. dowel to make it a snug fit in the wheel holes. This will keep the holes aligned. Use glue sparingly, because you don't want any excess squeeze-out here. Remove the dowel as soon as possible so it doesn't end up frozen in the axle hole.

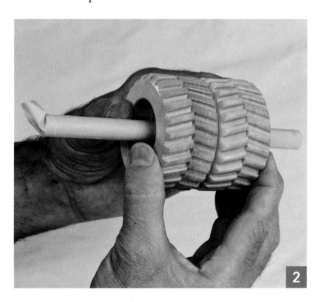

Body and Rear Frame

The single block of wood that forms the body will be pinned to the rear frame to create an articulated steering joint.

1. Rough out a block of wood large enough to yield the body, rear frame, and cab base.

2. Lay out those three parts. I used the templates (p. 100) for the profile and marked the axle holes with an awl.

3. Saw the outlines, all except the contour of the bumper (actually a weight mount) and grill area at the front of the body.

4. Lay out the front grill and bumper area on both sides.

5. Use the tread wedge fixture (p. 66) to cut the slightly pointed grill. Cut from each side, moving the wedge to the opposite side of the blade after the first cut. Stop the cuts ¼ in. before the intersection of the grill and the bumper. If you don't, the cut may go too deep on the bottom side.

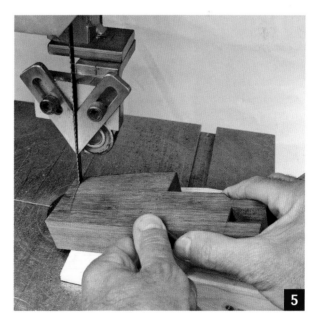

Body

TOP VIEW

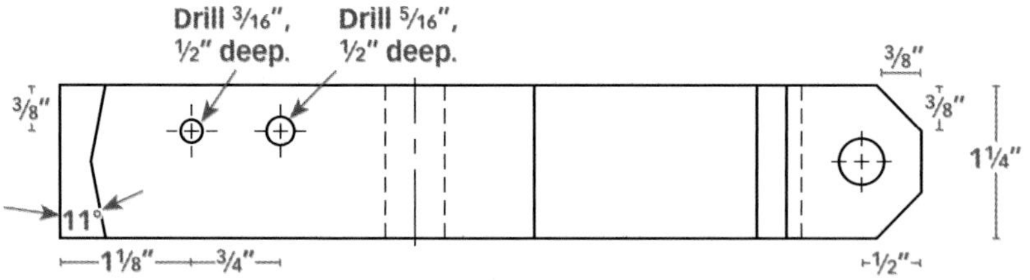

Drill 3/16", 1/2" deep.
Drill 5/16", 1/2" deep.
3/8"
11°
1 1/8"
3/4"
3/8"
3/8"
1 1/4"
1/2"

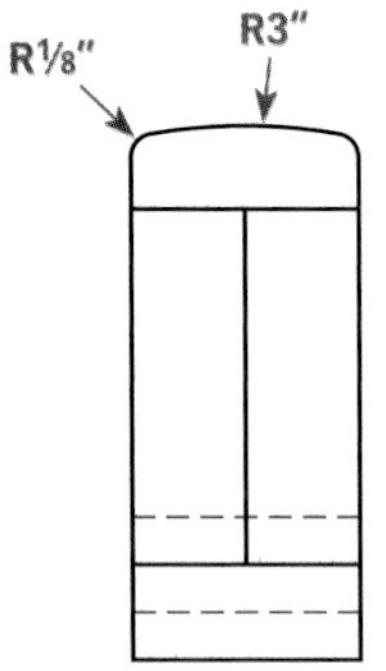

R1/8"
R3"

FRONT VIEW

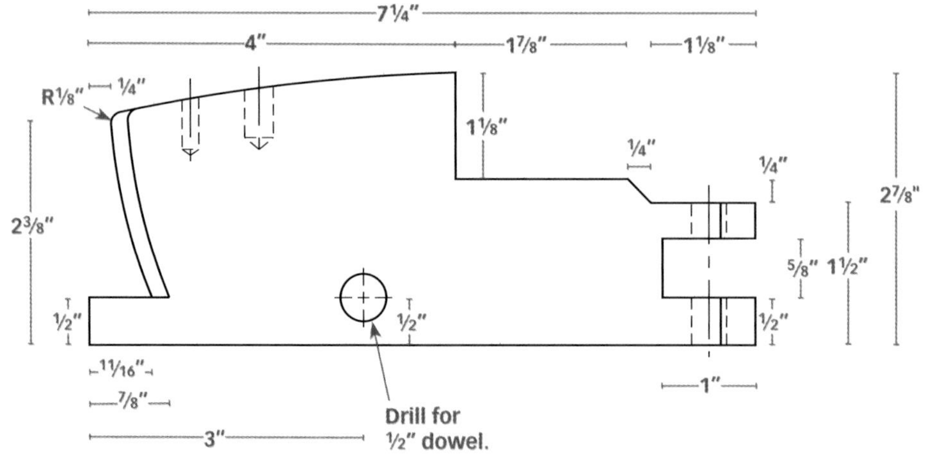

7 1/4"
4"
1 7/8"
1 1/8"
R1/8"
1/4"
1 1/8"
1/4"
1/4"
2 7/8"
2 3/8"
5/8"
1 1/2"
1/2"
1/2"
1/2"
1 1/16"
7/8"
3"
1"
Drill for 1/2" dowel.

SIDE VIEW

Rear Frame

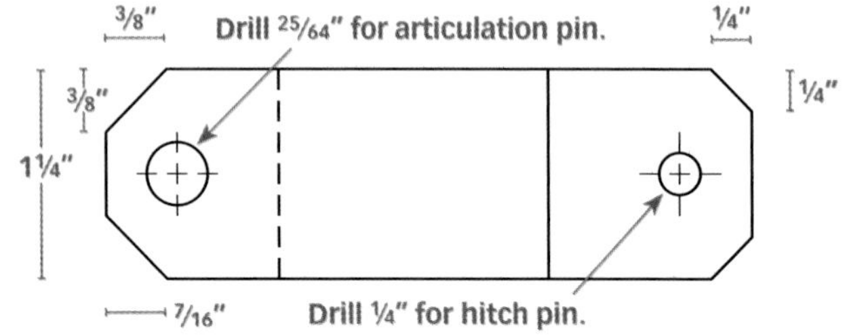

3/8"
Drill 25/64" for articulation pin.
1/4"
3/8"
1/4"
1 1/4"
7/16"
Drill 1/4" for hitch pin.

TOP VIEW

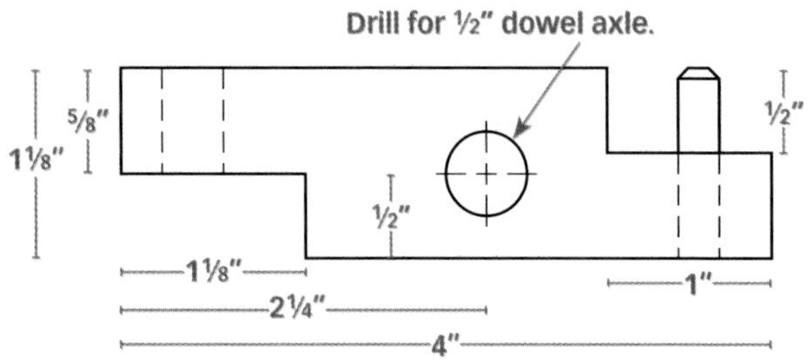

Drill for 1/2" dowel axle.
5/8"
1 1/8"
1/2"
1/2"
1 1/8"
2 1/4"
1"
4"

SIDE VIEW

6. Position the wedge fixture so it faces the blade. Cut the bumper top to the line.

7. Finish cutting the bottom of the grill contour with a hand saw, then file and sand the grill and bumper surfaces.

8. Drill the exhaust and intake holes, as well as the articulation hole. Mark and drill the articulation hole in the rear frame while you are at it.

9. Drill the axle hole. This will need to be a sliding fit on the ½-in. dowel axle. Use either a ³³⁄₆₄-in. or ¹⁷⁄₃₂-in. drill. If worst comes to worst, drill a ½-in. hole and then sand down the dowel to obtain the fit. While you have the drill set up, make the axle hole in the rear frame.

10. Sand away the sawmarks and break sharp corners. Make sure the deck area of the body piece is flat; finish is not important in this spot because the deck will cover it.

Cab Interior

The cab sits on a deck and consists of an interior (base) with seat and steering wheel and an exterior with sides, a back, and a roof. I used birch, which contrasts with the darker color of the purpleheart body and frame.

1. Cut the deck to size, sand, and glue it onto the body.

2. Fit the cab interior (cut out earlier along with the body and rear frame) to the deck and body. You may have to file and shape the front of the base or the firewall area of the body to get a close fit. This is important only at the top because a slight gap on the sides can be covered by the cab sides. When the

Deck

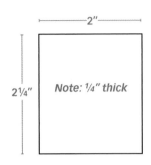

2"

2¼"

Note: ¼" thick

Cab Base

SIDE VIEW

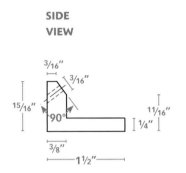

3/16"

3/16"

15/16"

90°

3/8"

1½"

11/16"

¼"

FRONT VIEW

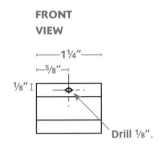

1¼"

5/8"

1/8" I

Drill ⅛".

Steering Wheel and Column

FRONT VIEW   **SIDE VIEW**

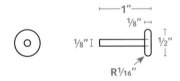

1"

1/8"

1/8" I

½"

R1/16"

Seat

FRONT VIEW   **SIDE VIEW**

7/8"

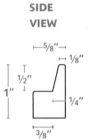

5/8"

1/8"

½"

1"

¼"

3/8"

Cab Interior Assembly

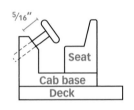

5/16"

Seat

Cab base

Deck

fit is good, glue the cab interior to the deck. Align the sides with the sides of the body.

3. To make the steering wheel, follow the instructions in Chapter 4, p. 72, but use the dimensions given in the cut list on p. 88. Drill the steering-

column hole. It should be about ½ in. deep and sized to fit a ⅛-in. dowel. I ended up using a 9/64-in. bit. This hole is centered on the angled dash of the cab base and is drilled at 90 degrees to the dashboard.

4. Make the seat. I use a piece of ⅝-in.-thick birch cut to ⅞ in. by 1 in. Mark out the contour on the end and carefully cut it on the bandsaw. It's the same procedure used to make the School Bus seats in Chapter 4 (see p. 68). Hold the seat in a clamp when sawing to keep fingers a safe distance from the blade. Sand to break all sharp corners.

5. Glue the steering wheel assembly into the dash, with the seat sitting loosely in place and aligned with the back of the cab base. This will help determine how far the steering wheel should stand away from the dash.

6. Glue the seat into place. I just press it firmly in place without clamping.

Cab Exterior

1. Cut the cab sides and back, making all three parts a bit oversize for now. When you lay out the pieces, orient the grain vertically. Lay out the window locations in the back and sides, either measuring directly or using the template on p. 100. Mark centers in each corner of the window for a hole to fit your coping saw or scrollsaw blade.

Tip

Some scrollsaw blades need only very small entry holes (³⁄₃₂ in.), whereas some coping saw blades need a ³⁄₁₆-in. hole. If you want sharper corners than a ³⁄₁₆-in. bit provides, drill two ⅛-in. holes side by side in one corner of the window layout. Join the holes with a small chisel to allow the coping saw blade to fit.

2. Put a dot of glue on the edge of the sides and press them together. Drill the holes in each window corner. Fit a coping saw blade through one hole and carefully saw out the windows. Do the same on the back.

Cab Assembly

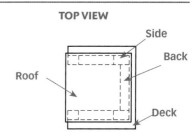

TOP VIEW

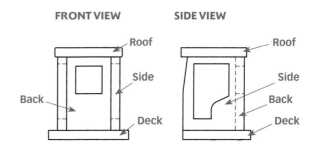

FRONT VIEW   **SIDE VIEW**

Cab Back   ### Cab Side

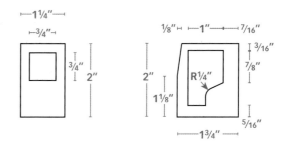

Cab Roof

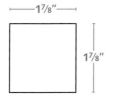

3. File the edges of the windows smooth. Bevel the edges first to minimize tearout.

4. Cut or sand the side pieces to their final dimensions, which will separate them. Finish-sand all the window surfaces and break any sharp corners.

5. Glue the sides and back onto the cab base, after a dry run to check fits and sizes. The sides should protrude slightly past the back.

In the photo below I have used an offcut of purpleheart in place of the roof to allow clamps to put some downward pressure on the sides. Two clamps are applying side pressure on the joint between the back and the sides. One more clamp is putting side pressure on the sides at their front edge.

6. When the glue has dried, sand the back surfaces flush and sand to level the top surfaces in preparation for the roof. When you sand the top, put a spacer under the side to keep the assembly square to the sanding disk. A slower but more reliable method is to use a sanding board.

7. Cut the roof, sanding off any sharp corners and edges. Glue it to the cab assembly so the overhang is uniform all around.

Intake and Exhaust Assemblies

1. Cut the two pieces of ¼-in. dowel to length. Cut the ⅜-in. dowels ½ in. overlong to make it easier to hold them for drilling. Square up one end of each dowel and mark the center on one end of each ⅜-in.-diameter dowel.

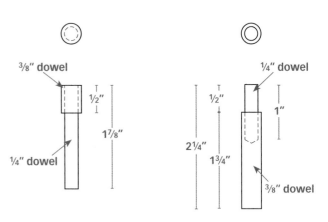

Ladder Sides   ## Ladder Rungs

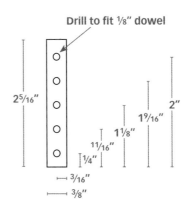

2. Drill ¼-in. holes ½ in. deep in the ends of the ⅜-in. dowels.

3. Glue the smaller dowels into the holes, using a toothpick to apply glue into the holes.

4. Saw off the extra ½ in. of dowel if you haven't already done so. Sand the hood area to prepare it for finishing. Now glue the exhaust and intake assemblies into the holes in the hood.

Ladders

These ladders are very similar to those on the Giant Loader in Chapter 1, but smaller. Use the instructions from the ladder section (p. 14), but follow the sizes shown in the cut list and the drawing on the facing page.

Assembly

It's now time to fit the articulation joint, and then the wheels and axles. The procedures are the same as those used for the Giant Loader. Also review the section describing the plastic washers I use to make the moving parts slide easier and last longer (see p. 16).

Hitch Pin

Cut the hitch pin dowel, then sand and bevel one end. Glue it into place so it protrudes from the bottom slightly. Sand the dowel flush after the glue is dry.

Articulation Joint

The halves of the articulation joint need to be a snug sliding fit. You also want to be sure that the axle holes are parallel when you pin the articulation joint together.

1. File and sand the projection on the rear frame to get a snug fit into the slot in the body. To test the fit, I use a piece of dowel 5 in. to 6 in. long, which allows me to install and remove it easily.

2. Once you can pin the articulation joint together, use two longer pieces of ½-in. dowel to double-check that the axle holes are parallel. If they aren't, file to correct the mating surfaces on the rear frame or the body to ensure that everything is square. If the joint becomes too loose, add a plastic washer to take up the space (or glue in a piece of veneer). If the joint's pivot hole is slightly off square, you may need to drill it out ¹⁄₆₄ in. larger, or file it slightly using a round file.

3. When everything fits nicely, remove the dowel and put paste wax into the pivot hole in the body using a cotton swab. Temporarily install the dowel for the articulation joint. Mark the length, remove it, and cut it about ⅟₁₆ in. too long. Sand the ends and bevel them slightly.

4. Put glue in the upper part of the hole in the body. Don't put any below the notch, or glue will be dragged into the hole in the rear frame, seizing up the joint.

5. Tap in the dowel until you have about ½ in. to go. Put glue on this ½ in., then tap the dowel in until only ⅟₁₆ in. protrudes.

6. When the glue has dried, file and sand the dowel flush if you wish. It's OK to leave the dowel slightly long.

Ladders

1. Position the ladders. They should contact the underside of the deck and protrude slightly past the bottom of the tractor body. Put a wheel in place temporarily so you can position the ladder about ¼ in. away from the wheel. The exact size of the gap is not critical.

2. Glue the ladders in place. Dab a bit of glue along the contacting edges of the ladder, but not so much that you will have squeeze-out in and under the rungs.

Wheels and Finish

1. Make the hubs. The axle itself as well as the wheels will spin freely. See Chapter 1, p. 25, for the procedure.

2. Assemble the wheels, axles, and hubs, again following the procedures in Chapter 1.

3. Finish the assembly as well as the wheels. I do these separately, as it is a little easier. See the notes on finishing on p. 3.

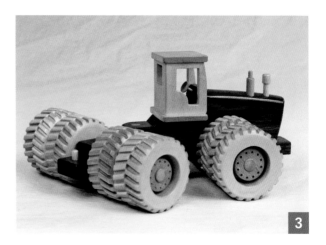

Compactors

These compactors are quite quick to make and fun for kids to tow around when playing with the tractor.

Compactor Frame

1. Cut two pieces of Baltic birch plywood to rough size. Lay out the frame profile, including the hole centers, on one piece. Glue the pieces together, putting the glue in areas that will be removed later.

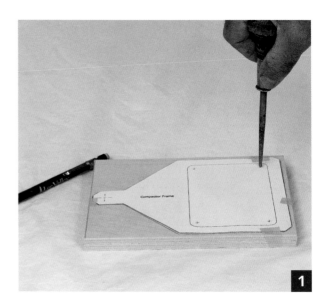

Compactor Assembly

TOP VIEW

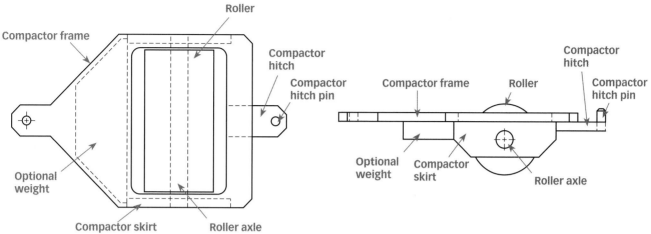

Roller

Compactor frame

Compactor hitch

Compactor hitch pin

Optional weight

Compactor skirt

Roller axle

SIDE VIEW

Compactor frame

Roller

Compactor hitch

Compactor hitch pin

Optional weight

Compactor skirt

Roller axle

Compactor Frame

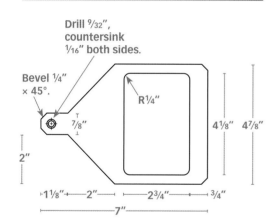

Drill ⁹/₃₂", countersink ¹/₁₆" both sides.

Bevel ¼" × 45°.

R¼"

⁷/₈"

2"

4⅛" 4⅞"

1⅛" 2" 2¾" ¾"

7"

Compactor Skirt

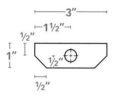

3"

1½"

½"

1"

½"

½"

Compactor Hitch

Drill for ¼" dowel.

¼" × 45°

⁷/₈"

1⅜"

1¾"

¼" ⅝"

Roller

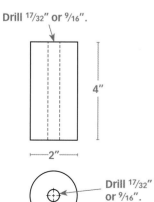

Drill ¹⁷/₃₂" or ⁹/₁₆".

4"

2"

Drill ¹⁷/₃₂" or ⁹/₁₆".

Optional Weight

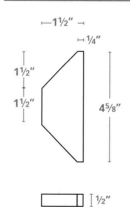

1½"

¼"

1½"

1½"

4⅝"

½"

2. Drill the holes in the corners of the cut-out area; brad point or Forstner bits work well here. Also drill the 9/32-in. hole for the hitch.

3. Cut out the center area with a coping saw. Put masking tape around the cut area to reduce tearout on the back side. After sawing, remove the tape and bevel the cut edges to reduce tearout when filing and sanding the cuts smooth.

4. Saw the outside contour, then smooth and bevel those cut surfaces.

Compactor Skirts

The compactor skirts serve as mounts for the roller axle.

1. Glue, drill, and cut these pieces the same way you did the compactor frames. You will need two pairs of skirts.

2. Glue the skirts to the frame. Slide a piece of ½-in. dowel through the hole in the skirts to help keep the parts aligned. Remove before the glue fully dries. Position the skirts 1/64 in. to 1/32 in. back from the inside edges of the frame. After the glue has dried, file and sand the inside edges flush with the skirts.

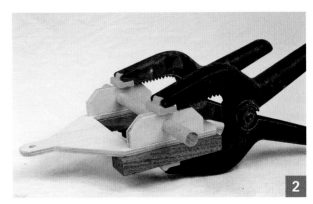

Compactor Hitch and Roller

The hitch is glued to the back of the frame. Make it using the same method you did for the frame: gluing the parts together, drilling, and then sawing the contour.

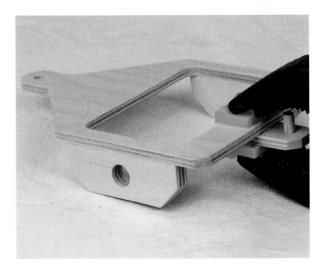

1. Cut the 2-in.-diameter roller dowels to length. They should be 1/32 in. to 1/16 in. shorter than the distance between the skirts. Sand the ends smooth and square, with bevels on the ends.

2. Mark the center. I use a combination square center head for this, but careful measurements will work, too.

3. Drill the hole for the ½-in. axle dowel in the center of each roller. The roller has to spin freely on the axle dowel, so drill the hole a bit larger than the dowel, or sand the dowel down. Make sure the roller dowel is exactly square to the drill press table, checking in two places 90 degrees apart. If you have a lathe and a Jacobs chuck accessory, use it to drill this hole.

4. Cut the ½-in. axle dowel 5 in. long, which should be ⅛ in. overlong. The dowel will protrude about 1/16 in. from each side. You can leave it proud or sand it flush.

5. Assemble the roller and axle. I put in one or two plastic washers in each end, depending on the amount of clearance that exists. The roller should turn freely, but not rub on the skirts.

Insert the axle dowel until only ⅜ in. remains to go. Apply glue to the exposed dowel, and to the open hole in the opposite skirt. Tap or push the axle dowel in the rest of the way until it is centered.

Compactor Weight

The weight helps keep the front compactor from lifting off the tractor hitch pin, especially when the second compactor is hooked up. It is not needed if you are only making one compactor. The most effective method is to have the weight on the front compactor only. It can be put on the top of the front compactor frame, or under as shown.

1. Choose a heavy wood for the weight. I used purpleheart to match the tractor, but any dense wood is fine.

2. Cut the weight to size, then file and sand to remove sawmarks and all sharp corners.

3. Glue the weight to the frame.

4. Give the compactor a final sanding, and finish it as you did the tractor.

Templates

For full-size template, enlarge by 300%.

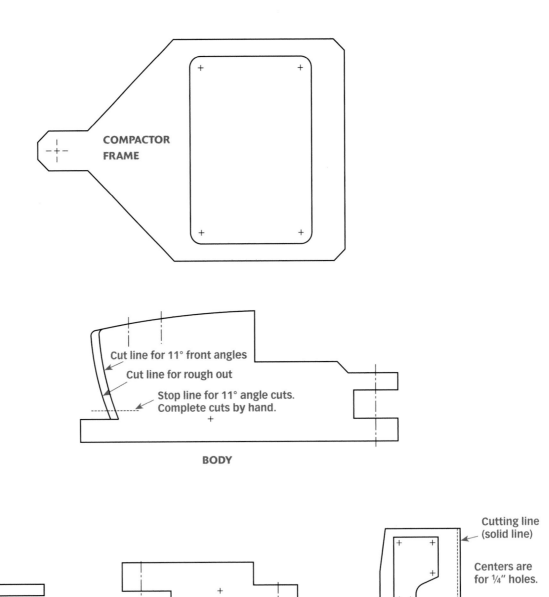

Note: Use wheel templates from School Bus.

CHAPTER 6

Heavy Equipment Transporter

*h**eavy equipment*** transporters haul extremely large machines on an oversize trailer. This toy version can haul the giant loader, mining truck, and grader, as well as the other oversize vehicles in this book. The truck has a simple frame that holds the hood, a hollow cab with seats, and a fifth-wheel hitch for the trailer. The truck has eight oversize wheels.

The trailer is extra wide, with 10 sets of 1½-in.-diameter factory-made dual wheels. It has folding ramps to help load whatever toy is to be hauled. The eight truck wheels are factory made, which I customized with additional angled crosscuts.

For "Giant Loader" see p. 4.

SIDE VIEW

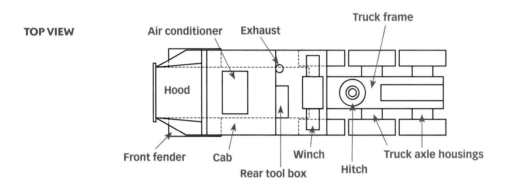

Air conditioner

Side tool box

Front fender

Rear tool box

Winch

Hitch ramp

Deck · Hitch · Truck frame

Truck axle housings

Bumper · Steps · Fuel tank · Rear fender

TOP VIEW

Air conditioner · Exhaust · Truck frame

Hood

Front fender · Cab · Rear tool box · Winch · Hitch · Truck axle housings

Truck Frame

TOP VIEW

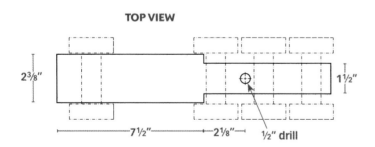

2³⁄₈″

1½″

7½″ · 2⅛″ · ½″ drill

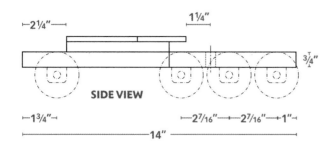

2¼″

1¼″

¾″

SIDE VIEW

1¾″ · 2⁷⁄₁₆″ · 2⁷⁄₁₆″ · 1″

14″

Deck Base

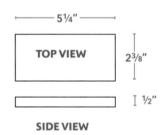

5¼″

TOP VIEW

2³⁄₈″

½″

SIDE VIEW

Deck

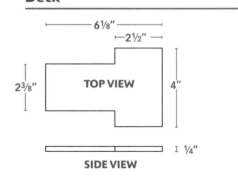

6⅛″

2½″

TOP VIEW

2³⁄₈″

4″

¼″

SIDE VIEW

HEAVY EQUIPMENT TRANSPORTER **CUT LIST**

PART NAME	FINISH DIMENSIONS L × W × T, IN.	NO. REQ'D.	NOTES
Truck Parts			
Truck frame	14 × 2 3/8 × 3/4	1	
Deck base	5 1/4 × 2 3/8 × 1/2	1	Baltic birch plywood
Deck	6 1/8 × 4 × 1/4	1	Baltic birch plywood
Hood	2 1/4 × 4 × 2 1/8	1	
Cab sides	2 1/8 × 3 5/8 × 1/4	2	Cut oversize, trim after assembly.
Cab back	3 1/2 × 2 1/8 × 1/4	1	Cut oversize, trim after assembly.
Cab roof	4 × 3 5/16 × 1/4	1	
Cab interior	3 1/2 × 3 3/8 × 1 3/8	1	
Seats	1 × 1 × 7/8	2	Can be 1 × 1 × 3/4 if need be.
Engine cover	1 3/4 × 1 × 3/4	1	
Air conditioner	2 × 1 1/4 × 1/4	1	
Front fenders	2 3/4 × 1 3/16 × 7/8	2	
Rear fenders	1 3/4 × 1 1/8 × 3/4	2	
Ladder sides	1 3/4 × 13/16 × 1/8	4	Baltic birch plywood; cut overlong, trim after assembly.
Ladder rungs	1/8 dowel × 3/4 long	8	Cut 7/8 in. long, trim after assembly.
Side tool boxes	3 1/2 × 5/8 × 1/2	2	Measure truck for exact length.
Fuel tanks	1 1/4 dowel × 2 3/4 long	2	Measure truck for exact length.
Truck axle housings	2 3/4 × 1 × 3/4	4	
Truck steps	3/16 dowel × 1/2 long	6	
Rear tool box	1 1/2 × 1 1/4 × 1/2	1	
Winch housing	1 1/2 × 1 1/8 × 1	1	
Winch	5/8 dowel × 3 1/2 long	1	
Hitches	1 1/4 dia. × 1/2 thick	2	Can be 1 1/4-in. dowel.
Hitch ramp	3 × 1 × 3/8	1	
Exhaust stack	3/8 dowel × 2 1/4 long	1	
Exhaust stack tip	1/4 dowel × 7/8 long	1	
Bumper	2 3/4 × 3/4 × 1/8 or 3/16	1	Can be Baltic birch plywood or solid hardwood.
Truck wheels	2 1/4 dia.	8	Factory-made wheels with treads
Truck axle pins	3/8 dia. × 2 long	8	Cut 2 1/2-in.-long factory-made pins to length.
Headlights	3/8 dowel × 3/8 long	2	Optional

continued

PART NAME	FINISH DIMENSIONS L × W × T, IN.	NO. REQ'D.	NOTES
Trailer Parts			
Trailer frame sides	25½ × 3⅛ × ½	2	Baltic birch plywood
Trailer frame gooseneck center	1¾ × ¾ × ⅝	1	Cut 2 × ¾ × ¾, trim after assembly.
Trailer frame stairs	3⁹⁄₁₆ × 2⅛ × ¾	1	
Trailer frame rear center	19½ × ¾ × ¾	1	Cut 20 × 1 × ¾, trim after assembly
Hitch pin	⅜ dowel × 1⅛ long	1	
Ramp mounts	1½ × 2³⁄₁₆ × ¾	2	
Ramps	3 × 1 × ½	2	
Ramp pivot	¼ dowel × 2³⁄₁₆ long	2	Cut 2⅜ long, trim after assembly
Trailer axle housings	4¼ × ¾ × ⅝	5	
Trailer wheels	1½ dia.	10	Factory-made duals; drill centers to fit ⅜ axle pins
Trailer axle pins	⅜ dia. × 2½ long	10	Factory made
Trailer deck tiedowns	¼ dia. axle pins	14	Cut shank ½ in. long
Trailer deck	17⅛ × 6¼ × ¼	1	Baltic birch plywood

Truck Frame

The frame is a ¾-in.-thick board that runs the length of the truck. The hood, cab, hitch, and axles are all attached to it.

1. Lay out the frame's profile and bandsaw it to shape. Leave the 2⅜-in.-wide section a bit oversize for now. Later, you'll sand it flush with the sides of the deck base.

2. Sand the 1½-in.-wide section smooth. Its exact size is not critical.

Deck Base

The deck base is a spacer block that supports the deck and cab assembly. I use ½-in.-thick Baltic birch plywood for this, but solid wood also works.

1. Cut the plywood to size, but leave about ¹⁄₁₆ in. extra on the width.

2. Sand one end smooth. It will face the back of the truck and be somewhat visible.

3. Glue the deck base to the frame. The smooth end aligns with the end of the wide section of the frame.

4. Sand the sides flush with the frame. I use a disk sander for this.

Deck

As with the deck base, I use Baltic birch plywood (¼ in. thick) for the deck, but solid wood also makes a good option. The winch, exhaust, and rear toolbox all go on the deck, as does the cab.

1. Cut the wood to size. Leave ¹⁄₁₆ in. or so extra on the 2⅜-in.-wide section for now.

2. Sand the edges of the wider section and round any sharp edges and corners.

3. Glue the deck to the deck base. Be sure the front edges of the two pieces are even. I use a pair of C-clamps, gently tightened, to keep the sides of the deck aligned with the sides of the frame and deck base.

4. When the glue has dried, sand the 2⅜-in. section flush with the deck base and frame. The deck won't be visible in this area, so you don't need to give it a fine sanding. However, if the deck is straight and square the side toolbox pieces will fit better.

Hood

The hood includes the front section of the cab but is made of a single block of wood. Shaping it requires

Hood

Cut ¹⁄₁₆" × ¹⁄₁₆" notches after cab assembly.

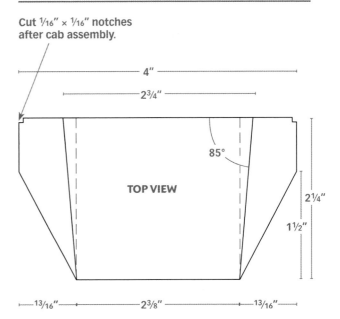

TOP VIEW

4"
2¾"
85°
2¼"
1½"
¹³⁄₁₆"
2⅜"
¹³⁄₁₆"

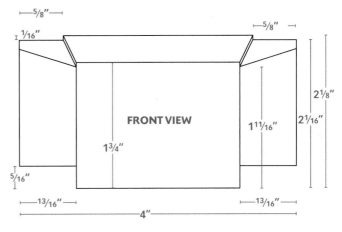

FRONT VIEW

⅝"
¹⁄₁₆"
⅝"
2⅛"
1¹¹⁄₁₆"
2¹⁄₁₆"
1¾"
⁵⁄₁₆"
¹³⁄₁₆"
¹³⁄₁₆"
4"

several cuts on the bandsaw, which in turn requires an angle jig (see the drawing on p. 106).

1. Cut the block of wood to size. Laminate thinner pieces if you don't have something the right size.

2. Smooth and square up the block. I used a disk sander, but a belt sander or sanding block will also work. Cutting the angles to shape the hood will be easier if you start with a square block.

3. Lay out all the lines and angles (see the top left photo on p. 106).

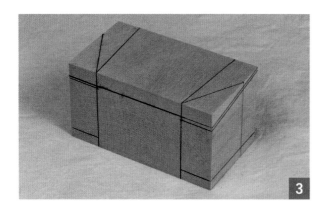

Hood Angle Jig

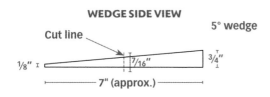

WEDGE SIDE VIEW

5° wedge

Cut line

⅛"   7/16"   ¾"

7" (approx.)

JIG TOP VIEW

4¾"

Ramp angles down.

Ramp angles down.

3½"

2½"   2½"   7/16"   10° wedge

⅛"   10"   1"

JIG SIDE VIEW

4. Make the hood angle jig. First, cut a small wedge to a 10-degree angle (⅜ in. up and 2¼ in. over) or close to it. Cut another wedge at a 5-degree angle; this one should be between 6 in. and 9 in. long. Cut the 5-degree wedge in half and glue the two pieces onto the 10-degree wedge so that the thickest and thinnest parts of the 5-degree wedge are next to each other (see the top photo at right). You can use the jig for all the angled cuts on the hood without having to tilt the bandsaw table.

5. The angles on the top of the hood are compound. To cut the angles on the sides, position the jig at 90 degrees to the blade. The angle on one side of the hood uses the wedge to the left of the blade; the angle on the other side uses the wedge on the right of the blade.

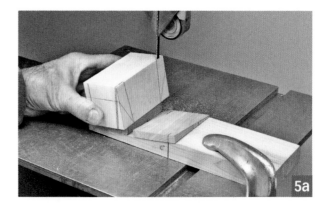

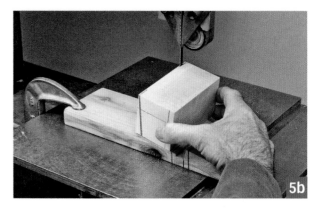

6. Cut the large angles on the front of the hood to give the piece its pointed profile. You don't need the angle jig for these cuts.

7. Cut down to the first angled cuts to remove a small wedge of wood. Use the angle jig for these cuts, but point the jig toward the blade.

8. Cut the top surface of the hood. This cut will be a little more than $\frac{1}{16}$ in. from the initial cuts on the edges.

9. Cut the small rectangular notches from the bottom of the hood sides. These provide space for the fenders.

10. Sand all surfaces flat, except for the front radiator area. You'll sand that after assembly. I use a disk sander for the larger surfaces and a small flat file on smaller areas. Try your best to keep all the surfaces flat. Don't do any hand-sanding yet, because that can leave parts slightly rounded.

11. Glue the hood to the frame. When the glue has dried, sand the front surfaces flat and even.

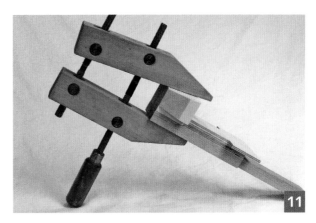

Cab Sides, Back, and Roof

Lay out the cab sides with the grain running vertically, to give the window posts strength. This means you will glue to end grain when you attach the roof, but it will be strong enough for a non-structural joint. The cab back has its grain running horizontally to provide a better glue surface for the roof.

1. Cut out the two sides, the back, and the roof. Shape both cab sides at once: Cut the two pieces a bit oversize, put a dot of glue on the excess wood, and clamp them together. Leave the back and the roof about $\frac{1}{16}$ in. oversize for now, too.

2. Use the template (p. 127) to copy the window locations onto the sides, or take the measurements from the drawing on p. 108.

Cab Sides

FRONT VIEW   **SIDE VIEW**

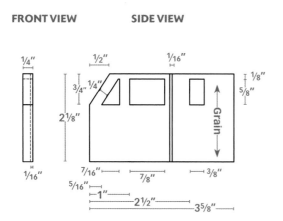

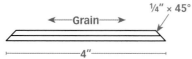

Cab Back

FRONT VIEW   **SIDE VIEW**

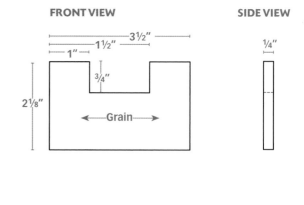

Note: A template is also provided for the cab sides at the end of the chapter.

Cab Roof

FRONT VIEW

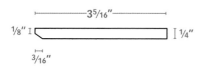

SIDE VIEW

Cab Assembly

TOP VIEW

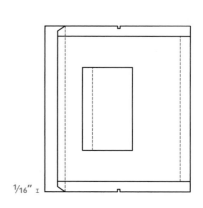

FRONT VIEW   **SIDE VIEW**

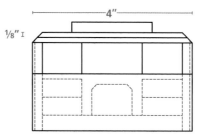

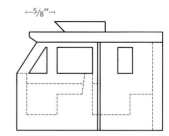

3. Mark a centerpoint in each window for small holes (⅛ in. to ³⁄₁₆ in.) so you can insert the blade of a coping saw or scrollsaw. Drill in each corner of the window.

4. Cut out the windows with a coping saw or scrollsaw. Repeat the window layout on the bottom side of the stack, drawing the lines tangent to the drilled holes. Leave a little margin for error, and keep an eye on the bottom side layout in case the blade is wandering.

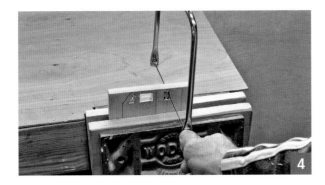

5. Carefully file the openings to get them close to finish quality. Begin by filing a slight bevel on the edges so the wood doesn't chip out.

6. Saw the outside profiles of the cab sides, leaving a bit extra all around. The sides should now separate.

7. Finish filing and sanding the window openings, with small bevels or rounds to break the corners and edges.

8. Finish-sand the angled front surfaces that form the windshield. It's better to finish the top, bottom, and back surfaces after assembly.

9. Cut out the window in the back on the bandsaw.

10. Mark and plane the angle on the front of the roof.

Cab Interior

On an earlier version of this toy I crafted a simpler interior, with a one-piece contour and a couple of bench seats. When my son saw it, he asked why I had put a church pew into a toy truck. That's why this version has a slightly more realistic interior.

1. Square up a block of wood for the cab interior, with the grain running across the width. If you want to save some work at the bandsaw and sanding later, you could build up the floor piece from end blocks glued to a ⅜-in.-thick board.

2. Lay out the profile and cut it to shape, using a clamp to hold it safely. Try to keep the floor section as flat as possible. File and sand the inside surfaces as needed.

3. Make the seats. I bandsaw a block long enough for both seats, cut the contour, and saw the block into two separate seats.

Front Seats

TOP VIEW

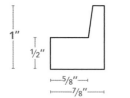

SIDE VIEW

Engine Cover

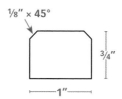

FRONT VIEW

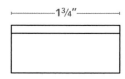

SIDE VIEW

Interior Assembly

TOP VIEW

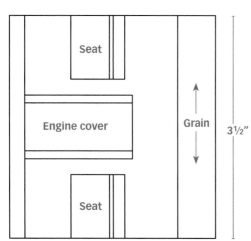

SIDE VIEW

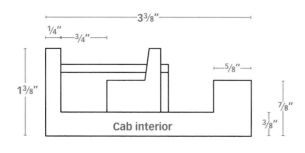

Air Conditioner

TOP VIEW

SIDE VIEW

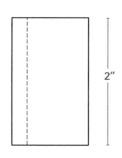

4. Sand the seats and glue them to the floor. Press them into place, but don't clamp them. Be sure they are positioned evenly and squarely; exact spacing is not critical, although you want the outside edges to overhang the floor by about ⅟32 in. You will sand them flush later.

5. Make the engine cover. (It is just a short section of axle housing, so you may want to jump to p. 114 and make an extra couple of inches of housing to use here.) Sand the cover and glue it in place.

Cab Assembly

1. Glue the back onto the interior assembly, with the sides and bottom protruding about ⅟32 in.

2. When the glue is dry, sand the sides and bottom flush. This will also even up the seats. I use a disk sander and a sanding board.

3. Glue one side into place. It should overhang a little bit on the bottom, front, and rear. When the glue is dry, attach the other side.

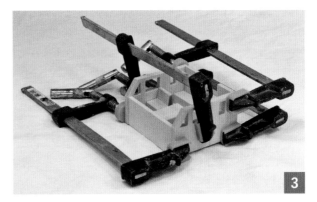

4. Sand the exterior surfaces to even up all the edges. Check the overall length and make sure the cab fits onto the frame. Also check that the cab front fits tightly against the rear surface of the hood. This can take a little fine-tuning unless both surfaces are exactly square and true.

5. Bandsaw ⅟16-in.-deep slots to delineate the doors.

6. I spray a finish on the interior at this point because it's now or never. (Never is an option). Mask the top edges that will be glue surfaces.

7. Glue on the roof. When the glue is dry, sand the side surfaces even and shape the side bevels.

8. Cut the air conditioner to size and sand an angle on the front. Exact sizes are not critical for this piece.

9. Glue the air conditioner to the roof. It should be square and centered, but the exact position is not critical.

10. Glue the cab to the frame. Check that it fits tight and sits squarely and evenly on the frame. Put ample glue on the front firewall area, so that a bit of glue will squeeze out in front of the doors. This will help hide any small gaps there.

11. When the glue is dry, bandsaw the 1/16-in.-deep slots to delineate the door fronts. I stand on the back side of the bandsaw for this, to ensure that I can see exactly where I put the slot.

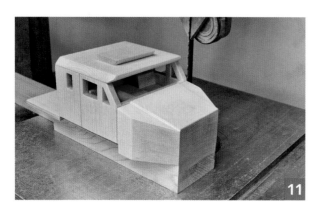

Fenders

You make the front and rear fenders in the same way and from the same wood, so it is easiest to make them all at once. I used yellowheart, to add a slight contrast to the cab and hood assembly.

1. Lay out the fenders on 7/8-in.-thick wood.

2. Cut them to shape and their final thickness. You can mark the exact thickness of the rear fender by holding it in place and tracing along the edge of the deck.

3. Sand as needed. You want a good flat surface on the rear fenders, where they touch the ladder. Check the fit and adjust as needed.

Front Fenders

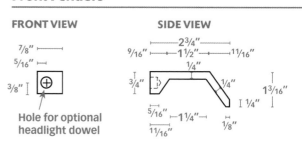

Rear Fenders

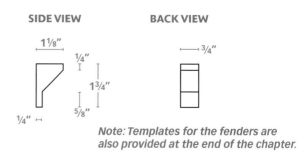

Note: Templates for the fenders are also provided at the end of the chapter.

Tank and Ladder Assembly

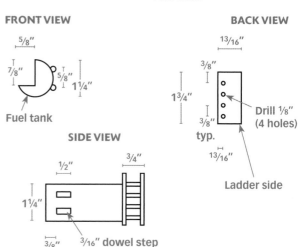

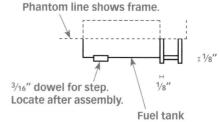

4. Sand to remove all sharp corners and exposed edges.

5. To position the front fender on the frame, make a small pencil mark in the center of the 1¼-in.-long flat section on the inside of the fender. Measure 1¾ in. from the front of the truck and make another small mark on the side of the frame, where the fender goes.

6. Glue one front fender in place against the frame and the underside of the hood, aligning the pencil marks.

7. When the glue has dried, glue on the second fender. Wait on the rear fenders until you have the ladders made, and then glue the ladders and fenders on at the same time.

Ladders

Follow the procedures in Chapter 1 (p. 14) to make these ladders, but use the dimensions shown in the cut list on p. 103. Glue the ladders to the sides of the truck frame, with the rear fenders butted up against them for reinforcement.

1. Glue one rear fender and ladder in place. Apply glue to the edge of the ladder and press it in place. Apply glue to the side of the fender that contacts the frame and to the front surface that contacts the ladder. Press the fender in place against the frame and the ladder. Hold it all in place for a few minutes while the glue begins to set, then put the truck aside.

2. When the glue joint is firm, glue the remaining ladder and fender to the other side.

Tool Boxes

The tool boxes improve the look and realism of the truck. Their exact size is not critical. I used yellowheart again, to match the cab and other components.

1. Cut the wood to size (see the drawing on p. 117). To get the exact length of the side tool boxes, measure the distance between the front fender and the ladder.

2. Sand as needed and round over one side of the rear tool box. Glue the side boxes to the frame against the underside of the cab. Glue the rear tool box to the deck, centered on the back of the cab.

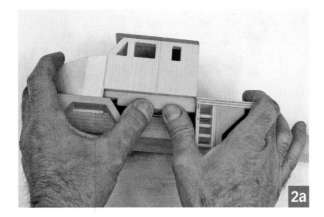

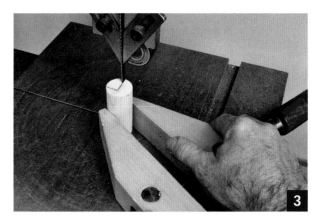

Fuel Tanks

I made the two fuel tanks from 1¼-in.-diameter dowel, but you could use a smaller dowel. The tanks are notched to fit against the frame.

1. Cut the dowel to length; measure from the front fender to the ladder for the exact dimension.

2. Sand as needed and lay out the notch on one end.

3. Cut the notch at the bandsaw, using a clamp as a handle and making sure the dowel is square to the saw table.

4. File and sand as needed, and then glue the tanks to the frame, one at a time.

Axle Housings

These are rectangular blocks that you drill for the axle pins after assembly. You may want to skip ahead and make the trailer axle housings now, too. Those are slightly different in size, but the parts are similar.

1. Rough out enough wood for five housings (see the drawing on p. 117); reserve one to use as a drill test piece.

2. Bevel the corners. This is just for looks, so the bevel's exact size and angle are not critical.

3. Cut the housings to length. I sometimes cut the front axle housing about ⅛ in. oversize, so that the front wheels protrude from the fenders slightly.

4. Sand as needed, but try to leave the glue surface as flat as possible.

5. Mark the hole location dead center on one end of one housing. Use an awl or center punch to mark the centerpoint clearly.

6. Find a drill size that matches the axle pins you have. This will be about $^{11}/_{32}$ in., but some pins vary quite a bit in diameter. Drill a test hole in a scrap block to check.

TIP

Make a simple fixture to drill the axle housings so that all axle holes will be identical. Square up a block of wood and attach two guides that are square to the table and spaced for a snug fit on the housing.

7. Clamp the spare axle housing into the fixture and align the drill bit on the centerpoint.

8. Drill a little more than half-way through. Feed the bit into the wood gently so it does not tend to wander. Stop and measure to ensure that the hole is centered side to side, within $^{1}/_{32}$ in. Adjust the fixture location as needed. Once you have started the hole, feed the drill in a little faster.

9. Flip the axle housing end for end and drill the other end.

10. When you are satisfied, drill the remaining axle housings. If you choose to drill the trailer axle housings now, you will need to use a $^{1}/_{4}$-in. shim to center those holes.

11. Temporarily install two wheels into the front axle housing and make sure the wheels are centered under the fenders. When you're satisfied with the location of the housing, glue it to the frame.

12. Glue on the three rear housings one at a time, making sure that each one is square and centered on the frame. Accurate spacing is also important here to make sure the wheels do not touch each other. The axle housings should be $2^{3}/_{8}$ in. apart, center-to-center. This provides a $^{1}/_{8}$-in. space between the wheels.

A spacer block can help with the setup, but use a square for accurate positioning.

Steps for Fuel Tank and Tool Box

The steps are small dowels with a flat sanded along one side for a glue surface (see the drawing on p. 112).

1. Sand or plane a small flat along a 3-in. or 4-in. length of dowel. I used one $^{3}/_{16}$ in. in diameter.

2. Saw six steps to length, sand the ends, and bevel the sharp corner on the round section.

3. Lightly clamp a scrap block onto the tanks to help align the steps. Mark a small line or dot to locate the center line of each step. The exact spacing is not critical.

4. Apply glue to the flat on each step, press into place, and hold for a minute.

Winch

The winch consists of a small block for the housing, which is drilled through for a dowel to represent the cable reels.

1. Cut the housing block to size.

2. Drill the block for a ⅝-in. dowel (a ½-in. dowel will also work). Use the axle housing fixture when you drill the hole.

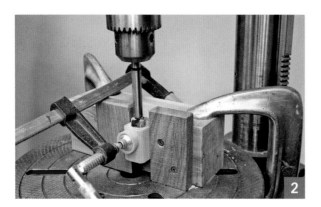

3. Round the top corners of the winch housing.

4. Cut the winch dowel to length and insert into the housing.

5. Glue the winch assembly to the deck. Its position is not critical, but I put it on center, with about ⅛ in. between the edge of the housing and the edge of the deck. Because the deck overhangs the frame here, slide a spacer under the deck to help absorb clamping pressure.

Exhaust Stack

1. Cut the two lengths of dowel.

2. Drill the ⅜-in. dowel to accept the ¼-in. dowel. I used the axle housing fixture again to do this.

3. Glue the ¼-in. dowel in the hole.

4. Sand a flat along the ⅜-in. dowel to make a glue surface.

5. Glue the exhaust assembly to the back of the cab. The location is not critical.

Side Tool Box

FRONT VIEW   **SIDE VIEW**

3/16" dowel for step.
Locate after assembly.

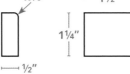

1/2"

1/4"

5/8"

1/2"

3 1/2"

Rear Tool Box

SIDE VIEW   **FRONT VIEW**

R 1/8"

1 1/2"

1 1/4"

1/2"

Truck Axle Housings

SIDE VIEW   **FRONT VIEW**

1"

1/2"

2 3/4"

3/8"

3/4"

1/8" × 45°

Drill 11/32" for axle pin.

Winch Housing and Winch Dowel

FRONT VIEW

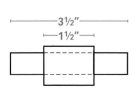

3 1/2"

1 1/2"

SIDE VIEW

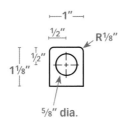

1"

1/2"

R 1/8"

1/2"

1 1/8"

5/8" dia.

Exhaust Stack

SIDE VIEW

1/4"

1/2"

2 5/8"

2 1/4"

3/8"

Hitch

TOP VIEW   **SIDE VIEW**

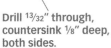

1/2"

1 1/4"

Drill 13/32" through,
countersink 1/8" deep,
both sides.

Hitch Ramp

TOP VIEW

1"

3"

SIDE VIEW

3/8"

3/16"

Bumper

SIDE VIEW   **FRONT VIEW**

3/16"

2 3/4"

3/4"

2 1/2"

1/8"

Headlights

I sometimes add two dowels in the fenders to represent headlights. If you decide to add this detail, here's how to do it.

1. Mark the headlight location using the measurements on the drawing on p. 112. The holes are not quite on center because the bumper covers a bit of the fender.

2. Drill holes that allow a ⅜-in. dowel to fit in easily. You can use either a drill press (with the table tilted 90 degrees) or a handheld drill for this. Put a bit of masking tape around the bit as a simple depth gauge.

3. Round the ends of a length of ⅜-in. dowel. Cut

the ends off to make the ⅜-in. pieces for the headlights. Bevel the cut corners slightly to help fit the dowels into the holes.

4. Put some glue in the holes and carefully press the dowels in place.

Hitch Parts

Two small parts fit on the frame: the hitch itself, which is a small disk drilled after it is glued in place, and a wedge-shaped block meant to help line up the trailer to the truck hitch. In this toy, the wedge has no function except to add a bit of realism.

1. Lay out the hitch ramp on a small block of wood.

2. Cut the slight taper and sand to remove any exposed sharp edges.

3. Glue the ramp to the frame. Clamping is not required here.

4. Drill a ½-in. clearance hole in the frame, which allows the hitch pin to pivot and tilt up and down a little as the truck and trailer drive over dips and rises.

5. Lay out the hitch on a piece of ½-in.-thick wood and drill the hole in the center.

6. Countersink the hole to about ½ in. or ⅝ in. diameter.

7. Cut out the disk. It can be round, like the one in the photos, or square or octagonal, depending on your preference. Sand the hitch to remove sharp edges and refine the shape.

8. Glue the hitch in place, centering it by eye over the clearance hole in the frame.

Bumper

The bumper attaches to the front of the frame. You can make it from ⅛-in.-thick solid wood or Baltic birch plywood; the thickness is not critical.

1. Lay out the bumper and cut it to size.

2. Sand any sharp edges or rough surfaces, but leave the glue surface flat.

3. Glue the bumper to the front of the frame. Firm hand pressure will hold it until the glue begins to set.

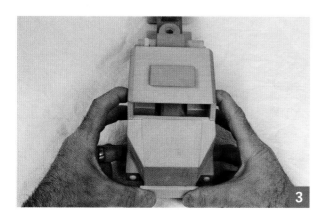

Wheel Treads

I think the factory-made wheels look much better if you add crosscuts to the treads. It gives a more aggressive look.

1. Use the template (p. 127) to mark out small lines where the crosscuts go.

2. Tilt the bandsaw table about 10 degrees. The exact angle is not important.

3. Make a stop block, so that each cut will be ¹⁄₁₆ in. deep. I cut the angled slot in the block with a handsaw and adjusted the depth when I clamped the block to the bandsaw table. Set a fence to keep the wheel centered on the blade.

4. Cut the slots, lining up the blade with the tread marks. The spacing won't be perfectly even, but the results will look good. Great, even.

Finish

I prefer to apply a finish before installing the wheels. This isn't absolutely necessary, but it does simplify the finishing process. If you choose to put the wheels on first, skip this step for now. As a rule, I spray on a urethane or Varathane varnish, something durable and nontoxic when cured.

1. Cut the axle pins to length, making sure that they are as long as possible without hitting each other inside the axle housing.

2. Push the pins into the housings. This keeps the spray out of the holes and finishes the axle pin heads in the process.

3. Spray the truck. I apply three or four coats of semigloss or satin finish, but high gloss is also fine. I sand after the first coat, and then only as needed after that.

4. Spray the wheels. Fortunately, factory-made wheels do not seem to need much sanding.

Wheel Installation

It's best to have the wheels a bit too loose rather than too tight. Use the wrench-shaped plastic spacer (see Chapter 1, p. 27), to set the clearance between the wheels and the frame.

1. Dry-fit the wheels to make sure they all spin. If one is a bit up off the ground, enlarge the wheel hole by about $\frac{1}{32}$ in. I often do this to allow for a little unevenness in a play surface.

2. Rub a little wax on the shaft of the axle pins, just below the head. This will help the wheel spin freely. Put a little wax on the end of the axle housing, too, but try to keep wax out of the hole. Have a softwood punch ready, in case a pin needs some gentle persuasion.

3. Put a soft rag on the table so the truck does not get scratched as you lay it on its side.

4. Put a generous amount of glue into the axle hole with a toothpick.

5. Slip the axle pin into the wheel, then apply a small amount of glue on the last $\frac{1}{2}$ in. of the pin. This may produce a little squeeze-out. Spin the wheel once or twice as the glue sets to keep it spinning freely.

6. Put the plastic spacer in place under the wheel. Gently push or tap the axle pin into place and leave the spacer in place.

7. As soon as the pin is in all the way, remove the spacer. Let the glue set for a few minutes before moving on to the next wheel.

Trailer

The trailer consists primarily of a frame, a deck, and some wheels. At the front of the frame is the short gooseneck center section; behind this is the stair section and the long strip that runs the length of the deck section.

Frame Sides

1. Cut a piece of $\frac{1}{2}$-in.-thick Baltic birch plywood to rough dimensions, large enough to fit both of the frame sides. Leave an extra $\frac{1}{8}$ in. all around and do the final cutting after assembly. You could cut two separate pieces if you like, but you save a little wood by laying them out head to toe on one piece.

Heavy Equipment Transporter

TOP VIEW

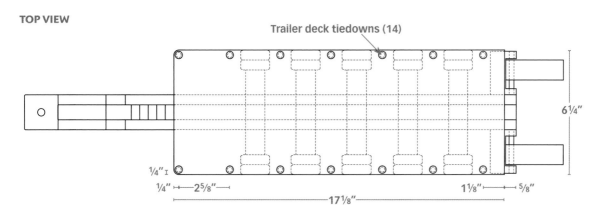

Trailer deck tiedowns (14)

6¼"

¼" I

¼" ↦ 2⅝" →

1⅛" → ⊢ ⅝"

17⅛"

SIDE VIEW

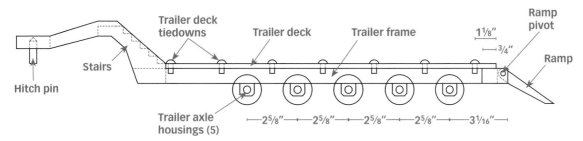

Trailer deck tiedowns

Trailer deck

Trailer frame

1⅛"

⊢ ¾" →

Ramp pivot

Ramp

Stairs

Hitch pin

Trailer axle housings (5)

2⅝" ⟷ 2⅝" ⟷ 2⅝" ⟷ 2⅝" ⟷ 3¹⁄₁₆"

Trailer Frame

TOP VIEW

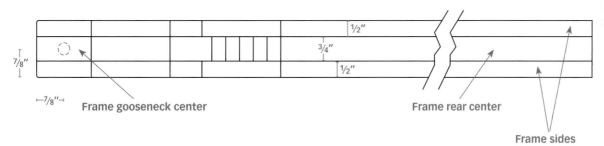

⅞"

½"

¾"

½"

⊢ ⅞" ⊣

Frame gooseneck center

Frame rear center

Frame sides

SIDE VIEW

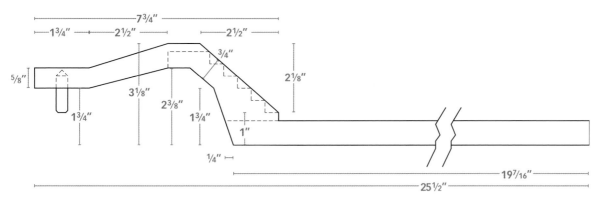

7¾"

1¾" ⟷ 2½"

2½"

¾"

2⅛"

⅝"

3⅛"

2⅜"

1¾"

1¾"

1"

¼" ⊢

19⁷⁄₁₆"

25½"

2. Lay out the profiles. Use the template (p. 127) for the gooseneck section at the front.

3. Cut the frame sides at the bandsaw, leaving about ⅛ in. extra all around to be trimmed off after assembly.

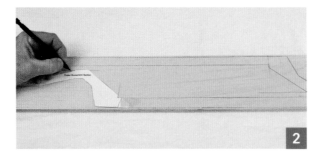

Frame Center Pieces

1. Cut a 20-in.-long strip of wood for the center of the frame and a 2-in. strip from the same piece of wood for the gooseneck center. Cut the long strip 1 in. wide and trim it after assembly. I used ¾-in.-thick yellowheart, only because I wanted it to match the yellowheart I used for some of the truck parts.

2. Sand the short gooseneck center on the end that will face the rear of the trailer. This is much easier to do now.

Frame Stairs

1. Cut a block for the stairs from the same piece of wood that yielded the frame center, or a piece of the same thickness.

2. Use the template on p. 127 (or the drawing on the facing page) to lay out the profile of the stairs.

3. Saw the steps carefully to the line, but leave the angled surfaces on the edge opposite the steps a little oversize. File and sand the steps, but not the other surfaces.

4. Test-fit the three center pieces on a side piece. The stairs fit atop the long center piece, and the gooseneck center goes at the front end of the gooseneck. You may need to cut ⅛ in. off the bottom of the stairs to compensate for the extra width of the long center piece. Otherwise, everything should fit.

Frame Assembly

1. Glue the center pieces to one of the frame sides.

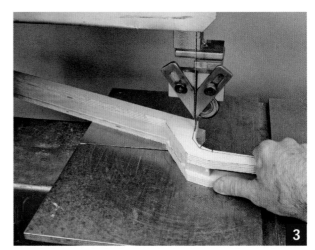

2. When the glue has dried, attach the other plywood side.

3. Saw the inner profile of the gooseneck close to the lines, removing most of the wood. File and sand to the lines.

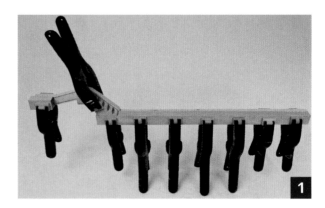

Trailer Frame Gooseneck Center

TOP VIEW

Drill for ³⁄₈″ dowel.

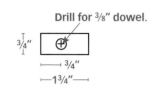

³⁄₄″

³⁄₄″

1³⁄₄″

½″ 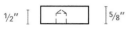 ⁵⁄₈″

SIDE VIEW

Trailer Frame Rear Center

TOP VIEW

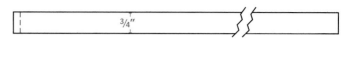

³⁄₄″

Cut 20″; trim angle after assembly.

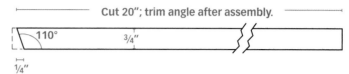

110° ³⁄₄″

¼″

SIDE VIEW

Trailer Frame Stair

TOP VIEW

³⁄₄″

3⁹⁄₁₆″

SIDE VIEW

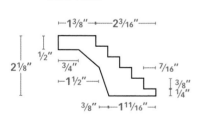

1³⁄₈″ 2³⁄₁₆″

½″

2¹⁄₈″ ³⁄₄″ ⁷⁄₁₆″

1½″ ³⁄₈″
¼″

³⁄₈″ 1¹¹⁄₁₆″

Ramp Mounts

TOP VIEW

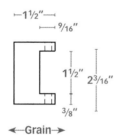

1½″

⁹⁄₁₆″

1½″ 2³⁄₁₆″

³⁄₈″

←Grain→

SIDE VIEW

¼″

³⁄₄″

³⁄₈″

Ramps

TOP VIEW

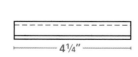

1″

SIDE VIEW

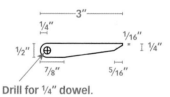

3″

¼″

½″ ¹⁄₁₆″ ¼″

⁷⁄₈″ ⁵⁄₁₆″

Drill for ¼″ dowel.

Trailer Axle Housings

SIDE VIEW

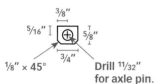

³⁄₈″

⁵⁄₁₆″ ⁵⁄₈″

³⁄₄″

¹⁄₈″ × 45°

Drill ¹¹⁄₃₂″
for axle pin.

FRONT VIEW

4¼″

4. Mark the center for the hitch pin on the gooseneck center. Drill the hole ½ in. deep.

5. Glue the hitch pin in the hole.

Deck

Make the deck from ¼-in. Baltic birch plywood. It has cut-down axle pins installed around the perimeter to help keep the large loads from rolling off. Kids can also steady various loads by wrapping elastic bands around the ends of the pins as tie-downs.

1. Cut the deck to size and lay out the centers for the holes for the tiedown pins.

2. Drill holes to fit the pins. To prevent tearout on the bottom of the plywood, place the deck over a piece of scrap, put masking tape along the bottom face, or both.

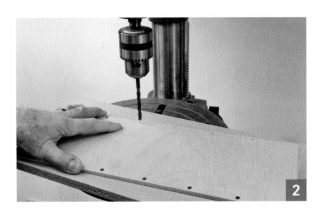

3. Cut the ends of the pins so only ¼ in. protrudes from the bottom of the deck. Sand and slightly bevel the ends.

4. Put a small bead of glue just under the heads of the pins, then push them into the holes.

Axle Housings

Follow the same procedures used to make the truck axle housings, but use the dimensions in the drawing on p. 123. Wait to drill the axle holes, though.

1. Use a ⅜-in. drill bit to enlarge the axle holes in the factory-made dual wheels. You will need these wheels to help fit the axle housings. I made a very simple V-block to keep the wheels centered when drilling. Only the first one needed to be lined up carefully.

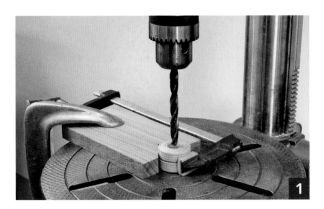

2. The trailer has ten dual wheels, spread out along the length of the frame, so the height of the axle holes is very important to ensure that all the wheels contact the ground. To determine the position of the holes in the axle housings, place the truck on a large level surface. Fit the trailer on the hitch pin and use shims to prop up the trailer so it's parallel to the level surface. The trailer hitch can be a fraction above the truck hitch; a little gap here is good.

3. Measure the height of the shims under the trailer. Here, it was 1¹⁄₁₆ in.

4. For 1½-in.-dia. wheels, the axle holes should be ¾ in. from the ground. Subtract ¾ in. from the 1¹⁄₁₆-in. shim height for the center of the axle holes—in this case, ⁵⁄₁₆ in. below the frame.

5. Carefully mark the center for the hole on one end of an axle housing or a practice piece. Put the housing in the fixture used to drill the truck axle housings. Add a ¼-in. spacer to account for the smaller size of the trailer housings. Drill the axle holes.

6. To check hole location after drilling, temporarily put the wheels into the axle housings. Sit the frame on the housings and hitch the trailer to the truck on a flat surface. If one or more wheels don't touch the ground, you may need to drill out the dual wheels for a little more clearance on the axle pins.

7. Glue the rearmost axle housing to the frame. Make sure it is in the correct location and square to the frame.

8. Glue on the remaining four housings. I made a small spacer to keep the spacing consistent.

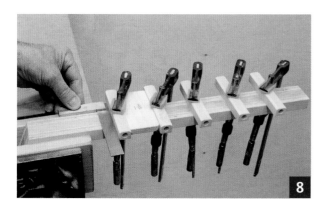

9. Glue the deck to the frame.

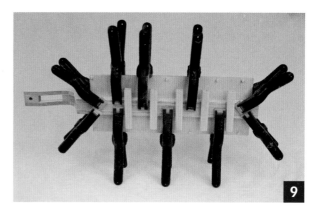

Ramp Mounts

These blocks are attached to the rear of the frame and the underside of the deck. They hold the ramps and allow them to swivel out of the way (see the drawing on p. 123).

1. On a piece of wood large enough for both ramp mounts, lay out their profile and the hole locations.

2. Cut out the notches as accurately as possible.

3. Drill the holes to fit a ¼-in. dowel.

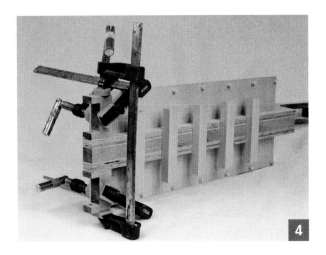

4

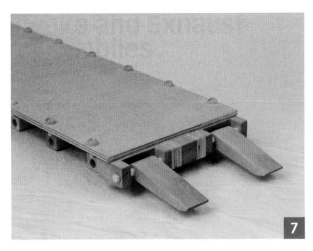

7

4. Attach the mounts. They should be glued to both the frame and the deck, aligned with the end of the frame.

Ramps

1. Cut the two ramps from a good close-grained hardwood. I used yellowheart.

2. On one edge, mark the hole center and the profile.

3. Drill the hole for the dowel for the ramp pivot. This hole should allow for a sliding fit on the dowel, but it can be somewhat snug. The ramp should not rattle about freely.

4. Saw or sand the angles at one end of the ramps. These angles are mainly for appearance.

5. Dry-fit the parts, using longer pieces of dowel to allow easy removal. You may need to file a little wood off the ramps or off the rear of the trailer to allow the ramps to pivot freely up past 90 degrees.

6. Cut the ramp pivot dowels.

7. Fit the ramp pivots and the ramps into the ramp mounts. Put some glue in the holes that abut the frame. Install the pivots and the ramp until the pivot has only about ¼ in. to go. Put glue on the end of the pivot, and push it in all the way.

8. When the glue is dry, trim the end of the pivots and sand them flush with the mounts.

Apply Finish, Install Wheels

I think it's easiest to spray on finish before attaching the wheels. But put the axle pins in their holes, as you did with the truck, to keep finish out of the holes. Use the plastic wrench-shaped spacer to help attach the wheels, again as you did with the truck wheels.

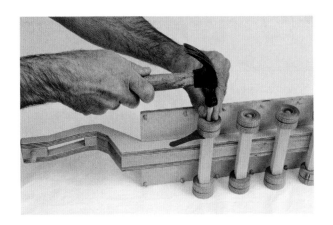

Templates

For full-size template, enlarge by 104%.

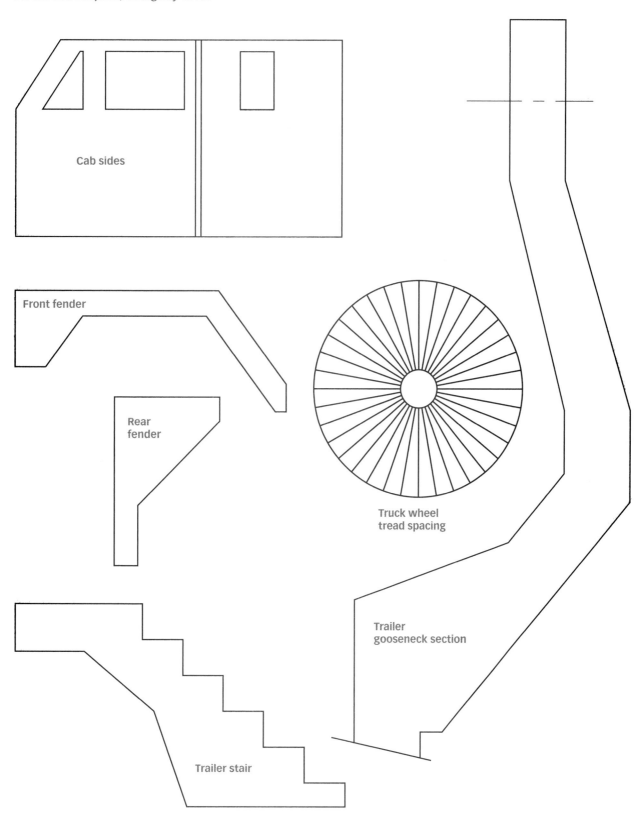

Cab sides

Front fender

Rear fender

Truck wheel tread spacing

Trailer gooseneck section

Trailer stair

CHAPTER 7

Wheeled Crane

*t**his heavy crane can** drive down a highway like a truck, then set up at a construction site and lift huge loads. Although the wood toy version can't match the real crane's 65-ton capacity, it does the same job.

The truck has outriggers that extend to keep it stable when the crane pivots to the side as it lifts large loads. The boom winch handle lifts the boom and locks in position, leaving the child free to use the other winch to raise and lower the load. When the lifting is done, the operator retracts the outriggers and sets the boom down in its docking station. The truck is ready to roll again.

Although the toy crane requires a number of small parts, they are easy to make. The end result is surprisingly robust. For this toy, I used birch and Baltic birch plywood for the lighter woods; the contrasting wood is padauk.

Frame Assembly

1. Rough-cut the wood for the frame (see the drawing on p. 131) and skid plate (see the drawing on p. 134). This will require a piece of wood at least 22 in. long.

2. Saw the skid plate and frame parts to length. Don't cut the angle on the skid plate yet; that's easier to do after assembly, and it is easier to attach the cab to the frame before you cut the angle.

Wheeled Crane Plan

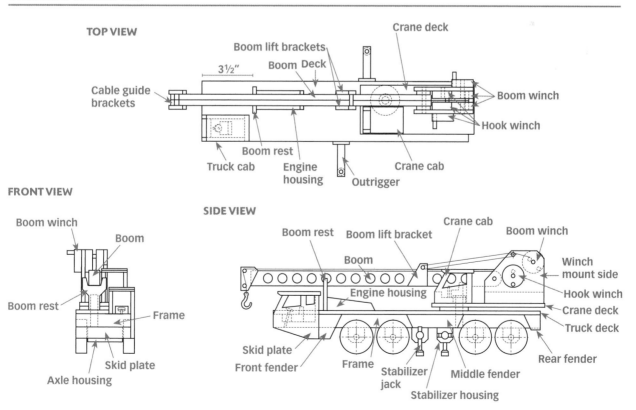

TOP VIEW

Boom lift brackets

Boom Deck

Crane deck

3½"

Cable guide brackets

Boom winch

Hook winch

Boom rest

Truck cab

Engine housing

Outrigger

Crane cab

FRONT VIEW

Boom winch

Boom

Boom rest

Frame

Skid plate

Axle housing

SIDE VIEW

Boom rest

Boom lift bracket

Crane cab

Boom winch

Boom

Engine housing

Winch mount side

Hook winch

Crane deck

Truck deck

Skid plate

Front fender

Frame

Stabilizer jack

Middle fender

Rear fender

Stabilizer housing

PART NAME	FINISH DIMENSIONS L × W × T, IN.	NO. REQ'D.	NOTES
Truck Parts			
Frame	18³⁄₈ × 3³⁄₄ × ³⁄₄	1	
Skid plate	3¹⁄₈ × 3³⁄₄ × ³⁄₄	1	
Deck	18³⁄₈ × 4 × ¹⁄₄	1	Baltic birch plywood
Cab base	2 × 1¹⁄₄ × ³⁄₈	1	
Cab left side	2⁷⁄₈ × 3¹⁄₈ × ¹⁄₄	1	
Cab right side	1³⁄₈ × 3¹⁄₈ × ¹⁄₄	1	
Cab back	1¹⁄₄ × 1¹⁄₄ × ¹⁄₄	1	
Cab roof	1⁷⁄₈ × 2³⁄₄ × ¹⁄₄	1	
Steering wheel	¹⁄₂ dowel × ¹⁄₈ long	1	
Steering column	¹⁄₈ dowel × 1³⁄₈ long	1	
Seats	⁷⁄₈ × ³⁄₄ × 1	2	Use one seat for truck, other for crane.
Engine housing	3¹⁄₄ × 1¹⁄₄ × ⁷⁄₈	1	
Boom rest	2¹⁄₈ × 1⁵⁄₈ × ¹⁄₄	1	Baltic birch plywood
Front fenders	1¹⁄₂ × 1¹⁄₂ × ³⁄₄	2	
Rear fenders	1 × 1¹⁄₈ × ³⁄₄	2	
Middle fenders	4 × ³⁄₄ × ³⁄₄	2	
Axle housings	2³⁄₄ × 1¹⁄₈ × 1	4	
Stabilizer housings	2 × 1¹⁄₈ × 1	2	
Outriggers	¹⁄₂ dowel × 4¹⁄₄ long	2	
Outrigger locating pins	¹⁄₄ dowel × ⁷⁄₈ long	2	
Stabilizer jacks	¹⁄₄ dowel × 1³⁄₄ long	2	
Jack feet	¹⁄₂ dowel × ³⁄₈ long	2	
Wheels	2¹⁄₄ dia.	8	Factory-made wheels with treads
Axles	³⁄₈ dowel × 4¹⁄₂ long	4	Cut 5-in. long, trim to fit truck and wheels.
Axle caps	³⁄₈ dowel caps	8	
Crane Parts			
Deck	7³⁄₄ × 3¹⁄₄ × ¹⁄₄	1	Baltic birch plywood
Turntable	2 dia. × ¹⁄₄ thick	1	Baltic birch plywood
Turntable pin	¹⁄₂ dowel × 2³⁄₈ long	1	Cut length to suit assembly.
Retainer rings	1 slab wheels × ³⁄₈ thick	2	
Cab base	2³⁄₈ × 1¹⁄₄ × ³⁄₄	1	Can be laminated from ³⁄₈-in.-thick stock.
Cab sides	2 × 2⁵⁄₈ × ¹⁄₄	2	

PART NAME	FINISH DIMENSIONS L × W × T, IN.	NO. REQ'D.	NOTES
Cab back	2 × 1¼ × ¼	1	
Cab roof	1⅞ × 2¼ × ¼	1	
Control levers	⅛ dowel × 1⅛ long	2	
Boom	18 × 1 × ¾	1	Can be any length between 16 in. and 20 in.
Cable guide brackets	1½ × 1¼ × ¼	2	Baltic birch plywood
Cable guide dowels	¼ dowel × 1¼ long	2	Cut ⅛ in. overlong
Boom lift brackets	1½ × 1¼ × ¼	2	Baltic birch plywood
Boom lift dowel	¼ dowel × 1¼ long	1	Cut ⅛ in. overlong
Boom spacers	1½ × 1 × ¼	2	Wood to match boom
Boom pivot dowel	¼ dowel × 1¾ long	1	Cut ⅛ in. overlong
Winch mount sides	4⅛ × 3½ × ¼	2	Baltic birch plywood
Winch mount base	4⅛ × 1¼ × ¾	1	
Winch disks	1½ slab wheels × ½ wide	6	Factory-made
Winch handles	¼ dowel × 1 long	2	
Winch axles	¼ dowel × ¾ long	2	
Winch handle axles	¼ dowel × 1¼ long	2	
Winch cable dowels	¼ dowel × 1¼ long	2	
Hook		1	Baltic birch plywood or laminated veneer
Boom lift cable	1/32 nylon braided string	1	Cut 36 in. long.
Hook lift cable	1/32 nylon braided string	1	Cut 36 in. long.

Frame

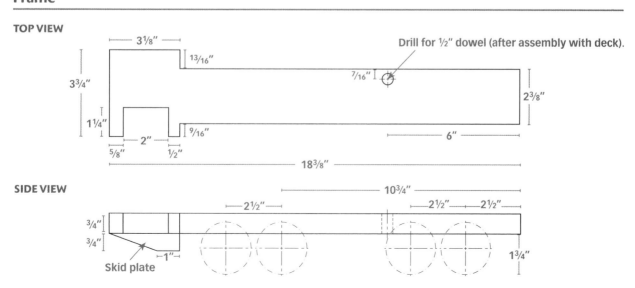

TOP VIEW

SIDE VIEW

Skid plate

3. Lay out the profile of the frame and saw it to shape, cutting as close to the lines as possible. Keep the ¹³⁄₁₆-in.-wide offcut to use for the middle fenders. The offcut will be just under ¾ in. wide, but the thickness will still be right for the fenders.

4. File and sand the cut surfaces to remove the sawmarks. Keep these surfaces as straight and square as possible for a good fit to the cab base and fender parts.

Deck

Make the truck deck and crane deck from Baltic birch plywood.

1. Lay out both pieces and cut them to size. File the notch in the truck deck straight and smooth for a good fit against the cab parts.

2. Lay out and cut the turntable. Sand it to the line. Glue the turntable to the crane deck.

Truck Deck

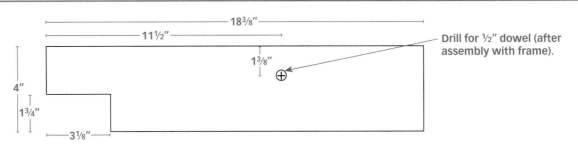

18³⁄₈″

11½″

1³⁄₈″

Drill for ½″ dowel (after assembly with frame).

4″

1¾″

3⅛″

Turntable Pin

½″ dowel

1″

³⁄₈″

2³⁄₈″

Retainer rings

Turntable

Drill for ½″ dowel (after assembly with deck).

2″

Crane Deck

Drill for ½″ dowel (after assembly with turntable).

1″

3¼″

1¾″

7¾″

3. When the glue has dried, drill the hole for the ½-in. dowel for the turntable pin. It should spin in the hole, but with minimal extra clearance. Drill a sample hole in some scrap to check the fit.

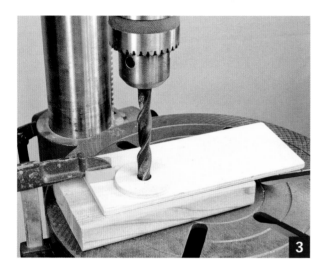

4. Sand all edges and round all sharp corners.

Truck Cab and Crane Cab

The two cabs (see the drawings on p. 134) are made much like the cabs on other vehicles, such as the Heavy Equipment Transporter in the previous chapter. Once you have completed the cab base, move on to the cab sides, back, and roof.

Truck Cab Base

1. Trace the frame notch onto a piece of ¼-in.-thick wood to size the truck cab base.

2. Saw the base slightly oversize, then sand the edges until the piece fits neatly in the frame notch.

3. Drill the hole for the steering column in the base. I gauge the 15° angle by eye, but mark the location with an awl. It's easiest to make this hole with a portable drill.

Steering Wheel and Seats

1. To make the steering wheel and steering column, refer to Chapter 4, p. 72. Use the sizes shown in the cut list on p. 130.

2. Make the seats for the truck and the crane cabs, referring to Chapter 4, p. 68. Again, use the sizes shown in the cut list.

Truck Cab Roof

TOP VIEW

1⁷⁄₈″

SIDE VIEW

2³⁄₄″

¹⁄₈″

³⁄₁₆″

Truck and Crane Seats

SIDE VIEW

³⁄₄″

¹⁄₄″

¹⁄₂″

1″

⁷⁄₁₆″

Truck Cab Assembly

TOP VIEW

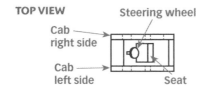

Cab right side

Steering wheel

Cab left side

Seat

SIDE VIEW

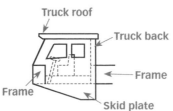

Truck roof

Truck back

Frame

Frame

Skid plate

FRONT VIEW

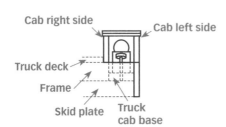

Cab right side

Cab left side

Truck deck

Frame

Skid plate

Truck cab base

Truck Cab Base

TOP VIEW

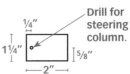

¹⁄₄″

Drill for steering column.

1¹⁄₄″

⁵⁄₈″

2″

SIDE VIEW

³⁄₈″

15°

Skid Plate

SIDE VIEW

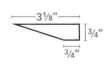

3¹⁄₈″

³⁄₄″

³⁄₄″

Truck Cab Left Side

SIDE VIEW

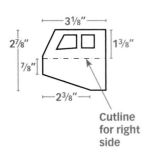

3¹⁄₈″

2⁷⁄₈″

1³⁄₈″

⁷⁄₈″

2³⁄₈″

Cutline for right side

Crane Cab Assembly

TOP VIEW

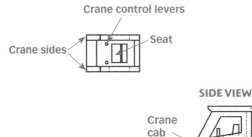

Crane control levers

Crane sides

Seat

FRONT VIEW

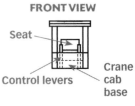

Seat

Control levers

Crane cab base

SIDE VIEW

Crane roof

Crane cab base

Back

Crane Cab Sides

SIDE VIEW

2⁵⁄₈″

1¹⁵⁄₁₆″

1¹⁄₄″

2″

Crane Cab Base

TOP VIEW

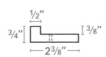

¹⁄₂″

³⁄₄″

³⁄₈″

2³⁄₈″

SIDE VIEW

1¹⁄₄″

1¹⁄₄″

Crane Cab Roof

TOP VIEW

2¹⁄₄″

1⁷⁄₈″

SIDE VIEW

¹⁄₈″

³⁄₁₆″

Note: Templates are also provided for the truck and cab sides at the end of the chapter.

Initial Truck Cab Assembly

1. Glue the skid plate block to the frame. Keep the front and side edges flush but don't cut the angle until you have attached the cab.

2. Put glue in the hole in the cab base and insert the steering wheel assembly. If necessary, sand the bottom flush after the glue has dried.

3. Glue the seat into place behind the steering wheel. The precise position is not critical; you just want the seat to look natural behind the steering wheel. Press it firmly in place, making sure it looks square to the rest of the cab area.

4. Glue and clamp the cab base into the frame notch and onto the skid plate.

5. Glue the truck deck to the frame. Align the front edges and check that the deck runs parallel to the frame. The deck overhangs the frame by ¼ in. on the cab side. Sand the front surfaces flush.

Crane Cab Base

1. The base uses 1¼-in.-wide wood. The truck cab back and the crane cab back are the same width, as is the winch mount base, so I cut stock for them at the same time. Make sure the grain runs along the length of the piece.

2. Lay out and saw the notch. (Or, if you like, make the base by gluing two blocks together.) Smooth the cut surface, taking care to keep it flat so the seat will fit well.

3. Lay out and drill the two holes for the ⅛-in. dowels that represent control levers.

4. Cut the ⅛-in. dowel pieces to length. Smooth and bevel the cut ends. Put some glue in the base holes and install these dowels. If the control levers protrude, sand the base smooth.

5. Glue the seat in place.

Cab Sides, Back, and Roof

1. Make the sides, back, and roof parts for both cabs. Follow the instructions on p. 107, but use the sizes shown in the cut list on pp. 130–131 and the drawing on p. 134 (also see the templates on p. 150). The left and right sides of the truck cab are different sizes, but the window and roof contours should line up.

2. Dry-fit the cabs to make sure the parts fit together well.

Truck Cab Glue-Up

1. Glue the left side of the truck cab to the truck frame. The bottom of the side should line up with the bottom of the skid plate. Check that the back surface of the side is square to the frame and that the top edge is parallel to the frame.

2. Glue the right side and the back to the truck frame. Clamp as needed. The photo above right shows a 1¼-in.-wide spacer, slightly wedge-shaped, that I used to press the right side against the edge of the deck. The clamp across the frame ensures that the left side of the cab won't be pushed away from the frame.

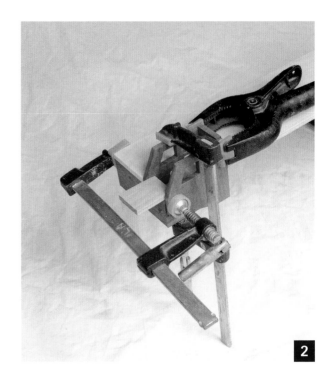

3. When the glue has dried, carefully sand the top surfaces flush so they provide a flat, even surface for the roof.

TIP

Finish as you go. Spray-finish the interior now, when it's easiest. Then attach the roof. That means masking off the deck area and the top edges where the roof attaches. It's also a good idea to finish the wheels and dowel caps before installing them.

4. While the finish dries, cut the crane cab roof and the truck cab roof to size. Sand the bevels in the front edges, then finish-sand both roofs.

5. When the finish has dried, remove the masking tape and glue the truck cab roof in place. Keep the overhang even on the sides and back. Clamp as needed.

2. After the glue has dried, glue the back and the other side to the cab base and let the glue dry.

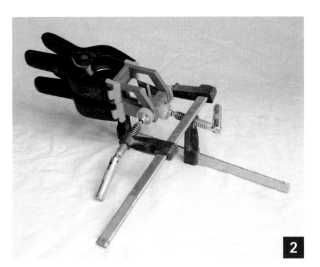

3. Remove the clamps and sand the top, bottom, and back surfaces flush. I either use the disk sander or a sanding board. Do the final sanding on the outside surfaces of the sides and back.

4. As with the truck cab, it is a good idea to spray-finish the interior of the cab after masking off the top edges.

5. Glue the roof in place, keeping the overhang even on the sides and back.

6. Glue the cab assembly into place on the crane deck. The location is not critical; I have it flush with the side edge of the deck and about 3/16 in. back from the front of the deck.

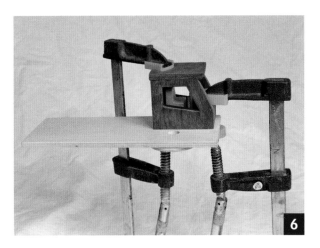

Skid Plate Angle

1. When the glue for the truck cab has dried, cut the angle on the front of the skid plate, using the angle of the cab side as a guide.

2. Sand the skid plate to remove sawmarks.

Crane Cab Glue-Up

1. Dry-clamp the sides and back into place to make sure the fit between the sides and back will be tight. When you are satisfied, glue one side to the cab base.

Winch Mount Sides and Base

1. Rough out two rectangular pieces of ¼-in. Baltic birch plywood, making them about ½ in. oversize.

2. Spot-glue the two pieces together, with the best sides to the inside. Put glue only in places that will be cut off later.

3. Lay out the profile on one side, using the template on p. 150 or the measurements from the plan below.

4. Drill the four ¼-in.-dia. holes in the winch mount sides. The two at the top and front are sized for a snug fit; the other two, drill for a clearance fit (¹⁄₆₄ in. over dowel size) so the winch axles will spin freely but not rattle around.

5. Saw the profile, keeping the two parts together as long as possible. Then pin the sides together with two short pieces of dowel and sand the edges to the line. Break all sharp corners and edges.

6. Glue one side to the base. When the glue has dried, glue on the second side. Slide dowels through the holes to ensure that they are aligned. Use a square to check the alignment of the edges on the front and top surfaces. Sand the bottom surfaces flush.

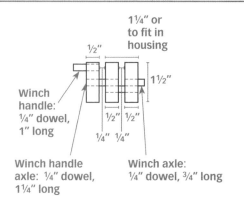

Winch Mount Sides

SIDE VIEW

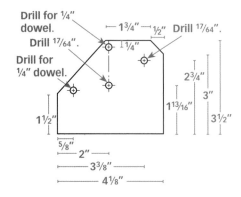

Drill for ¼" dowel.
Drill ¹⁷⁄₆₄".
Drill for ¼" dowel.
1¾" — ½" Drill ¹⁷⁄₆₄".
1¼"
2¾"
3"
1¹³⁄₁₆"
3½"
1½"
⁵⁄₈"
2"
3³⁄₈"
4⅛"

Note: A template is also provided for the winch mount sides at the end of the chapter.

Winch Handle Disks

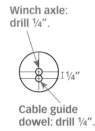

Handle: drill ¼".
Handle axle: drill ¼".
⁹⁄₁₆"

Winch Drum Disks

Winch axle: drill ¼".
1¼"
Cable guide dowel: drill ¼".

Winch Parts

1¼" or to fit in housing
½"
1½"
½" ½"
¼" ¼"
Winch handle: ¼" dowel, 1" long
Winch handle axle: ¼" dowel, 1¼" long
Winch axle: ¼" dowel, ¾" long

Winch

The crane's two winches are each made from three disks. Two form the winch; the third is the crank with a handle. The winch cable dowel is offset between the winch disks so that it acts as a cam as you spin the winch. In this way, the winch "locks" in one place on each rotation.

You can make the disks by slicing up 1½-in.-dia. dowel, or you can buy factory-made 1½-in. slab wheels. I prefer the ready-made wheels because they are very even in thickness and the holes are exactly square to the faces.

1. Carefully lay out the hole for the handle on one disk. Mark the center for the cable guide dowel holes on the remaining two disks. These holes should be as close as possible to the center holes without actually touching. I aim for a ¹⁄₆₄-in. to ¹⁄₃₂-in. space between the two holes. All holes are to be a snug fit on ¼-in. dowel.

2. Use a short length of dowel to pin the two winch disks together, marking them so you can keep them matched up later. Drill the cable dowel holes. Be sure the bit is square to the work.

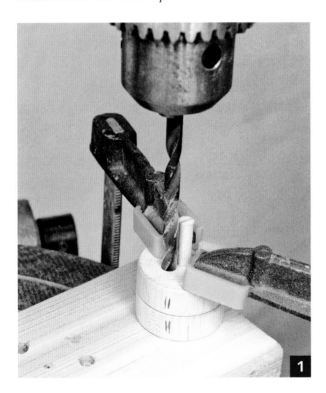

3. Make six small plastic washers, which act as slippery wear plates between the winch disks and the winch housing. The washers allow the winch to spin much more freely and make the mechanism more durable. See p. 16 for instructions on making the washers. Make them about ¾ in. in diameter, so they are not visible from the side.

4. Cut the cable guide dowel to a length that fits inside the winch mount assembly, with ¹⁄₃₂-in. to ¹⁄₁₆-in. clearance. Dry-assemble it with the winch disks. To keep the disks aligned, slide a length of ¼-in. dowel into the center axle holes. Check that this assembly fits into the winch mount assembly with the washers in place. There should be enough clearance for the disk assembly to spin freely.

5. It is safest to glue the cable guide dowel into one winch disk, with the dowel ending up flush with the outside of the disk. Let the glue dry. Then glue the second winch disk onto the dowel until the end surfaces are flush; slide a length of dowel through the axle holes to keep the parts aligned. Quickly, before the glue sets, add two washers to the axle dowel and check the fit between the axle housing sides. Adjust until there is ¹⁄₆₄ in. to ¹⁄₃₂ in. of clearance.

6. Cut the winch handle dowels and the winch axle dowels, then sand and bevel the ends slightly. Glue the handle dowels into the winch handle disks.

7. Take one winch assembly, put glue into the axle holes, and place it in the winch housing. Slide the axle dowels into place. Later, you can either leave them proud or sand them flush with the sides of the winch housing.

8. Glue the second winch into place. I usually have the handles on opposite sides, but you could have them both on the same side if you think that may work better.

9. Glue the winch assembly to the crane deck. Its exact location is not critical: I set it flush at the rear of the deck and $1/32$ in. to $1/16$ in. in from the side of the deck.

Axle Housings

To make the axle housings, follow the instructions on p. 54 but use the sizes shown here.

1. Cut a strip of wood 16 in. long, which is enough to make four axle housings and two stabilizer housings.

Axle Housings

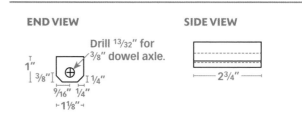

END VIEW

Drill $13/32$" for $3/8$" dowel axle.

1" · $3/8$" · $1/4$" · $9/16$" · $1/4$" · $1/4$" · $1\frac{1}{8}$"

SIDE VIEW

$2\frac{3}{4}$"

Front Fenders

TOP VIEW

$3/4$"

SIDE VIEW

$1\frac{1}{2}$"
$1\frac{1}{2}$"
$3/4$"

Middle Fenders

TOP VIEW

$3/4$"

SIDE VIEW

4"
$3/4$"
$3\frac{1}{8}$"
$7/16$"

Rear Fenders

TOP VIEW

$3/4$"

SIDE VIEW

$1\frac{1}{8}$"
1"
$5/8$"

2. Shape all the housings and drill the necessary holes. Glue the axle housings into place using the locations shown on the frame drawing (p. 131). Keep them centered on the deck and square to the frame.

Stabilizers

When the crane pivots to the side it will tend to tip, especially if the child is using it to lift a heavy load with the boom at a low angle. As on a real crane, outriggers with stabilizing jacks slide out from the frame to help keep the crane upright.

On this toy crane, when you extend the outriggers, locator dowels on the inside end fit in horizontal slots on the stabilizer housings. That keeps the jacks vertical. When you retract the outriggers, they are rotated 90 degrees so the jacks fit into the horizontal slot at the outer end of the housing.

Stabilizer Housings

FRONT VIEW   **END VIEW**

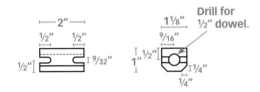

Outriggers

SIDE VIEW

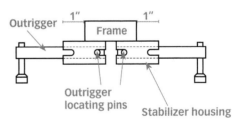

Stabilizer Jacks

TOP VIEW

SIDE VIEW

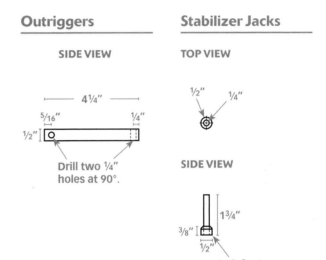

Stabilizer Assembly

TOP VIEW

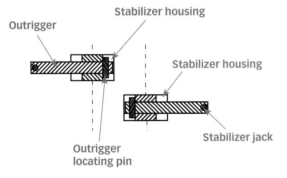

FRONT VIEW

SIDE VIEW

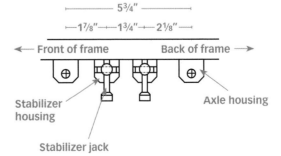

1. Lay out the cross holes at each end of the stabilizer housings. Drill a ⁹⁄₃₂-in.-dia. hole, which produces a sliding fit on a ¼-in. dowel.

2. Saw in from the ends to form the slots. File and sand the housings to remove all sharp corners.

3. Cut the dowel for the outriggers and bevel the ends slightly. Check that the outriggers slide freely in the stabilizer housings, sanding them down if needed. Lay out the end holes in the outriggers.

4. Drill one hole in each outrigger, sized for a snug fit on a ¼-in. dowel. Cut the short outrigger locating pin dowels ⅞ in. long, then sand and bevel the ends slightly. To glue the locating pin dowel into the outriggers, install the dowel until it has about ¼ in. to go. Put glue in the hole on one side and on the last ¼ in. of dowel on the other end. Push the dowel in the rest of the way.

Test-fit the outriggers into the stabilizer housings. They should slide freely, and the locating pin dowels should fit easily into the housing slots.

5. Drill a hole in the other end of each outrigger for the jack. Make sure the locating pin dowel is horizontal to ensure that the two holes are perpendicular to each other. A drill-press vise is handy for this, but clamping the dowel to scrap plywood on the drill-press table is a good alternative. The ¼-in. jack dowels should fit snugly in their holes.

Jacks

The easiest way to make these parts the correct size is to temporarily install the wheels on the crane.

1. Place the crane on a flat surface and use an offcut to lift the stabilizer housing up against the frame. Add shims to lift the wheels off the ground by about ¹⁄₃₂ in. Slide a jack dowel into the outrigger. Mark the location of the jack dowel in the outrigger, then cut the dowel ⅛ in. to ³⁄₁₆ in. above the mark. Sand a slight bevel on one end.

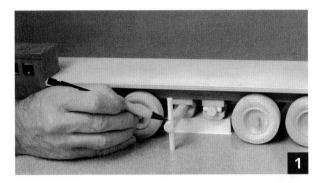

2. To make the feet, drill a ¼-in. hole in the end of a ½-in. dowel that is about 2 in. long. Mount the dowel vertically in the drill press and drill about 1 in. deep.

3. Sand the bevel on one end, then cut it ³⁄₈ in. long. Sand and bevel the new end, then cut the second foot ³⁄₈ in. long. Glue the feet to the jack dowels.

4. Place the outrigger dowels into the stabilizer housings, then glue the jacks in place.

5. With the wheels still temporarily installed, dry-clamp the stabilizer assemblies to the frame. Check that the outriggers rotate and travel in and out without interfering with each other or with the wheels. When you're satisfied, glue and clamp the stabilizers into place, keeping them square to the frame.

Crane Deck Attachment

1. Drill the ½-in.-dia. pivot hole through the truck frame and deck. It is best to lay out and drill this hole from the underside of the frame to be sure that the hole is centered between the axle housing and the outrigger.

2. Make the two retainer rings. These will attach to each end of the ½-in. turntable pin to keep the crane in place on the truck frame (see the drawing on p. 132). The simplest retainer ring is a 1-in. factory-made wheel with its axle hole drilled out to ½ in. You can also cut ³⁄₈-in.-long slices from a 1-in. dowel.

3. Drill the center of the disks to fit snugly onto a ½-in. dowel. Clamp the disks to plywood scrap on the drill-press table to ensure that the holes will be square to the disks.

4. Dry-assemble the crane deck, truck frame, a length of ½-in. dowel, and the retainer rings. You may need to sand a flat on the top retainer ring to make room for the cab; I had to do that for this crane. To reduce friction and wear, make a 1³⁄₄-in.-dia. plastic washer for this turntable joint and a ⁷⁄₈-in.-dia. washer to fit between the frame and the bottom retainer ring.

Hold the parts together to mark the necessary length of the dowel. You can cut the dowel so that it protrudes about $1/16$ in. on each end, or you can make it flush with the retainer rings. I like the dowel to sit proud of the retainers, so I cut it $1/8$ in. oversize.

5. Glue the top retainer ring to the turntable pin. When the glue has dried, rub wax along most of the length of the pin; leave the last $5/8$ in. or so where you will be attaching the second retainer. If you don't use the plastic washers, wax the mating surfaces of the turntable.

6. Put a bit of glue under the top retainer to attach it to the crane deck.

7. When the glue is dry, install the pin, with the plastic washer in place, through the crane deck and truck deck, and then glue the second retainer to the bottom end of the pin. Press the retainer in tightly so there is minimal clearance and hold it for 2 or 3 minutes until the glue starts to set. With no washer, you will need to allow $1/64$ in. to $1/32$ in. of clearance. With a washer, the crane will pivot smoothly with virtually no clearance.

Boom Assembly

The length of the boom can vary. It has to extend past the front of the truck, so 16 in. is the minimum. If you make it longer, the crane can lift objects higher but will be more likely to tip over. I made this boom 18 in. long, but you could certainly extend it to 20 in.

1. Cut the boom to size. Round over the corners at the tip to keep the cable string sliding smoothly. Leave the other corners sharp until you have attached the brackets.

2. Lay out and drill the side holes.

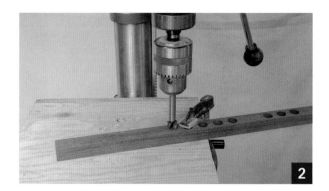

Boom Assembly

TOP VIEW

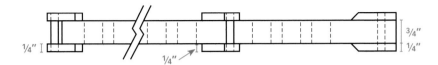

SIDE VIEW

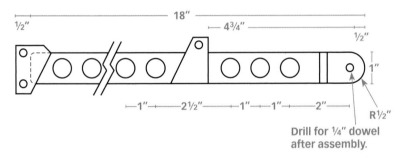

Drill for ¼" dowel after assembly.

Cable Guide Brackets

SIDE VIEW

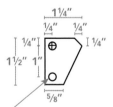

Drill for ¼" dowel after assembly (2 holes).

Boom Lift Brackets

SIDE VIEW

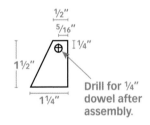

Drill for ¼" dowel after assembly.

Boom Spacers

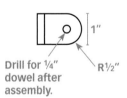

Drill for ¼" dowel after assembly.

R½"

Note: Templates are also provided for the brackets at the end of the chapter.

Cable Guide and Boom Lift Brackets

1. Cut two pieces of Baltic birch plywood 1½ in. wide and about 3½ in. long. These will be enough for the cable guide and boom lift brackets.

2. Lightly glue the two pieces together near the edges, where they will be cut apart later.

3. Lay out the two brackets (see the drawing on p. 145). Drill the holes to fit your ¼-in. dowel.

4. Cut the parts to size, leaving the end cuts last so the two pieces of wood stay attached as long as possible. Sand the cut edges and break any sharp corners.

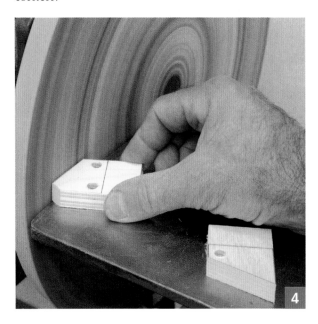

5. Glue the brackets to the boom. It is best to glue one side on, let the glue dry, and then glue the mate to the other side. Line up the holes using short lengths of ¼-in. dowel, and check for square each step of the way.

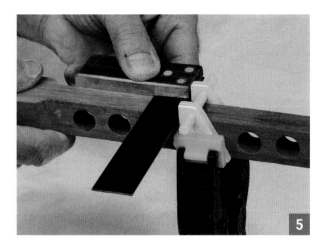

Boom Spacers

1. I used padauk for the spacers so they would match the boom. Lay out and cut the two small spacers. Make them about ¹⁄₁₆-in. oversize for now. Don't round the ends yet.

2. Sand the bevels, then glue the spacers to the boom.

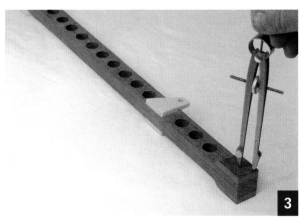

3. After the glue has dried, sand the side surfaces flush, then lay out the location of the hole and the radius for the end.

4. Drill the hole to fit a ¼-in. dowel, then saw and sand the rounded end.

Dowel Installation

1. Cut the three dowels for the brackets on the boom as well as the longer one for the boom pivot joint. Cut them about ⅛-in. overlong for now.

2. Install the three dowels into the brackets; sand the ends flush when the glue has dried.

3. Install the boom in the winch housing assembly. You can either leave the dowel slightly proud of the housing sides or sand it flush.

Boom Rest and Engine Housing

1. Lay out the boom rest using the template on p. 150 or measurements from the plan below. Saw the contour about 1/16-in. oversize, then sand to the lines and bevel all sharp corners.

2. Cut the engine housing, and again sand and break the sharp corners.

3. Glue the engine housing in place, centering it under the boom. The position front to back is not critical; there should be about 3½ in. from the front of the truck to the front of the housing. Press the engine housing firmly in place by hand.

4. When the glue has dried, put the boom rest into position and glue it to the deck and the front of the engine housing. I don't clamp this piece but hold it in place firmly for 2 minutes or so.

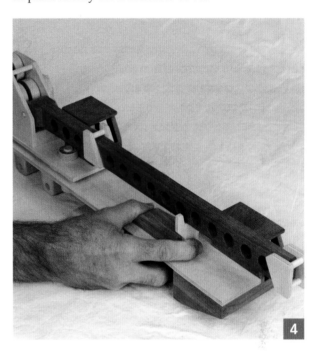

Boom Rest

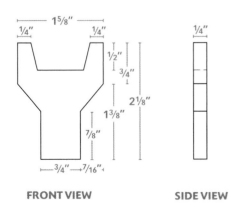

FRONT VIEW   **SIDE VIEW**

Engine Housing

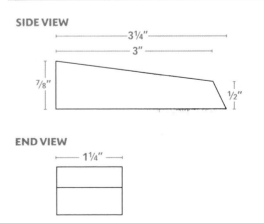

SIDE VIEW

END VIEW

Fenders

1. Lay out and cut the fenders (see the drawing on p. 140). Cut the middle fender from the scrap left over when you made the frame sides. It should be a perfect fit into the space between the stabilizer housings and the deck.

2. Sand and fit the fenders to the frame. Fit the front fenders carefully, so they sit against both the deck and the skid plate.

3. Glue the fenders into place. It is a good idea to slip the wheels into place temporarily to be sure that the middle fender is approximately centered between the wheels. The fenders can be pressed into place by hand or clamped if needed.

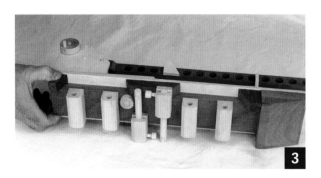

Finishing

See the notes on finishing on p. 3. I spray-finished the crane assembly separately from the wheels and dowel caps, then assembled the parts when the finish had cured. I used a satin finish, which ends up being closer to semigloss on the padauk but is satin on the birch.

Wheel and Axle Assembly

The crane uses 2¼-in. treaded wheels, but with cross treads cut in. See p. 119 for instructions regarding the wheels.

1. To determine the correct length for the axle dowels, cut a length of ⅜-in. dowel about 5 in. long and put a dowel cap on one end. Assemble this dowel axle and two wheels into an axle housing and then mark the length of the axle where it meets the second wheel.

2. Measure how far the dowel goes into the axle cap and add that distance after the line you just marked. Cut four dowels to this new length and slightly bevel the ends.

3. Glue an axle cap to one end of each axle.

4. When the glue has dried, fit one axle and two wheels into an axle housing. Put glue into the remaining axle cap and press it into place. I use a small wrench-shaped plastic spacer (see p. 27) to ensure a little clearance. Repeat for the remaining axles and wheels.

Hook

You can make the hook from Baltic birch plywood or a lamination of hardwood veneer. I had a variety of veneer left over from other projects and decided to make the hook from those scraps.

1. If you laminate your own material, be sure to alternate grain direction. I used contrasting light and dark veneer for a slightly industrial look.

2. Use the template on p. 150 to lay out the hook. Because pencil lines are hard to see on dark wood, I taped the template onto the veneers.

3. Drill a small hole for the cable and a larger one for the inside curve of the hook before you cut the profile. It is much easier to hold at this stage.

4. Cut the profile using a coping saw or a scrollsaw. Round all the sharp corners. Sand the hook smooth and apply finish.

Cable

I use nylon cord that is about ¹⁄₃₂ in. thick. It is very strong and quite slippery, which makes it ideal for sliding smoothly as you operate the winches. However, it's hard to tie a durable knot. I am not great with knots, so I tie the cord to the winch and hook with a simple slip knot and then apply a bit of epoxy to the knot when the cord is in place.

The crane boom lift mechanism requires winding the cord around the boom lift bracket then back in order to increase the mechanical advantage and reduce the amount of lift gained with each turn of the winch.

1. Tie the cord to the winch dowel and then up and over the cable-raising dowel. Slip it under the boom lift dowel, back around the cable-raising dowel, then return again to slip it under the boom lift dowel (for the second time), and return to tie to the cable-raising dowel. This gives you four wraps. The boom should now move up and down easily, with the cam effect allowing it to stop at a variety of angles.

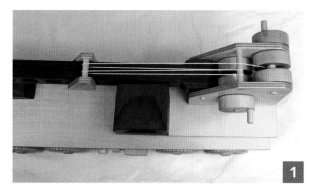

2. The hook cable is simpler, running from the hook winch along the boom, under the boom lift dowel, and then over the dowels at the boom end. Tie the hook on and, if need be, use a bit of epoxy to make the knot permanent.

You should now be able to raise and lower the boom easily, and you should be able to lock it at a chosen height when you let go of the winch handle and pull down on the hook.

Templates

For full-size template, enlarge by 128%.

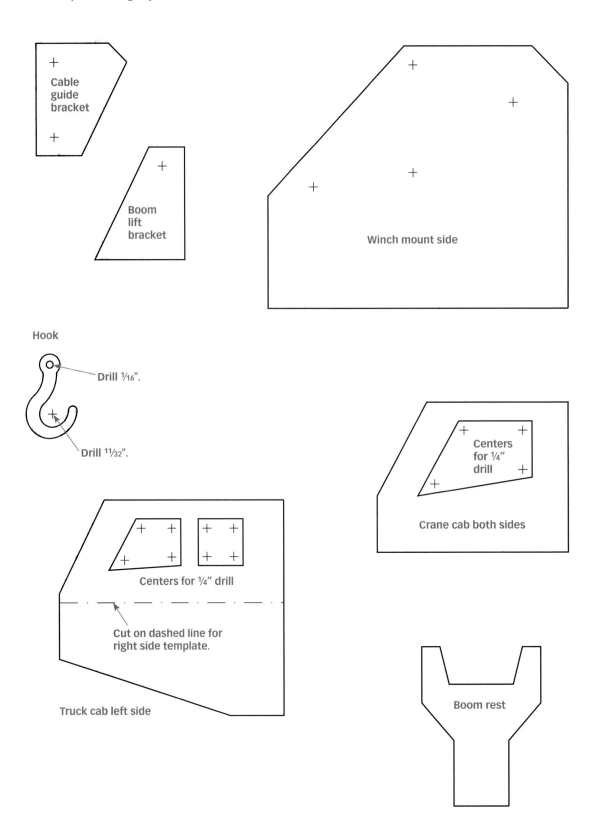

Cable guide bracket

Boom lift bracket

Winch mount side

Hook

Drill ¹⁄₁₆".

Drill ¹¹⁄₃₂".

Centers for ¼" drill

Crane cab both sides

Centers for ¼" drill

Cut on dashed line for right side template.

Truck cab left side

Boom rest

CHAPTER 8

Fire Truck

V*ery few toys* are as popular as fire trucks. The real ones have towering ladders, powerful water nozzles, flashing lights, sirens, and—not least—firefighters themselves who risk their lives to help others. This toy combines many features from different types of fire engines. It has the multiple axles used by the heaviest of the hydraulic platform trucks, large off-road tires used by some fire trucks in wilderness areas, and a turntable tower ladder with the bucket suspended at the end.

Fire Truck Plans

TOP VIEW

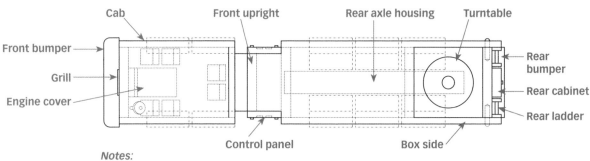

Bucket pivot dowel

Bucket nozzle

Ladder bucket

Ladder pivot dowel

Winch mount side

Turntable

Retaining ring

Cable-raising dowel

Pivot pin

TOP VIEW (without ladder)

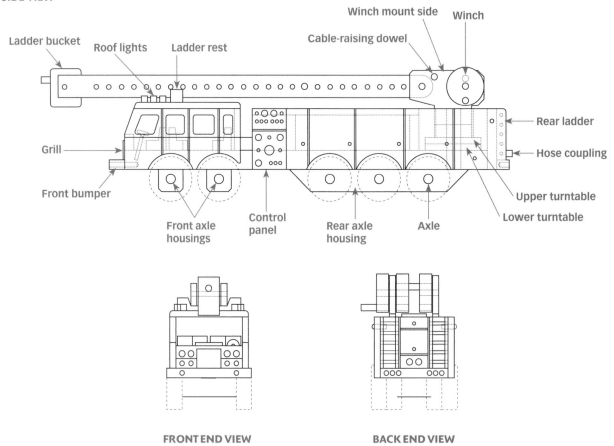

Cab

Front upright

Rear axle housing

Turntable

Front bumper

Grill

Engine cover

Rear bumper

Rear cabinet

Rear ladder

Control panel

Box side

Notes:
Some hidden lines removed for clarity.
Wheels shown as phantom lines.

SIDE VIEW

Ladder bucket

Roof lights

Ladder rest

Winch mount side

Cable-raising dowel

Winch

Rear ladder

Hose coupling

Grill

Front bumper

Front axle housings

Control panel

Rear axle housing

Axle

Upper turntable

Lower turntable

FRONT END VIEW

BACK END VIEW

PART NAME	FINISH DIMENSIONS L × W × T, IN.	NO. REQ'D.	NOTES
Frame	14¾ × 2¾ × ¾	1	Dark wood, such as padauk
Box top	6¾ × 2¾ × ¼	1	Dark wood, such as padauk
Cab roof	4⅜ × 3¼ × ¼	1	Dark wood, such as padauk
Divider	2¼ × ½ × ½	1	Dark wood, such as padauk
Front upright	2¼ × 1⅜ × ⅜	1	Dark wood, such as padauk
Middle uprights	2¾ × 1⅜ × ⅜	2	Dark wood, such as padauk
Back upright	2¾ × 2⅜ × ⅜	1	Dark wood, such as padauk
Rear axle housing	7¼ × ⅞ × 1	1	Dark wood, such as padauk. Size assumes dual wheels will be used; widen piece accordingly for single wheels.
Front axle housings	2⅛ × 1 × ⅞	2	Dark or light wood
Cab sides	4¾ × 2⅜ × ¼	2	Make bottom from dark wood, top from light wood.
Cab back	2¾ × 1⅝ × ¼	1	Make bottom from dark wood, top from light wood.
Cab dashboard	2¾ × ⅝ × ⅜	1	Dark wood, such as padauk
Engine cover	2 × 1⅛ × ⅝	1	Dark or light wood
Steering wheel	½ dowel × ⅛ long	1	Cut to length after shaping.
Steering column	⅛ dowel × 1⅛ long	1	
Seats	⅞ × ¾ × ⅝	6	Light wood
Roof lights	¼ dowel × ⁷⁄₁₆ long	6	Use pairs of yellowish, red, and light woods, or stain the wood.
Ladder rest	2¾ × ½ × ⅜	1	Light wood
Control panels	2⅜ × 1⅜ × ¼	2	Light wood
Panel dark gauges	¼ dowel × ³⁄₁₆ long	4	Use dark wood, such as walnut. Cut ⅛ in. overlong, trim after assembly.
Panel small knobs	⅛ dowel × ⅜ long	10	Use light wood. Cut ⅛ in. overlong, trim after assembly.
Panel discharge dowels	¼ dowel × ½ long	6	Use light wood. Cut ⅛ in. overlong, trim after assembly.
Panel inlet dowels	⅜ dowel × ½ long	2	Use light wood. Cut ⅛ in. overlong, trim after assembly.
Box sides	8⅞ × 2⅜ × ¼	2	Dark wood, such as padauk
Box handle dowels	⅛ dowel × ¼ long	10	Cut ⅛ in. overlong, trim after assembly.
Box lights	³⁄₁₆ dowel × ⅝ long	2	
Rear cabinet	2 × 1⅛ × ⅜	1	Light wood
Rear cabinet knobs	⅛ dowel × ⁵⁄₁₆ long	2	
Rear discharge dowels	¼ dowel × ½ long	2	
Rear ladder sides	2 × ⅜ × ⅛	4	Baltic birch plywood
Rear ladder rungs	⅛ dowel × ¾ long	10	Cut ⅛ in. overlong, trim after assembly.
Rear bumper	2¾ × ½ × ⅜	1	Dark wood, such as padauk
Rear lights	³⁄₁₆ dowel × ½ long	6	

continued

PART NAME	FINISH DIMENSIONS L × W × T, IN.	NO. REQ'D.	NOTES
Front bumper	3½ × ⅝ × ⅜	1	Dark wood, such as padauk
Front bumper horns	3/16 dowel × 1 long	2	Cut ⅛ in. overlong, trim after assembly.
Headlights	¼ dowel × 5/16 long	4	
Front flashing lights	¼ dowel × ⅜ long	4	Make two from reddish wood, two from light colored wood.
Grill	1 × ¾ × 1/16	1	Use very dark or very light veneer.
Ladder sides	15⅜ × ¾ × ¼	2	Light wood
Ladder rungs	3/16 dowel × 1½ long	26	Cut ⅛ in. overlong, trim after assembly.
Ladder cable rung	¼ dowel × 1½ long	1	Cut 2 in. overlong, trim after shaping grooves.
Ladder bucket	1½ × 1¼ × ⅞	1	Light wood
Bucket nozzle	¼ dowel × ¾ long	1	
Bucket pivot dowel	3/16 dowel × 1½ long	1	Cut ⅛ in. overlong, trim after assembly.
Ladder pivot dowel	¼ dowel × 2 long	1	Cut ⅛ in. overlong, trim after assembly.
Cable-raising dowel	¼ dowel × 2 long	1	
Hose couplings	¼ dowel × 2 long	2	
Winch base	1½ × 1½ × ½	1	
Turntables	¼ thick × 2¼ dia.	2	Baltic birch plywood
Pivot pin	½ dowel × 2⅜ long	1	
Retaining ring	½ thick × 1⅜ dia. disk	1	Use 1½-in.-dia. factory-made wheel.
Winch mount sides	3 × 2⅝ × ¼	2	Baltic birch plywood
Winch disks	1½ slab wheels × ½ wide	3	Use factory-made wheels.
Winch handle	¼ dowel × 1 long	1	
Winch axle	¼ dowel × 13/16 long	1	Cut 1/16 in. overlong, trim after assembly.
Winch handle axle	¼ dowel × 15/16 long	1	Cut 1/16 in. overlong, trim after assembly.
Winch cable dowels	¼ dowel × 17/16 long	2	Cut 1/16 in. overlong, trim after assembly.
Wheels	1¾ dia. × ⅝ wide	10	Factory-made wheels with treads
Axles	½ dowel × 3¼ to 3½ long	5	Cut length to fit truck.

The ladder raises and lowers with a winch that locks in place at different angles and can be swiveled full circle. The large cab has six seats. The wheels are factory-made, with the centers drilled out to hold a stronger axle. I used local maple and reddish padauk to mimic the red and white colors of a full-size fire truck. And I used a gloss finish because it seems to me that a fire truck should be bright and shiny.

Frame and Cab Interior

The frame and box top are the same width, so it makes sense to cut both pieces now.

1. Lay out the frame profile on ¾-in.-thick wood; the box top on ¼-in.-thick stock. Cut them to width and length.

2. Lay out the notch for the control panels in the sides of the frame. Cut to the line, then file and sand the edges.

3. Trace this notch onto the box top, with the front end of the top offset 5¼ in. from the front end of the frame. Saw and file this notch, checking that it is the same final width as the frame notch.

Frame

TOP VIEW

Drill for ½" dowel after turnbuckle attached.

2¾"   2"   ¼"   7/8"   15/16"
3/8"
4¾"   1⅜"
6⅝"
14¾"

SIDE VIEW

Drill all wheel wells after sides are attached.

¾"   R1"
3/8"
1⅞"   2"   4½"   2"   2"

Box Top

TOP VIEW

2¼"   2¾"   ¼"
1⅜"
6¾"

Frame Assembly

SIDE VIEW

5¼"   6¾"   2¾"
3/8"   3/8"
1"
3/8"   3/8"
Front upright   1¼"
½"   Box top   1⅜"   Back upright
Middle uprights
½"
¾"   Divider
Frame   Front axle housing   Rear axle housing

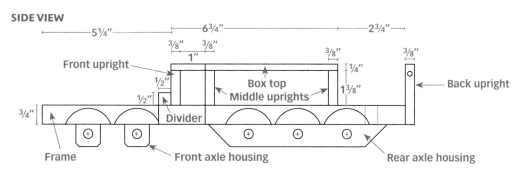

Front Axle Housing

1"
½"   Drill ¹³/₃₂"
3/8"   7/8"
⅛" × 45°

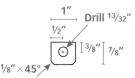

Rear Axle Housing

7¼"   Drill ¹³/₃₂"
7/8"   3/8"
7/8"   2"   2"   1⅝"

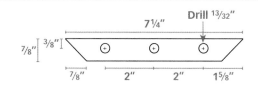

Engine Cover

TOP VIEW

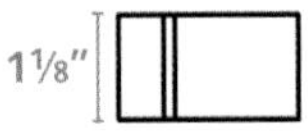
1 1/8"

SIDE VIEW

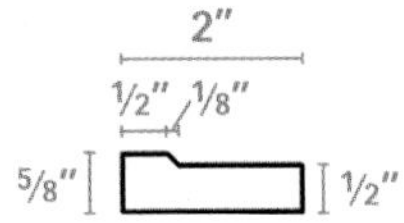
2"
1/2"
1/8"
5/8"
1/2"

Seats

TOP VIEW

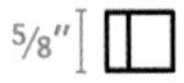
5/8"

SIDE VIEW

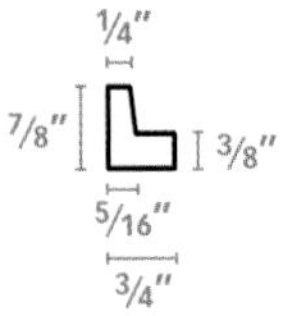
1/4"
7/8"
3/8"
5/16"
3/4"

Steering Wheel and Column

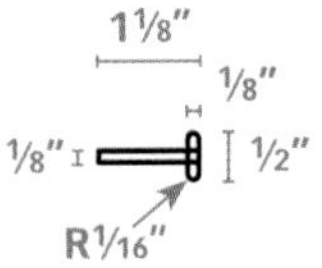
1 1/8"
1/8"
1/8"
1/2"
R1/16"

Cab Back

FRONT VIEW

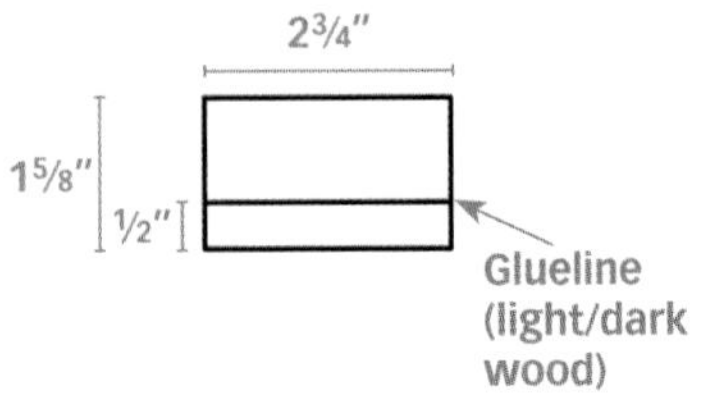
2 3/4"
1 5/8"
1/2"
Glueline (light/dark wood)

Cab Left Side

(Right side is mirror image)

TOP VIEW

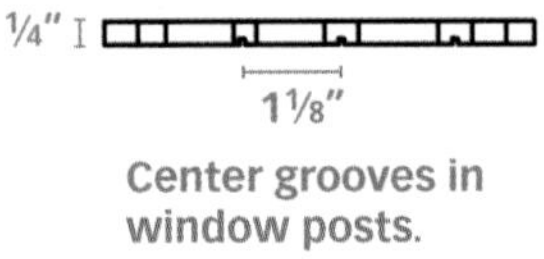
1/4"
1 1/8"
Center grooves in window posts.

SIDE VIEW

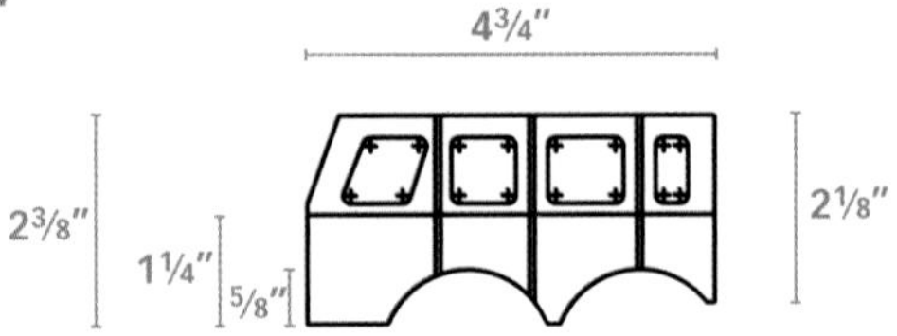
4 3/4"
2 3/8"
1 1/4"
5/8"
2 1/8"

Note: A template for the cab sides is provided at the end of the chapter.

Cab Interior Layout

TOP VIEW

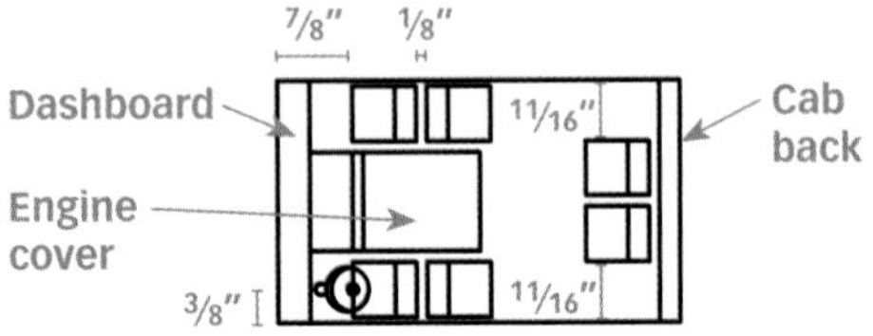
7/8"
1/8"
Dashboard
Engine cover
3/8"
11/16"
11/16"
Cab back

SIDE VIEW

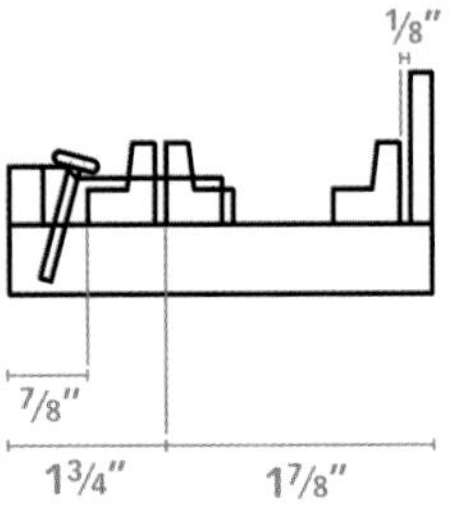
1/8"
7/8"
1 3/4"
1 7/8"

Cab Roof

TOP VIEW

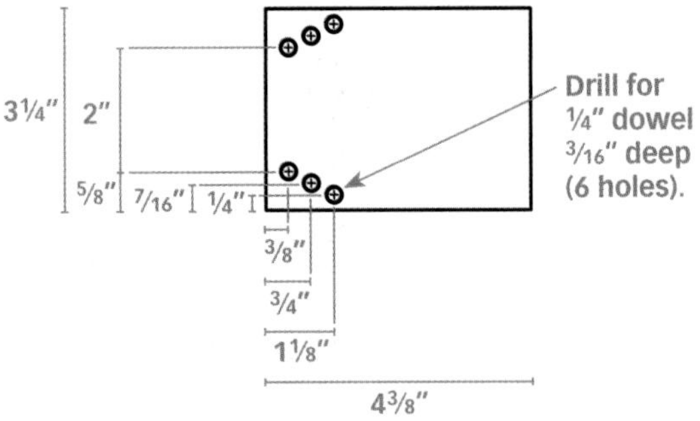
3 1/4"
2"
5/8"
7/16"
1/4"
3/8"
3/4"
1 1/8"
4 3/8"
Drill for 1/4" dowel 3/16" deep (6 holes).

SIDE VIEW

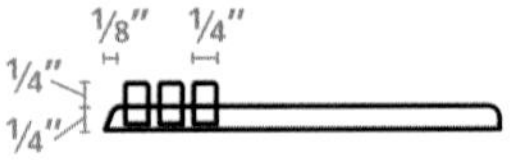
1/8"
1/4"
1/4"
1/4"

Ladder Rest

FRONT VIEW

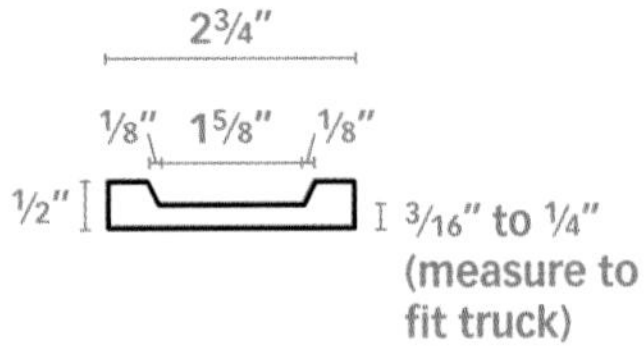
2 3/4"
1/8"
1 5/8"
1/8"
1/2"
3/16" to 1/4" (measure to fit truck)

Engine Cover

1. Lay out the engine cover profile on the side of a 2-in.-long block of wood. Use a clamp to grip the small block as you cut, then file and sand to the line. Square the front end where it meets the dashboard.

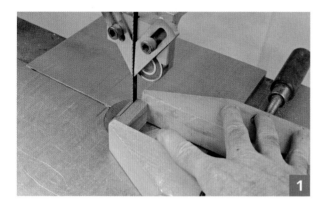

2. Glue the cover to the frame, centered side to side and set back ⅜ in. from the front of the frame. Press the cover into place by hand for a couple of minutes.

Seats

1. Make these seats by following the same process described on p. 68, but use the sizes shown in the drawing on the facing page.

2. Glue on the seats, pressing each one into place by hand. Be sure each seat is square to the frame.

TIP

When gluing parts like the seats, use a suction joint. Apply glue and press the part in place. Move it back and forth slightly several times. This will draw the glue into the wood. Be sure the part is positioned properly, then let go.

Steering Wheel and Column

1. Make the steering wheel and column following the same process described on p. 72. Use the sizes shown here.

2. Mark the steering column hole in the frame. Use an awl to make a deep mark to maintain the angle of this hole. I use a portable drill, with a drill bit that lets me fit the dowel without any hammering.

3. Dry-fit the steering assembly in case you need to shorten the column to have the steering wheel height look appropriate next to the seat. When you are satisfied, put a bit of glue in the hole and insert the steering assembly.

Crosswise Components

The dashboard, divider, the cab back, the uprights, and the rear bumper all need to be flush with the frame edges. I glue them on and sand the sides flush, and then attach the cab sides and box sides.

1. Cut out these pieces, making them 1/32 in. to 1/16 in. overlong so they overhang the frame slightly. Cut all but the back upright to their finished height. Leave the back upright slightly overlong.

2. Glue the dashboard into place against the engine cover. Have the edges overhang the frame slightly.

3. Glue the front upright (see the drawing on p. 155) to one side of the divider, exactly centered and the bottom edges flush. Sand the ends flush and to the 2¼-in. length. Adjust this as required to be an exact fit between the notches cut at the control panel area.

4. Edge-glue two pieces of light and reddish wood together for the cab back. Sand the glue seam flush. Glue the cab back to the other side of the divider, with the divider exactly centered and the bottom edges flush.

TIP

For a nearly invisible glueline, clamp the two woods for the cab back together so that their inside faces are toward each other. Plane the edge of both pieces at once. When you unfold the two pieces, their edges should match precisely.

5. Sand the bottom of this assembly to make it flat and even. Glue it in place on the frame so the front of the divider lines up with the front edge of the notch.

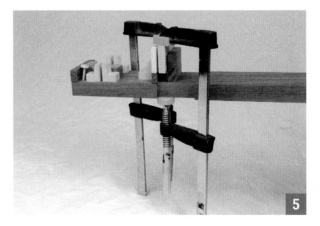

6. Glue the middle and rear uprights into place, again making sure that they overhang the frame slightly on each side.

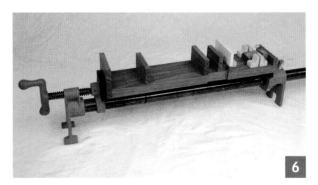

7. Glue the box top in place. Use a square to check that the notch cutout in the top aligns with the notch in the frame.

8. Glue the rear bumper into place (see the drawing on p. 163).

9. When the glue is dry, sand the sides of the assembly flat and flush with the frame. Take care to keep the sides square to the frame. I use a sanding board for this, but you could use a belt sander to remove most of the excess first.

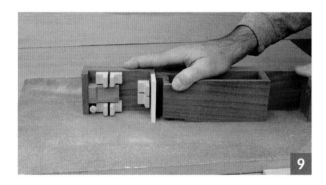

Cab Sides

I chose pieces of maple and padauk that were the closest to the colors I wanted and with the least dramatic grain patterns.

1. Cut the strips of wood. The lower part will end up 1¼ wide; the upper part, 1⅛ in. wide. I cut both pieces about ⅛ in. over width and 1 in. overlong and trim them after gluing.

2. As you did for the cab back, edge-glue the two pieces of wood. If you use ¼-in.-thick stock, align

the thicknesses carefully. It's OK if the cab sides end up slightly less than ¼ in. thick after sanding.

3. When the glue is dry, sand or plane the surfaces flat and smooth. Cut the wood in half to make the two cab sides. Leave them ½ in. or so overlong for now; as in other projects, glue the pieces together at the waste ends so you can shape both sides at once. Keep the gluelines aligned when doing so.

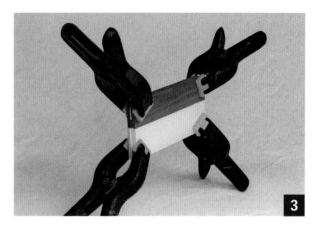

4. Lay out and cut the cab windows and side profile using the method outlined on p. 107, but use the template on p. 174. You will cut the wheel wells later.

5. Finish-sand the sides and glue one to the frame. When the glue is dry, attach the second side, carefully aligning it with the first.

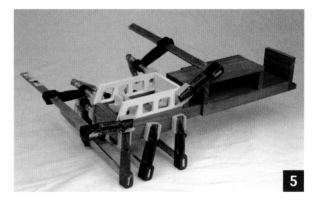

6. Sand the top of the cab assembly flat. I use a sanding board, although you could carefully use a belt sander if you have to remove more than 1/32 in. of wood.

Spray Finish

Before proceeding with assembly, pause for the first installment of finishing. To prevent sanding dust from the reddish wood getting embedded in the white maple, spray a seal coat on the cab exterior once it is complete. Do the same for the control panel, the next part of the assembly. Spray the cab interior now, because it is nearly impossible to finish after you attach the roof.

Box Sides

The box sides are detailed to resemble a real fire truck's storage box, with grooves and dowel handles for the compartments.

1. Lay out the sides, using the template on p. 174 or measurements from the drawing. You will drill the wheel wells later.

2. Cut the sides to size, leaving about ¹⁄₃₂-in. extra on the top and bottom. Remove the excess after assembly.

3. Mark out and drill the five handle holes, sized to fit the ⅛-in. dowel that forms the handles.

4. Round over the outside edge at each end, then glue the sides to the truck frame assembly. Keep the front edge even with the upright, but let the sides overhang the top and bottom slightly.

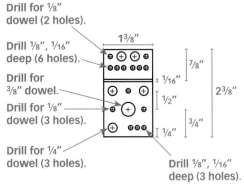

Box Sides

SIDE VIEW

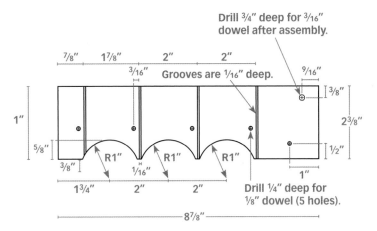

7⁄8″ 1 7⁄8″ 2″ 2″ 3⁄16″ Grooves are 1⁄16″ deep. 9⁄16″
Drill ¾″ deep for ³⁄₁₆″ dowel after assembly.
3⁄8″ 2 3⁄8″ 1″ 5⁄8″ 1⁄2″
R1″ R1″ R1″ 3⁄8″ 1⁄16″ 1 3⁄4″ 2″ 2″ 1″
Drill ¼″ deep for ⅛″ dowel (5 holes).
8 7⁄8″

Control Panels

SIDE VIEW

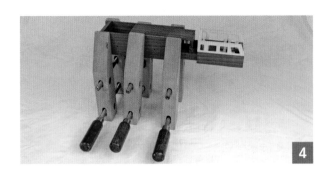

Drill for ⅛″ dowel (2 holes).
Drill ⅛″, ¹⁄₁₆″ deep (6 holes).
Drill for ³⁄₈″ dowel.
Drill for ⅛″ dowel (3 holes).
Drill for ¼″ dowel (3 holes).
1 3⁄8″ 7⁄8″ 1⁄16″ 2 3⁄8″ 1⁄2″ 3⁄4″ 1⁄4″
Drill ⅛″, ¹⁄₁₆″ deep (3 holes).

Where not specified, hole locations are symmetrical side to side.

Note: Templates are also provided at the end of the chapter.

5. Sand the top and bottom surfaces of the cab and box sides to make them flush with the underside of the frame and the top of the box.

6. On the top edges of the sides of the back box and the cab, mark the location of the small notches that outline the doors on the cab sides. Cut the notches at the bandsaw, using the method outlined on p. 111.

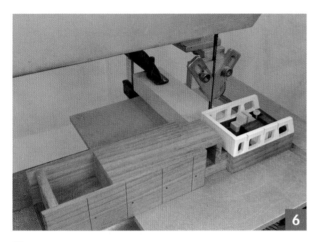

7. Drill the ³⁄₁₆-in. hole for the box light.

Control Panels

The control panels have a series of holes and dowels representing the water inlet couplings, outlet couplings, control knobs, and pressure gauges. I used black walnut dowel for the inset gauges, but if you have a plug cutter you can use any wood that you have on hand.

1. Cut the two control panels to size and round over the outside edges.

2. Lay out the hole centers using the control panel template on p. 174 or the drawing on the facing page.

3. Following the drawing, drill nine ¹⁄₈-in.-diameter holes ¹⁄₁₆ in. deep. Drill the other holes all the way through.

4. Cut the dowels as needed. Better to have them too long than too short, as any excess can be trimmed off the back later. I sand each end of the dowels and bevel the sharp corners slightly.

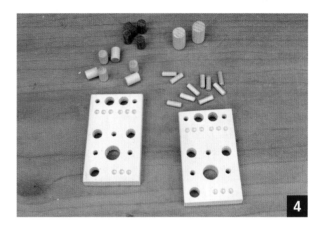

5. For the top two large gauges, recess the dowels ¹⁄₃₂ in. to ¹⁄₁₆ in. from the front. To install them, start the dowel into the hole from the back. Put a little glue on the dowel and tap or push it in until it has the look you are after. Don't put glue in the hole, because inserting the dowel will push the glue forward and obscure the end of the dowel.

6. To install the remaining dowels, put glue in the holes. Tap or push the dowels in place, allowing them to protrude the desired amount (¹⁄₁₆ in. for most dowels, ¹⁄₄ in. for the larger inlet dowel).

7. When the glue is dry, sand the back surface flush and smooth.

8. Glue the control panels into place one at a time. I hold them by hand for a couple of minutes instead of clamping, but they can be carefully clamped top and bottom if necessary.

Cab Roof

This rectangular piece will finish the cab.

1. Cut the roof to size, leaving it about ¹⁄₃₂ in. to ¹⁄₁₆ in. oversize all around.

2. Sand a bevel on the front to match the profile of the cab sides' windshield area.

3. Finish-sand the underside of the roof and glue it into place. Have a slight overhang on the sides and back, but line up the front angled edges.

4. When the glue is dry, sand the edges flush and round over the sides and back. This is a good time to spray a seal coat of finish on the outside of the cab if you are using contrasting woods.

Wheel Wells

Form the wheel wells by drilling holes with a 2-in. Forstner bit. This requires clamping a sacrificial block to the frame, drilling the flat-bottomed holes, and removing the block to reveal the arcs in the truck sides and frame.

1. Make two sacrificial boards, each 2 in. or 3 in. wide, at least ¾ in. thick, and 12 in. long. (You need one board for each side of the truck, or a board the same width as the frame.)

2. Clamp the board to the truck frame so it's flush at the front and flush on the side to be drilled. Lay out the hole centers as shown on the drawing on p. 155.

3. The wheels I have are slightly more than ⅝ in. wide, so I drill the front wheel wells about ⅝ in. deep. The axle housing will protrude into the wheel well ⅟16 in. to ⅛ in, allowing the wheel to protrude

slightly. If you want the wheels flush with the truck sides, drill the wheel wells ⅟16 in. to ⅛ in. deeper than the width of the wheels. Either way, set a stop on the drill so all wheel wells are the same depth.

4. Drill the rear wheel wells deep enough to allow the dual wheels to protrude the same amount as the front. If you are not using duals, then make the wells the same depth as the front.

5. Repeat the process for the second side.

6. Remove the sacrificial block and sand the wheel wells to round the sharp edges.

Front Bumper and Lights

1. Cut the front bumper to size. Mark the radius on the corners of the front bumper, then sand to the line. Round over any sharp edges that will be exposed after assembly.

2. Lay out the hole centers. Drill these holes through the bumper and into the frame. The dowels that fit in the holes represent truck horns, but they also help hold the bumper in place.

Lay out the holes on the frame on either side of the grill area, using an awl to make large center marks. The larger top holes represent flashing strobe lights, usually white and red on each side. The smaller lights represent conventional headlights.

Rear Bumper

BACK VIEW

After assembly, drill for
3/16" dowel (6 holes).

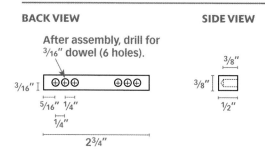

3/16"

5/16" 1/4"

1/4"

2 3/4"

SIDE VIEW

3/8"

3/8"

1/2"

Front Bumper

TOP VIEW

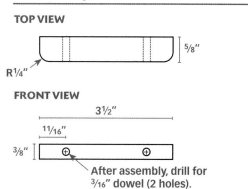

5/8"

R 1/4"

FRONT VIEW

3 1/2"

11/16"

3/8"

After assembly, drill for
3/16" dowel (2 holes).

Rear Cabinet

END VIEW

Drill for
1/8" dowel,
1/4" deep
(2 holes).

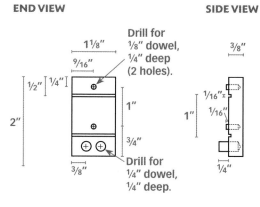

1 1/8"

9/16"

1/2" 1/4"

2"

1"

3/4"

3/8"

Drill for
1/4" dowel,
1/4" deep.

SIDE VIEW

3/8"

1/16"

1"

1/16"

1/4"

Rear Ladders

SIDE VIEW

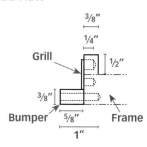

3/8"

3/16"

2"

1/4"

3/8"

1/4"

Drill for 1/8" dowel
(5 holes).

END VIEW

3/4"

1/8"

1/8" dowel, 3/4" long
(5 pieces)

Truck Front

FRONT VIEW

Drill for
3/16" dowel,
1/4" deep
(4 holes).

7/8"   1"

1/4" 3/8"

Drill for 1/4" dowel,
1/4" deep (4 holes).

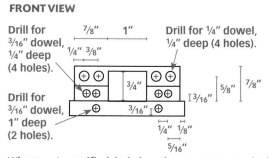

3/4"

Drill for
3/16" dowel,
1" deep
(2 holes).

3/16"

3/16"

1/4" 1/8"

5/16"

5/8" 7/8"

Where not specified, hole locations are symmetrical side to side.

SIDE VIEW

3/8"

1/4"

Grill

1/2"

3/8"

Bumper   5/8"   Frame

1"

Truck Rear

SIDE VIEW (with both sides removed)

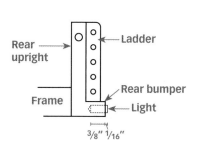

Rear
upright

Ladder

Frame

Rear bumper

Light

3/8" 1/16"

BACK VIEW

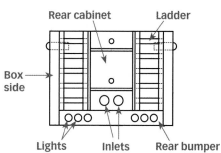

Rear cabinet   Ladder

Box
side

Lights   Inlets   Rear bumper

3. Glue the front bumper to the truck frame, flush at the bottom and centered side to side. Clamp it lightly.

4. When the glue is dry, drill the ³⁄₁₆-in. and ¼-in. holes front and back. Finish-sand the bumpers.

5. Cut the eight pieces of ³⁄₁₆-in. dowel for the front and rear bumpers. Make them equal to or just shorter than the depth of the holes. Sand the ends of the six rear lights to round them. I do this using the drill press (see the bottom left photo on p. 72).

6. Cut dowels ³⁄₈ in. long for the front lights. Round the ends if you want rounded lights or sand them flat with slight bevels.

7. Smear a generous amount of glue on the sides of the holes and install the dowels. Have them protrude about ⅛ in. for the rear lights, about ¹⁄₃₂ in. for the front horns.

8. Sand the front dowels flush with the bumper.

Roof Lights

This detail represents flashing red, yellow, and white lights.

1. Lay out the hole centers, following the plan on p. 156. Drill the holes ³⁄₁₆ in. deep, just short of penetrating the roof.

2. Make the lights. Cut short lengths of ¼-in. dowel and stain them the colors you prefer. Or use a plug cutter to make pieces of different woods.

3. Put glue in the holes and install the lights.

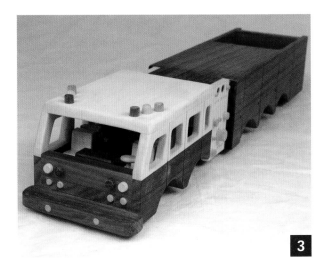

Rear Cabinet

1. Make the rear cabinet the same way you did the control panels. Follow the instructions on p. 161, but use the sizes shown in the drawing on p. 163.

2. After you have glued in the dowels, lay out the location of the ¹⁄₁₆-in. notches that outline the cabinet doors. Saw the notches with a bandsaw, just as you did for the cab and rear box.

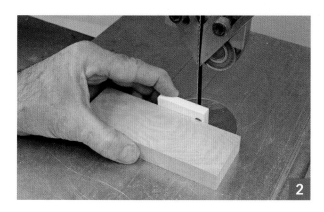

3. Glue the cabinet in place, centered on the back of the truck. The bottom of the cabinet rests on top of the bumper.

Rear Ladders

To make the ladders, follow the instructions on p. 14, but use the dimensions given in the drawing on p. 163. The ladders should fit between the rear cabinet and the box sides with about ¹⁄₁₆ in. to spare.

1. Use a sanding board to flatten the edges that attach to the box sides.

2. Put glue sparingly along the two edges that contact the back of the truck, and more generously along the side that is pressed against the box side.

3. Hold the ladder firmly in place for 2 minutes or so, until the glue begins to set. Repeat for the second ladder.

Grill

Make the grill from a piece of dark veneer, 1 in. long and ³⁄₄ in. wide.

1. Cut the small rectangle, being careful to keep the corners square. If you don't, any off angles will show up when you attach the piece.

2. Glue the grill in place, centered on the truck front. Use a scrap block and clamp to hold it flat.

Winch Assembly

The winch raises and lowers the ladder. It has a cam design that allows it to "lock" in place in each winch revolution. The string cable is wound twice to give

Winch Base

Drill for ½" dowel.

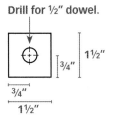

3/4"
1½"
3/4"
1½"

Upper and Lower Turntables

Drill for ½" dowel.

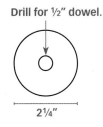

2¼"

Winch Mount Sides

SIDE VIEW

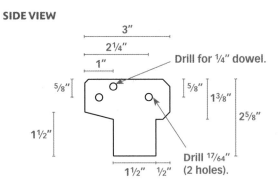

3"
2¼"
1"
Drill for ¼" dowel.
5/8"
5/8"
1³/8"
2⁵/8"
1½"
1½" ½"
Drill ¹⁷/64" (2 holes).

Note: A template for the winch mount sides is provided at the end of the chapter.

Retaining Ring

TOP VIEW

Drill for ½" dowel.

SIDE VIEW

1³/8"

½"

Winch Parts

WINCH HANDLE DISK

Winch handle: drill ¼".

9/16"

Winch handle axle: drill ¼".

1⁷/16" or to fit in housing

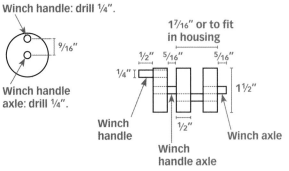

½" 5/16" 5/16"
¼"
1½"
½"
Winch handle
Winch handle axle
Winch axle

WINCH DRUM DISKS (2)

Winch axle: drill ¼".

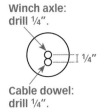

¼"

Cable dowel: drill ¼".

Winch Assembly

TOP SECTIONAL VIEW

Winch section shown rotated 90° for clarity

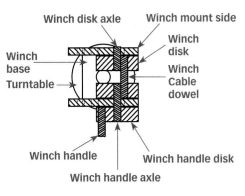

Winch disk axle
Winch mount side
Winch disk
Winch base
Turntable
Winch Cable dowel
Winch handle
Winch handle disk
Winch handle axle

FRONT VIEW

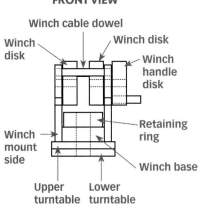

Winch cable dowel
Winch disk
Winch handle disk
Winch mount side
Retaining ring
Winch base
Upper turntable
Lower turntable

SIDE VIEW

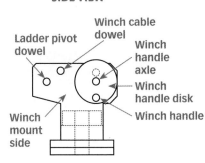

Ladder pivot dowel
Winch cable dowel
Winch handle axle
Winch handle disk
Winch handle
Winch mount side

the winch additional mechanical advantage, and allows the kids playing with it to lock the ladder at several angles between horizontal and vertical.

Winch Base

Rip the stock 1½ in. wide. Cut enough for the base and for a second identical piece that will be used as a spacer. The ripped edges need to be exactly parallel; otherwise the ladder may bind. Mark those sides. Saw the two pieces 1½ in. long.

Winch Turntables

The lower turntable is glued to the truck frame. The upper turntable is attached to the winch mount and spins with the ladder.

1. Use a compass to mark circles on ¼-in. stock. After you have drawn them, use an awl to enlarge the center mark for accurate drilling.

2. Saw the circles and then sand to the line. Sand away all sharp edges.

3. Glue and clamp the bottom surface of the upper turntable (the side that does not have the hole center marked on it) to the winch base, centering the base on the turntable.

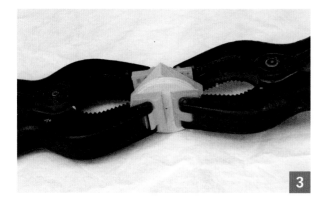

4. Glue and clamp the lower turntable to the truck frame. Have the hole center facing up, and center the turntable in the back of the truck.

5. When the glue is dry, drill the hole in the lower turntable and frame. The hole should provide a snug fit for a ½-in. dowel pivot pin.

6. Drill the upper turntable and base assembly. Clamp it to the drill-press table or hold the square base in a drill-press vise. The pivot pin needs to turn freely in this hole, so either drill it to $^{33}\!/_{64}$ in. or later sand the pivot pin dowel where it fits the winch base.

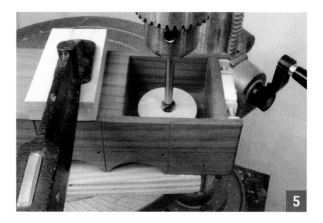

TIP

You can make a simple spindle sanding tool from a length of dowel and a strip of sandpaper. Saw a slot in the last inch or so of a 3-in.-long dowel (in this case $^{3}\!/_{8}$ in. dia.). Start a strip of sandpaper in the slot, and then wrap it around, spinning the dowel in the same direction it rotates in the drill press. When the dowel is chucked up, insert it into the hole that needs sizing and start the drill press at a low or medium speed. This custom spindle sander can be adapted to just about any diameter and depth of hole.

Winch Mount Sides

These parts are made following the same general method used for the cab sides and ladder sides.

1. Cut the winch mount sides about ½ -in. oversize all around.

2. Glue the two parts together with just a dab of glue in each corner, which will be cut off later.

3. Use the template on p. 174 to mark the outline and hole locations.

4. Drill the holes and then cut the profile.

5. Use scrap dowels to hold the pieces together. Sand the profile to the lines and remove all sharp corners.

6. Glue one side to the winch base and allow it to dry.

7. Clamp the second side into place. Use a square to be sure the sides line up, and make sure a ¼-in. dowel fits through the holes.

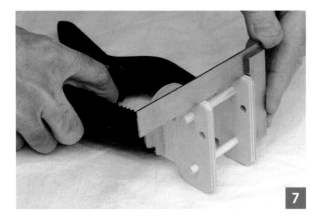

More Spray Finish

At this point, I generally spray finish into the turntable and winch mount recess at the rear of the truck. I also spray the winch mount assembly. To keep finish away from glue surfaces, fit scrap dowels into the winch mount holes. Mask off external areas of the truck and then finish areas that will be hard to reach later.

Retaining Ring and Pivot Pin

1. For the pivot pin, cut a ½-in. dowel 2½ in. long; trim it after assembly if necessary.

2. If the dowel is a tight fit in the winch base and turntable, sand the hole to enlarge it very slightly, or sand that area of the dowel until the winch assembly spins freely. Leave the fit snug on the end that will be glued into the truck frame.

3. Make the retaining ring. I generally use a 1½-in.-diameter factory-made flat wheel. Sand it

down to about 1⅜ in. diameter, which will allow it to spin inside the winch assembly. Drill the center hole for a snug fit on the pivot pin dowel.

4. Make a large plastic washer for the turntable, as explained on p. 16. The turntable washer should be 1¾ in. to 1⅞ in. in diameter. Make another about 1¼ in. in diameter to go under the retaining ring.

5. Dry-fit the assembly to be sure the winch mount spins freely and to check the length of the pivot pin. Mark a line to indicate how far to insert the dowel into the turntable and frame when gluing it.

6. When all is good, glue the dowel into the truck frame and lower turntable.

7. Rub some wax onto the section of dowel that contacts the winch mount, but not on the top section that will be glued to the retaining ring. Slide the larger plastic washer and the winch mount assembly into place.

8. To get a good rotating fit for the winch and ladder mechanism, make a horseshoe-shaped spacer from thin plastic or heavy paper (see p. 27). Place the spacer over the pivot pin. If the assembled mechanism is too tight, you will need to drill out and remake the pivot assembly. The spacer allows you to fit the parts together tightly and then slip the spacer out to provide a little room for movement.

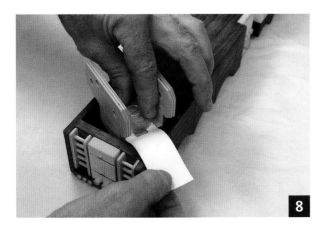

9. Put glue in the retaining ring hole. Smear a very small amount of glue on the pivot pin, then install the smaller plastic washer. Firmly press the ring onto the pivot pin. Hold the parts tight for a couple of minutes and then set them aside. After a few minutes, gently remove the spacer and rotate the winch mechanism a little to ensure that glue squeeze-out is not making the joint seize up. Let the glue dry.

Rear Axle Housing

The plan assumes that you will use dual wheels at the rear. If you don't want duals, the rear axle housing will have to be about 2½ in. wide.

1. Measure the truck to determine the exact width of the axle housing. It should be ¹⁄₁₆ in. to ⅛ in. wider than the distance between the wheel wells.

2. Cut the angles and then sand away any sharp exposed corners.

3. Lay out the centers for the axle holes and then drill as shown in the drawing on p. 155. A ¹³⁄₃₂-in. bit allows the axle dowels to spin freely and gives the axles a little room to move up and down so all wheels will contact the ground.

The holes must be the same distance from the frame, so clamp the axle housing against a fence. Make sure the base of the housing is exactly parallel to the drill so that the holes end up parallel to the frame. Drill one hole, then slide the axle housing along the fence without moving the drill or drill-press table.

Front Axle Housing

To make these axle housings, follow the instructions on p. 54, but use the sizes shown in the drawing on p. 155.

1. To determine the exact length, measure the distance between the front wheel wells and add ¹⁄₁₆ in. Drill the ¹³⁄₃₂-in. holes.

2. Dry-fit the housings with the wheels in place to make sure the wheels end up centered in the wheel wheels. Mark the final axle housing locations, then glue the housings to the frame.

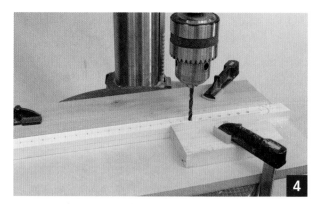

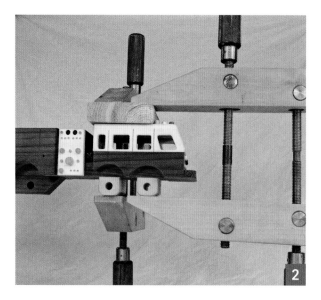

Ladder

Make the ladder much like the two small ones. This one is a little more difficult to assemble because of its size and the number of rungs.

1. Cut the sides but make them at least 1 in. overlong. Glue them together at the ends so the drilled holes will align exactly side to side. Mark the edges so you can keep them oriented when gluing the rungs in place.

2. Mark the hole locations and the radius at the bottom end.

3. Select a drill bit that provides a slightly loose fit for the ³⁄₁₆-in. dowel rungs.

4. Set up a drill-press fence like the one for the rear axle housing. Use it to drill the 26 rung holes as well as the two ¼-in. holes.

5. Saw the ladder sides to length, one end square and one rounded. Pin the sides together with a few short dowel pieces to sand the rounded end smooth.

6. Cut the ³⁄₁₆-in. rung dowels all ⅛-in. overlong.

7. Cut the ¼-in. ladder cable rung dowel about 2 in. overlong so you can grip it in the drill chuck when forming the cable grooves. (The grooves help keep the lifting strings parallel.) Measure from the center to mark out the groove locations.

8. Chuck the dowel in the drill press with the groove area ¼ in. to ³⁄₈ in. away from the chuck. Use a round file to form the grooves. This is a bit easier if you can steady one hand on the table.

9. Cut the cable dowel to length, keeping the grooves centered. Bevel the ends slightly.

10. To prepare for the assembly, make two wood spacers that are the length of the ladder and sized to fit between the ladder sides (see the photo on the facing page); this will keep the sides parallel and correctly spaced. Round or bevel the spacers' corners very slightly to keep any glue squeeze-out away.

Ladder

TOP VIEW

SIDE VIEW

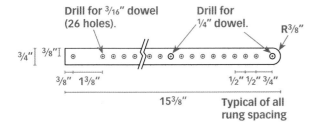

Drill for 3/16" dowel (26 holes).

Drill for 1/4" dowel.

R3/8"

3/4" · 3/8"

3/8" · 13/8"

1/2" 1/2" 3/4"

153/8"

Typical of all rung spacing

Ladder Bucket

TOP VIEW   **SIDE VIEW**

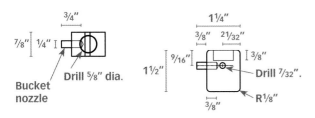

3/4"

7/8" · 1/4" I

Bucket nozzle

Drill 5/8" dia.

11/4"

3/8" 21/32"

11/2" · 9/16" I 3/8"

Drill 7/32".

3/8" R1/8"

Make another simple fixture to speed the assembly. Saw a 1/16-in.-deep dado into a block of wood to make a depth stop when you push the dowels into the ladder side. Or glue 1/16-in. strips about 3/8 in. apart on a piece of scrap.

The ladder's width will be just under 1 in., but measure to be sure the assembled ladder will fit into the winch mount with 1/32 in. to 1/16 in. of clearance. Have a small mallet ready in case the dowels need persuading.

11. Dry-assemble the ladder and clamp the spacers in place on each side of the rungs. Check again to be sure the ladder fits the winch mount and that the rungs are square to the sides. Make sure the sides are oriented the same way they were when drilled.

Ladder Cable Rung   ## Ladder Rungs

11/2" · 1/4" I R1/8"

3/16"

O ← 1/4"

11/2"

O ← 3/16"

TIP

Choose a glue that has a long open time (the time between applying the glue and assembling the parts) and a long closed time (the maximum time needed to get the clamps on and adjust the parts). Waterproof glues generally have longer open and closed times, as do some epoxies. I use Titebond III, which provides 10 minutes open time and 15 minutes closed time. That's about twice as much as most carpenters' glues.

12. Glue half the rungs into one side. Put glue in the holes and slide the rungs into place. Have the rungs protrude 1/16 in. from one side (use the fixture for this) and keep them generally parallel to each other. Glue in the remaining rungs. Save the 1/4-in. cable-raising dowel for later.

Before the glue's closed time is up, place the other ladder side onto the rungs. Don't use any glue; the second side just keeps the rungs aligned while the glue dries.

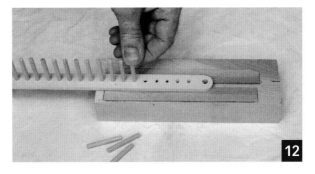

13. When the glue is dry, remove the second side and put glue in all the dowel holes. Press the side into place until all the dowels are started in their holes. Place the spacers on each side of the rungs and clamp along the length of the ladder.

14. When the glue is dry, sand the dowel ends flush with the ladder sides. Round over any sharp corners and edges.

Ladder Rest

The ladder rest also provides a cross rib to strengthen the roof.

1. Determine the distance between the ladder and the cab roof when the ladder is horizontal. Pin the ladder in place on the winch mount and use spacers to get the ladder parallel to the roof. The thickness of the spacers is the thickness of the base of the ladder rest (shown as 3⁄16 in. to 1⁄4 in. on the drawing on p. 156).

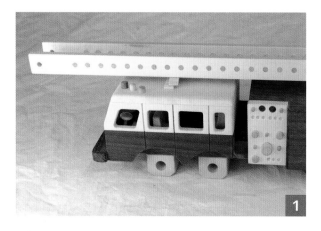

2. Lay out the contour and saw the ladder rest to shape. Sand away all exposed sharp corners and edges.

3. Glue the rest to the roof. The position is not critical, but the rest should be centered and square to the roof. Press it into place without clamping.

Winch

This winch is almost identical to the one on the Wheeled Crane in Chapter 7. Follow the instructions on p. 139 to make and install the winch parts, but use the sizes shown in the drawing on p. 166.

Bucket

The bucket must pivot freely and be bottom-heavy so it remains vertical as the ladder moves up and down. The bucket should fit between the ladder sides with at least 1⁄16 in. total clearance. Adjust the thickness shown on the drawing on p. 171 to your ladder as needed. The pivot hole is 1⁄32 in. off center to compensate for the weight of the bucket nozzle.

1. Cut the block to size and mark the hole locations. Drill the holes. They should not quite intersect, so check the depths carefully as you drill. Sand to round over the lip of the 5⁄8-in.-diameter hole.

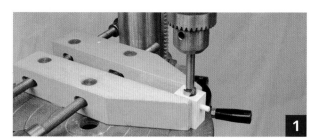

2. Sand to round the corners and break any sharp edges.

3. Cut the bucket nozzle and glue it into place. Apply glue into the hole but not to the dowel itself.

Ladder Attachment

Now it's time to fit the ladder and bucket in place.

1. Cut the bucket pivot dowel and cable-raising dowel about ⅛ in. overlong. Put the bucket in place on the ladder and start the dowel; stop with about ¼ in. to go. Put glue in the hole and on the remaining length of dowel. Slide the dowel in until it protrudes on the other side.

2. When the glue is dry, sand the dowel flush.

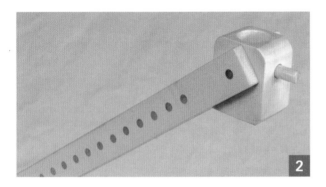

3. Repeat this process to attach the ladder to the winch mount sides and then to install the cable-raising dowel.

Wheels and Axles

I use a solid axle for this truck to ensure durable wheels and axles. It is best to have the wheels and axles a little loose, so allow 1/32 in. to 1/16 in. of extra length in the axles for side to side movement.

1. Slide a length of axle dowel through the wheels and axle housing; mark the length required. I add about ¼ in. to the length, which allows me to round

off the axle ends and have them protrude ⅛ in. past the wheel face. That's only for looks. You could just as well cut the axles to length and make the ends flush with the wheels.

2. Round the ends of the axles if desired. I rough this out on a disk sander, and then use the drill press as a vertical lathe for the final forming and sanding.

3. Put the wheels on the axles to spray on the finish. This keeps finish from getting in the glue area and seals the axle ends. That makes it easy to remove squeeze-out when you glue the wheels to the axles.

4. Glue one wheel to one end of each axle. (For dual rear wheels, glue a pair of wheels to the axle.) Be quite generous with the glue in the wheel hole,

and apply glue sparingly to the axle.

When the glue is dry, remove squeeze-out and wax the axle center where it will be enclosed by the axle housing. Add ¾-in.-dia. plastic wear washers here to help the wheels spin freely.

5. Place the wheel and axle into the housing and glue on the other wheel or pair of wheels. Use a small wrench-shaped spacer (see p. 27) to be sure the second wheel doesn't sit tight against the axle housing.

String the Winch

The winch uses a rather slippery nylon string, available at any hardware store.

1. Tie the string to the winch dowel, then dab on a bit of clear glue (I used melamine glue) to keep the knot together. Wrap the string twice around the lift dowel and the cable-raising dowel, which increases the mechanical advantage. This makes the ladder easier to lift and provides more locking angles where the ladder will rest. If you want even more mechanical advantage, increase the number of wraps to three.

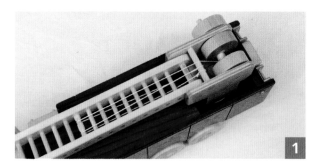

2. Tie the string around the winch cable dowel, then run it up over the cable-raising dowel and out to the ladder cable dowel, and then down under the ladder and back toward the winch. It pops up just before the ladder pivot dowel and wraps back around the cable-raising dowel. Run it out to the ladder cable dowel again, then back under the ladder, up over the ladder pivot dowel again and tie it to the cable-raising dowel. Dab on glue to hold this knot, too.

Templates

For full-size template, enlarge by 161%.

CAB SIDES

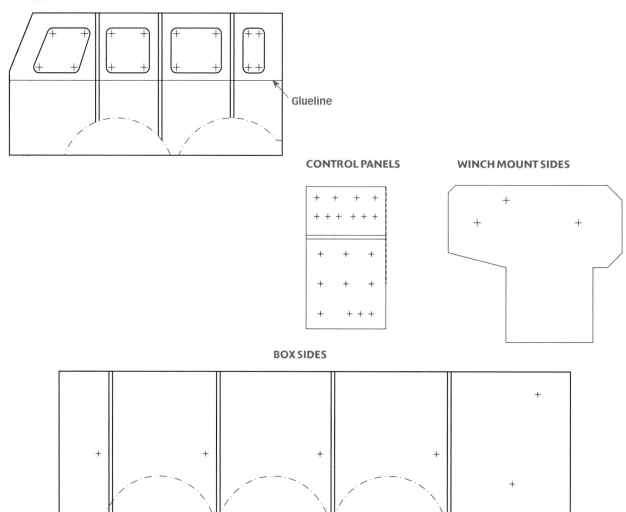

Glueline

CONTROL PANELS

WINCH MOUNT SIDES

BOX SIDES

CHAPTER 9

Skid-Steer Loader

i *recently had to drive* through a highway construction project. There among the large equipment was a tiny Bobcat® skid-steer loader, scraping and moving gravel near a bridge. It was useful and necessary to the project, going where the big machines couldn't. Similarly, this little toy is a lighthearted contrast to the huge machines in the rest of this book. It's close in scale with the others, so kids can use it alongside the large toys. A simple dowel handle is all it takes to lift and tilt the bucket.

I used wenge for the dark components and birch for the light ones. The factory-made treaded wheels are 1-in.-dia. maple, attached with standard factory-made axle pins.

TOP VIEW

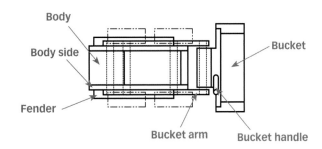

Body

Body side

Fender

Bucket

Bucket arm

Bucket handle

SIDE VIEW

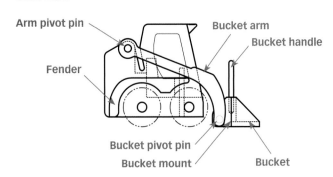

Arm pivot pin

Bucket arm

Bucket handle

Fender

Bucket pivot pin

Bucket mount

Bucket

FRONT VIEW (bucket removed for clarity)

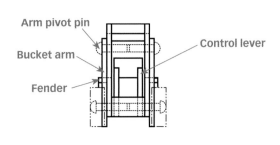

Arm pivot pin

Bucket arm

Fender

Control lever

SKID-STEER LOADER CUT LIST

PART NAME	FINISH DIMENSIONS L × W × T, IN.	NO. REQ'D.	NOTES
Body	2⅝ × 1¹⁵⁄₁₆ × ⅞	1	Could use ¾-in.-thick material.
Body sides	2⅜ × 2⅝ × ⅛	2	Baltic birch plywood
Roof	1⅜ × ⅞ × ¼	1	Wenge
Bucket arms	3⁷⁄₁₆ × 1¼ × ⅛	2	Baltic birch plywood
Bucket back	2 × ⅝ × ⅛	1	Wenge
Bucket bottom	2 × ¾ × ⅛	1	Wenge
Bucket ends	¾ × ¾ × ¼	2	Make from two layers of ⅛-in. Baltic birch plywood.
Bucket mount	1⅛ × ¾ × ½	1	Use same wood as body.
Bucket handle	⅛ dowel × 1⅜ long	1	
Control levers	⅛ dowel × 1⅜ long	2	
Seat	¾ × 1 × ¾	1	
Fenders	2⅛ × 1 × ¼	2	Baltic birch plywood
Wheels	1 dia.	4	Factory-made wheels with treads
Axles	⁷⁄₃₂ axle pins	4	Factory-made; cut length to suit.
Bucket and arm pivot pins	⁷⁄₃₂ axle pins	4	Factory-made; cut length to suit.

Body

TOP VIEW

Drill for 1/8" dowel (2 holes).

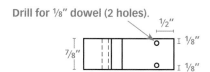

7/8" 1/2" 1/8" 1/8"

SIDE VIEW

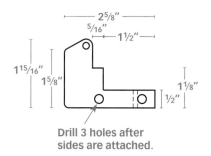

2 5/8"
5/16"
1 1/2"
1 15/16"
1 5/8"
1 1/8"
1/2"

Drill 3 holes after sides are attached.

Control Levers

TOP VIEW

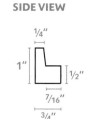

1/8"

SIDE VIEW

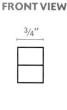

1 3/8"

Roof

SIDE VIEW

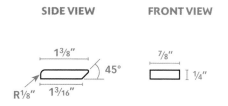

1 3/8"
45°
R 1/8"
1 3/16"

FRONT VIEW

7/8"
1/4"

Seat

SIDE VIEW

1/4"
1"
1/2"
7/16"
3/4"

FRONT VIEW

3/4"

Body

The body section encompasses the frame, cab floor, and engine housing. The roof is exactly the same width as the body, so make it now out of the same block of wood. Drill the holes in the body later, after you attach the sides.

1. Lay out the shape on a block of 7/8-in.-thick wood, using the template on p. 179 or measurements from the plan shown above. You can use 3/4-in.-thick wood if that's what you have on hand. Saw the body and roof to shape, leaving them about 1/32-in. oversize all around. Set the roof aside for now.

2. File and sand to smooth the sawcuts in the area that will form the interior of the cab. Wait to sand the back and bottom surfaces until you have attached the sides. As shown in the photo at right, keep the floor as flat as possible to provide a good surface for the seat.

3. Drill the 1/8-in.-dia. holes for the control levers. Drill a sample hole in a scrap to test your dowel size.

4. Cut the two control lever dowels to length. Sand and bevel the ends.

TIP

When making small dowel parts, sand and bevel both ends, even though only one will be seen. Too often in the assembly process I accidentally reverse a dowel, so the "bad" end is exposed and the sanded end hidden. Having a bevel on the glue end also makes the dowel easier and quicker to install.

5. Use a toothpick to apply some glue in each hole, then push or tap the control levers into place.

6. If necessary, sand the bottom flush.

Seat

Make the seat by following the instructions in Chapter 4, p. 68. Use the dimensions shown in the drawing on p. 177.

1. Fit the seat to the floor in the body piece. You may have to adjust the fit unless both seat and body are exactly square.

2. Apply a little glue to the body, then press the seat into place and hold it for a couple of minutes.

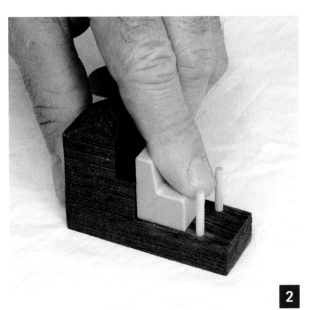

Body Sides

The sides are made of ⅛-in. Baltic birch plywood.

1. Cut the two pieces at least ½ in. oversize, then glue them together using three or four dabs of glue in the waste wood near the edges.

2. When the glue has dried, lay out the contour, using the template on the facing page. Use an awl

to clearly mark the hole centers and to lightly dot the arc that forms the back of the window.

3. Drill the ¼-in. holes that form the corners of the window, as well as the ⅛-in. hole at the end of the slot that forms the back of the cab outline.

4. Put masking tape on the back side to reduce tearout, then cut the window opening with a coping saw or scrollsaw.

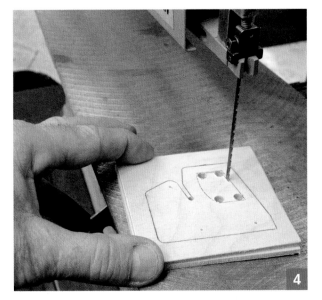

5. File a slight bevel on the edges of both sides of the window opening. This will reduce chipout as you file and sand to smooth the opening. Sand to round all the windows' sharp edges.

6. When you have finished the window opening to your satisfaction, saw out the outside contour, leaving it ⅟32-in. to ⅟16-in. oversize for now. Plan the cuts so that the two pieces stay glued together as long as possible.

7. Sand the front and back window edges, as well as the ⅛-in.-wide slot that separates the cab from

Templates

Templates shown at 100%.

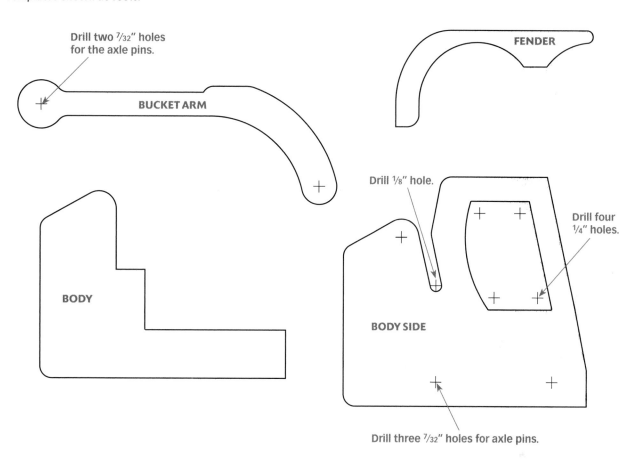

Drill two ⁷/₃₂" holes for the axle pins.

BUCKET ARM

FENDER

Drill ¹/₈" hole.

Drill four ¼" holes.

BODY

BODY SIDE

Drill three ⁷/₃₂" holes for axle pins.

the rear engine sections. Leave the top, bottom, and back oversize; you'll sand them flush after you glue the sides to the body.

8. Glue one side to the body, clamping it as needed. Both body and side are about ¹/₃₂-in. oversize at this point, so the edges should line up quite well.

9. When the glue has dried, attach the second side. Use a square to check the alignment with the first side.

10. While the glue dries, sand the roof piece and shape the front bevel. I use a disk sander for this.

11. Apply glue to the sides of the roof and slip it in place between the sides. You may need to spring them apart very slightly, but that is easy to do. Have the sides extend about ¹/₃₂ in. past the roof. Clamp it lightly.

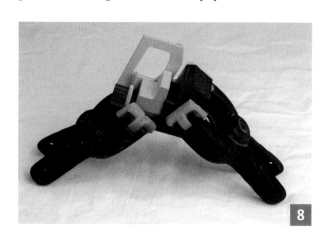

8

11

12. When the glue has dried, sand the roof, back, and bottom surfaces flush. Sand the roundovers and remove all sharp edges.

13. Drill the three ⁷⁄₃₂-in. holes for the axles. Drill a hole in scrap first to be sure the axle pins fit snugly. Ideally, you should be able to push them into place easily, but they won't fall out if you hold the wood upside down.

TIP

Drill bits come in four common sizing systems: fractional, number, letter, and metric. Fractional size sets usually include sizes from ¹⁄₁₆ in. to ½ in. Numbered drills go from 1 to 80, sized from 0.228 in. (just under ¼ in.) to 0.0135 in. (just under ¹⁄₆₄ in.). Because there are 80 drill sizes within this range, you can usually find the exact size for the fit you want.

Letter drills are slightly larger than numbered drills and labeled A through Z, sized from just under ¼ in. to just under ⁷⁄₁₆ in. Metric sets usually come in 0.1 mm increments or 0.5 mm increments from 1 mm (just over ¹⁄₃₂ in.) to 12 mm (just under ½ in.). Fairly inexpensive high-speed drill bit sets are available in each of these sizing systems; sometimes a set will include fractional, numbered, and letter drills.

Bucket Arms

The bucket arms are made following the same general procedures you used for the body sides.

1. Cut two strips of Baltic birch plywood for the bucket arms, making them at least ½ in. oversize. Glue them together at the corners so that you can cut and drill both arms at once.

2. Use the template on p. 179 to lay out the shape and the hole centers.

3. Drill the ⁷⁄₃₂-in. holes for the axle pins that connect the arms to the body and bucket.

4. Use a bandsaw, scrollsaw, or coping saw to cut out the bucket arm shapes. Cut them ¹⁄₃₂ in. oversize and then sand to the lines, rounding over any sharp edges and corners.

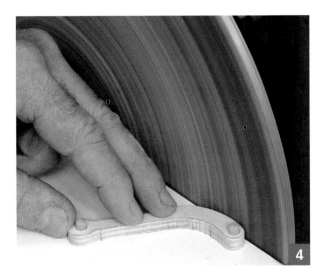

TIP

When shaping two pieces at once, like the bucket arms, leave the pieces attached in a couple of places. Smooth the cut edges and then finish sawing to separate the pieces. Pin the pieces together with dowels in the drilled holes while you finish smoothing the edges.

Fenders

Use Baltic birch plywood for the fenders. Follow the same procedure as for the bucket arms, gluing two oversize pieces together, marking and cutting the shape.

1. Saw the wheel well shapes first, leaving the rest to hold the parts together, and then sand the curves. I chuck a small drum sander into the drill press and sand as close to the line as possible. Once the fender is in place over the wheels, any irregularities in the curve will become apparent. This probably won't bother the child playing with the toy, but it might bother the builder.

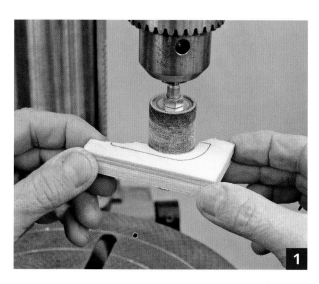

2. Finish cutting out the fenders, and then sand the tops and backs. Round over any sharp edges on the sides that will be exposed.

3. Temporarily install the wheels (without glue) and use them as a placement guide to glue the fenders in place, one side at a time. The top of the fender should line up with the bottom of the window in the cab, although this is not critical. The gap between the wheels and fender should be about $1/16$ in. Press the fenders into place and hold them by hand for a minute or two until the glue starts to set.

4. Remove the wheels and clean off any glue squeeze-out.

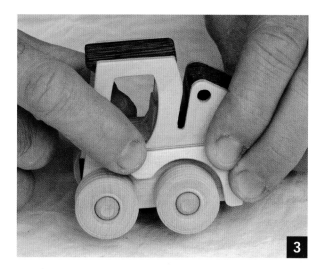

Bucket

Begin with the mount that connects the bucket to the bucket arms. Then add the ends and back.

Bucket Mount

1. Cut this small block to its rectangular shape. Make it $1/64$ in. to $1/32$ in. larger than the width of the body assembly.

2. Saw the angle, using a clamp to hold the block.

3. Sand the bucket mount, rounding the back edges on a disk sander, then break any sharp corners that will be exposed after assembly. Don't drill the hole yet; wait until you have assembled the bucket.

Bucket Mount

SIDE VIEW

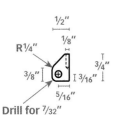

Drill for ⁷/₃₂″ axle pin.

R¼″
½″
¹/₈″
³/₈″
³/₄″
3/₁₆″
⁵/₁₆″

FRONT VIEW

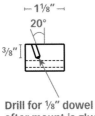

← 1¹/₈″ →
20°
³/₈″

Drill for ¹/₈″ dowel after mount is glued to the bucket back.

Bucket Back

TOP VIEW

¹/₈″ I

FRONT VIEW

Drill for ¹/₈″ dowel after mount is glued to the bucket back.

20°
⁵/₈″
2″

Bucket Bottom

TOP VIEW

³/₄″
2″

SIDE VIEW

¹/₈″ I

Bucket End Left Side

(Right side is mirror image.)

TOP VIEW

¹/₈″ I
¹/₈″

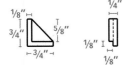

¹/₈″
³/₄″
⁵/₈″
³/₄″

¼″
¹/₈″ I
¹/₈″

SIDE VIEW   **FRONT VIEW**

Bucket Assembly Parts

TOP VIEW

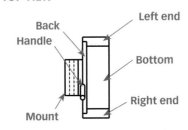

Back
Handle
Left end
Bottom
Right end
Mount

SIDE VIEW

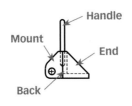

Handle
Mount
End
Back

FRONT VIEW

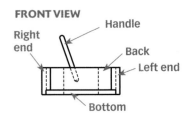

Right end
Handle
Back
Left end
Bottom

Bucket Bottom and Back

1. Cut these two pieces from ¹/₈-in. stock, making them slightly overlong. I used wenge again. At least one long edge of the back and bottom needs to be perfectly straight to form a good glue joint where they meet.

2. Glue the bucket mount to the bucket back. Center the mount side to side and have it extend ¹/₈ in. below the back. This forms a ¹/₈-in. rabbet for the bucket bottom.

2

3. Glue the bottom to the back. I press the parts into place by hand, using a small offcut block (padauk in the photo) to hold them square. The off-cut has a bevel sanded onto one corner to provide space for glue squeeze-out.

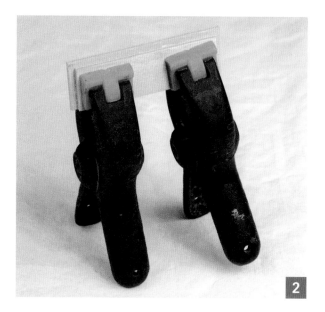

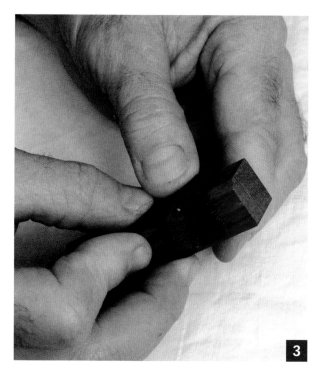

4. When the glue has dried, sand the back and bottom surfaces flush, and sand the ends even and square.

Bucket Ends

1. Accurately cut two pieces of ⅛-in. Baltic birch plywood. Make one ⅞ in. wide by 3 in. long and the other 1 in. wide by 3⁵⁄₁₆ in. long. I cut these at the bandsaw and then carefully sand to the lines using a disk sander.

2. Glue and clamp them together with an offset of ⁵⁄₃₂ in. on the ends and one side. This offset will form a rabbet for the bucket bottom and back. Remove any glue squeeze-out from the rabbet.

3. When the glue has dried, hold the bottom/back assembly in the rabbet to mark the diagonal cutline.

4. Saw the triangular ends, leaving about ¹⁄₃₂ in. extra to be sanded down after assembly.

5. Glue the ends on one at a time. Apply glue to the rabbet in one end piece and hold it firmly against one end of the bottom/back assembly for a couple minutes. When the glue has dried, glue on the other end.

6. After the glue has dried, sand the diagonal edge until it just meets the bottom and back edges. I use a disk sander for this, working very carefully. Hand-sand the surfaces and break all sharp edges.

7. Drill the pivot-pin hole to fit your axle pins. Hold the bucket with a clamp, checking carefully that the bucket is square to the table and parallel with the drill bit.

8. Locate the hole for the handle pin, using an awl to make a large center mark. The hole is 7/8 in. from the end of the bucket and centered on the glueline between the mount and the bucket back. It should be about 1/2 in. deep, sized to be a snug fit for a 1/8-in. dowel. The angle is not critical, but if you angle the pin too steeply it can interfere with the bucket arm.

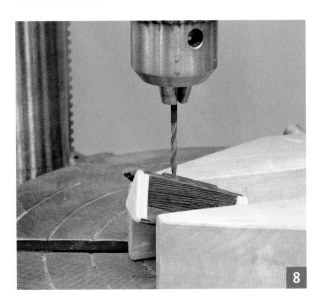

9. Put glue in the hole, as well as a tiny amount around the end of the dowel. Push the dowel into place.

Finishing

See the section on finishing on p. 3.

Cut the axle pins to length and use them to temporarily plug the holes in the body and bucket. This keeps finish out of the holes and allows you to apply the finish to the axle pin heads along with the rest of the toy. Spray-finish the wheels, body, bucket, and bucket arms separately. Let the finish dry overnight.

Final Assembly

Make a small spacer to set the amount of clearance needed between the wheels and the body. I use a small wrench-shaped piece of plastic (see p. 27).

1. Dry-fit the wheels to the body and be sure all the wheels turn when you push the skid-steer along a flat surface. If one wheel does not touch the ground, remove the wheels and drill out the axle holes, making them 1/32-in. oversize. You may also need to sand down the circumference of the axle pin heads.

2. Put a little paraffin or other wax just under the heads, where the wheels will turn. Put some wax on the body sides around the axle holes and on the inside surfaces of the wheels.

3. Slide one pin into a wheel and put a tiny bit of glue on the end of the pin. Put a more generous amount of glue in the hole in the body. Press the pin firmly into place, with the wrench spacer between the wheel and the body. After several minutes, when the glue has begun to set, remove the spacer and install the next wheel.

4. Let the glue dry and then install the wheels on the other side.

5. When all the wheels are secure, attach the bucket arms to the body and bucket. Apply wax to the sliding surfaces on the ends of the arms and the ends of the bucket mount. Dry-fit the arm and bucket assembly, checking that it raises, lowers, and tilts without binding. When the fit is good, put glue in the holes in the body as well as the holes in the bucket, then press the four axle pins into place. This fit can be quite snug, so I don't use the spacer. The

mechanism needs to be able to move, of course, but does not need to spin freely.

As the glue dries, move the bucket up and down gently to ensure that any squeeze-out does not freeze the bucket or bucket arm joints.

5a

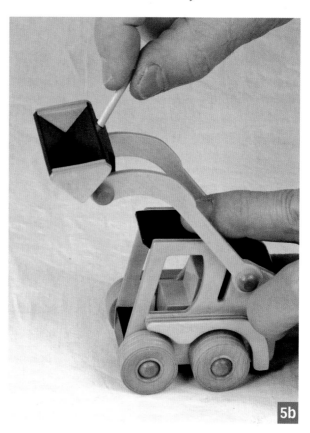

5b

appendix

Tools and Machinery

You will need some sort of workplace, of course, but you will not need a professional-level shop—although that would be nice. I have neither a large shop nor very expensive tools. I began the book working in a small detached building. In the midst of the project, my wife and I moved to a house that didn't have a separate shop. I put my tools and machinery in the garage and finished the toys there.

Long ago, when I was still a machinist apprentice, I built a tablesaw, bandsaw, and wood lathe. When you look though the photos in the book, you will see that these machines are uncomplicated. My tablesaw developed motor difficulties as I worked on the last couple of chapters, so I used the bandsaw with a clamped-on fence to rip the wood for the projects. If you don't have a tablesaw, the bandsaw will suffice quite nicely.

Essential Machines
- Drill press
- Bandsaw
- Disc sander, belt sander, or both

Nice to Have but Not Required
- Tablesaw
- Scrollsaw
- Portable electric drill

Essential Hand Tools
- Steel rule
- Square
- Awl
- Coping saw
- Brad-point drill bits
- Forstner bits
- Flat files (small smooth cut and small bastard cut)
- Round file about ¼ in. in diameter
- Small chisel
- Sandpaper in a variety of grits up to 220-grit or 320-grit
- Drum sanding set for the drill press
- Woodworking vise
- Hand plane
- Compass
- Spring clamps, C-clamps, and at least one bar or pipe clamp.

Sources of Supply

I buy wood, tools, and other supplies primarily from Rockler®, Westwind Hardwoods, Lee Valley®, and Bear Woods and have had good luck with each of those companies. There are many other reputable businesses. I have listed a few here, in alphabetical order.

Bear Woods Supply
www.bearwood.com
800-565-5066
P.O. Box 275
Cornwallis, Nova Scotia B0S 1H0
Canada
Toy parts, dowels, 1¾-in. treaded wheels

Lee Valley Tools Ltd.
www.leevalley.com
800-871-8158
P.O. Box 1780
Ogdensburg, NY 13669-6780

P.O. Box 6295, Station J
Ottawa, Ontario, K2A 1T4
Canada
Tools, toy parts, dowels, veneer

Rockler Woodworking and Hardware
www.rockler.com
800-279-4441
4365 Willow Drive
Medina, MN 55340
Tools, machines, planed hardwood ⅛ in. to ¾ in. thick, toy parts

Stockade Wood and Craft supply
www.stockade.ca
800-463-0920
785 Imperial Road North
Guelph, Ontario N1K 1X4
Canada
Toy parts, dowels

Westwind Hardwood Inc.
www.westwindhardwood.com
800-667-2275
P.O. Box 2205
Sydney, British Columbia V8L 3S8
Canada
Good variety of hardwoods

Woodcraft®
www.woodcraft.com
800-225-1153
P.O. Box 1686
Parkersburg, WV 26102-1686
Tools, machinery, dowels, hardwood

Woodworker's Supply®
www.woodworker.com
800-645-9292
1108 North Glenn Rd.
Casper, WY 82601
Tools, toy parts, dowels

Woodworks Ltd.
www.craftparts.com
800-722-0311
4521 Anderson Blvd.
Haltom City, TX 76117
Dowels, 1¾ in. treaded wheels

Workshop Supply Inc.
www.workshopsupply.com
800-387-5716
P.O. Box 160
100 Commissioners St. East
Embro, Ontario N0J 1J0
Canada
Tools, toy parts, dowels

metric equivalents

INCHES	CENTIMETERS	MILLIMETERS	INCHES	CENTIMETERS	MILLIMETERS
⅛	0.3	3	13	33.0	330
¼	0.6	6	14	35.6	356
⅜	1.0	10	15	38.1	381
½	1.3	13	16	40.6	406
⅝	1.6	16	17	43.2	432
¾	1.9	19	18	45.7	457
⅞	2.2	22	19	48.3	483
1	2.5	25	20	50.8	508
1¼	3.2	32	21	53.3	533
1½	3.8	38	22	55.9	559
1¾	4.4	44	23	58.4	584
2	5.1	51	24	61	610
2½	6.4	64	25	63.5	635
3	7.6	76	26	66.0	660
3½	8.9	89	27	68.6	686
4	10.2	102	28	71.7	717
4½	11.4	114	29	73.7	737
5	12.7	127	30	76.2	762
6	15.2	152	31	78.7	787
7	17.8	178	32	81.3	813
8	20.3	203	33	83.8	838
9	22.9	229	34	86.4	864
10	25.4	254	35	88.9	889
11	27.9	279	36	91.4	914
12	30.5	305